Psychology AS

The Teacher's Companion for AQA 'A'

Michael Griffin

•

Rosalind Geillis

•

Consultant editor

Cara Flanagan

United Kingdom: Folens Publishers, Waterslade House, Thame Rd, Haddenham, Buckinghamshire HP17 8NT.

www.folens.com

Ireland: Folens Publishers, Greenhills Road, Tallaght, Dublin 24.

Email: info@folens.ie

Editor:	Geoff Tuttle
Project development:	Rick Jackman (Jackman Publishing Solutions Ltd)
Concept design:	Patricia Briggs
Layout artist:	The Manila Typesetting Company
Illustrations:	The Manila Typesetting Company
Software architecture and design:	Haremi Ltd
Cover design:	Patricia Briggs
Cover photographer:	Chris Cardwell
Cover image of dog:	courtesy of Clifton Photographic Company

First edition published 2004 by Nelson Thornes
Second edition first published 2010 by Folens Limited

British Library Cataloguing in Publication Data.
A catalogue record for this publication is available from the British Library.

ISBN 978-1-85008-396-2

ACKNOWLEDGEMENTS

The authors and publisher would like to thank the following for permission to reproduce copyright material:

p.3, © These images are copyright of Maxim Malevich/Fotolia and Varina Patel/ Fotolia; p.9, © Marco Birn/Fotolia; p.10, © Maksym Yemelyanov/Fotolia; p.13, © javarman/Fotolia; p.107, © Sean Gladwell/Fotolia, © Magnum/Fotolia; p.108 and 155, © Mr_Vector/Fotolia; p.112 and 175, © Antonis Papantoniou/Fotolia; p.117, © Andres Rodriguez/Fotolia; p.118, © robynmac/Fotolia, © ioannis kounadeas/Fotolia; p.119, © LiveStock/Fotolia, © elvira gerecht/Fotolia, © Cristian Ciobanu/ Fotolia, © Irina Redko/Fotolia, © AlenaT/Fotolia; p.121, © chrisharvey/Fotolia; p.122, © Lisa F. Young/ Fotolia, © julien tromeur/Fotolia, © AKS/Fotolia; p.123, © Lom/Fotolia, © and emily2k/Fotolia; p.124, © zentilia/Fotolia; p.125, © Marion Wear/Fotolia, © Eric Isselée/Fotolia, © Goran Bogicevic/Fotolia; p.126, © Lars Lindblad/Fotolia, © AKS/Fotolia, © ioannis kounadeas/Fotolia; p.127, © Leo Blanchette/ Fotolia, © designer_things/Fotolia; p.128, © Sundikova/Fotolia; p.129, © xmasbaby/Fotolia; p.134, © moodboard/Fotolia, © Ashwin/Fotolia, © bsilvia/Fotolia, © Yuri Arcurs/Fotolia, © Yuri Arcurs/Fotolia; p.137, © mikes/Fotolia, © Andres Rodriguez/Fotolia, © ioannis kounadeas/Fotolia; p.139, © Pefkos/ Fotolia; p.140, © cardiae/Fotolia; p.145, © James Steidl/Fotolia, © subnurbs/Fotolia; p.149–150, © Stephen Coleman/Fotolia; p.152, © kamphi/Fotolia, © Fotolia IV/Fotolia, © govicinity/Fotolia, © i love images/Fotolia; p.153, © Sean Prior/Fotolia; p.156, © Fotolia IV/Fotolia; p.160, © ioannis kounadeas/Fotolia; p.161, © Edyta Pawlowska/Fotolia; p.164, © kmit/Fotolia, © Emil Iliev/Fotolia; p.165L - © Bettman/Corbis; p.165R - © Getty Images; p.170, © PinkShot/Fotolia, © Mr_Vector/Fotolia; p.171, © NiDerLander/Fotolia; p.173, © Dmitriy V/Fotolia, © publicist/Fotolia; p.175, © Pétrouche/ Fotolia, © Dawn Hudson/Fotolia, © Ala/Fotolia; p.181, © absfred/Fotolia; p.184, © WOGI/Fotolia; p.185, © jeff Metzger/Fotolia; p.186, © jeremybaile/Fotolia, © Kapu/Fotolia, © Mikko Pitkänen/Fotolia, © Michael Flippo/Fotolia; p.187, © Aleksandar Jocic/Fotolia, © Photosani/Fotolia, © Alex/Fotolia, © pressmaster/Fotolia, © paulo cruz/Fotolia, © Kirill Zdorov/Fotolia; p.188, © Alexey Afanasyev/Fotolia; p.189, © piumadaquila.com/Fotolia; p.194, © Adem Demir/Fotolia, © photoGrapHie/Fotolia, © Lars Lindblad/Fotolia, © picsfive/Fotolia; p.195, © Tasosk/Fotolia; p.197, © Keo/Fotolia; p.200, © Kristina Afanasyeva/Fotolia; p.205, © Photoroller/Fotolia; p.206, © Shutterbug/Fotolia, © schmetfad/Fotolia; p.212, © Dariusz Kopestynski/Fotolia; p.213, © WOGI/Fotolia; p.214, © bilderbox/Fotolia, © DN/ Fotolia, © Philip Date/Fotolia, © Kwest/Fotolia; p.215, © ioannis kounadeas/Fotolia; p.222, © Christos Georghiou/Fotolia, © bilderbox/Fotolia, © digerati/Fotolia; p.223, © Julydfg/Fotolia, © Feng Yu/Fotolia; p.225, © JJAVA/Fotolia, © iQoncept/Fotolia; p.227, © JLV Image Works/Fotolia, © Carole Mineo/Fotolia, © Nigel Monckton/Fotolia, © Cool Graphics/Fotolia, © kameel/Fotolia, © Rafa Irusta/Fotolia; p.229, © Cory Thoman/Fotolia; p.232, © Feng Yu/Fotolia; p.233, © Tatyana Okhitina/Fotolia, © Maxim Pavlov/ Fotolia, © lookata/Fotolia, © AKS/Fotolia; p.240, © frenta/Fotolia, © triling/Fotolia; p.241, © Robert Mizerek/Fotolia; p.242, © Fotolia VI/Fotolia; p.247, © Cory Thoman/Fotolia; p.248, © David Mathieu/ Fotolia, © Friax74/Fotolia, © sabri deniz kizil/Fotolia; p.249, © Vladislav Ociacia/Fotolia, © robodread/ Fotolia, © Mikhail Basov/Fotolia, © V. Yakobchuk/Fotolia, © Ralf Kraft/Fotolia, © ioannis kounadeas/ Fotolia, © fliegenwulf/Fotolia, © Stephen VanHorn/Fotolia, © Jan Matoška/Fotolia, © Doctor Kan/ Fotolia, © Arsha/Fotolia, © AlienCat/Fotolia; p.253, © RTimages/Fotolia; p.255, © i love images/Fotolia, © Fredy Sujono/Fotolia; p.265, © candan/Fotolia; p.268, © picsfive/Fotolia, © Ewa Walicka/Fotolia, © Danny Hooks/Fotolia.

Sections 1–3, Handouts 1–25, © This icon is copyright of © rolffimages/Fotolia; Handouts 26–36 - © mipan/Fotolia; Handouts 45–57 - © treenabeena/Fotolia; Handouts 58–68 - © Barbo333/Fotolia; Handouts 69–80 - © ioannis kounadeas/Fotolia; Handouts 81–91 - © Michael Brown/Fotolia; Handouts 92–101 - © Alexandra Thompson/Fotolia; Handouts 102–110 - © jeff Metzger/Fotolia; Handouts 111–118 - © DeanMurray.com/Fotolia; Handouts 119–125 - © Web Buttons Inc/Fotolia; Handouts 126–131 - © 25/Fotolia; Handouts 132–136 - © PASQ/Fotolia; Handouts 137–146 - © Vladislav Kochelaevskiy/Fotolia; Handouts 147–155 - NamraTurnip/Fotolia; Handouts 156–162 - © Carsten Reisinger/Fotolia; 163–183 - © AKS/Fotolia.

Handouts 17 and 64: Jo Gotts, a user of psychexchange.co.uk, for her permission to use her wonderful 'brief summaries' idea.

Handouts 117 and 164: Alana Clogan, for her ability to write silly stories custom made for the learning of psychology!

Page 48–49: Psi Chi, the National Honour Society in Psychology.

CONTENTS

DEDICATIONS

Michael:

To my still gorgeous, long-suffering *newly wedded Wife* Alana! Also thank you to the Griffins (especially Lewis for his ideas) and Clogans (best in-laws you could ask for) who always showed an interest in the project and never once looked bored when I talked about it!

Rosalind:

To Shawn, friends and family. I know there is more to life than Psychology lessons, honest!

INTRODUCTION

Mike Griffin

Mike Griffin: This is now the second *Teacher's Companion* we have produced and the feedback from the AS version has been fantastic, thank you. The material in this A2 version is largely different in both content and execution but I am sure you will find some familiar themes and rationales for our worksheets and ideas for delivery. For those new to these resources and to myself, I would like to offer the warning that I am actually only in my third year of teaching and I'm always conscious of the fact that many using this pack will have much more experience than me! So let me try and justify my role as author! I have been incredibly lucky during my short teaching career and have come across some amazing teaching ideas – which I continue to 'borrow' and adapt for my own lessons. Initially, I did my PGCE at Keele University in 2006–2007 which was an incredibly good foundation to start on. The course tutor, Yvonne Hill, gave us a fantastic introduction to teaching techniques and really encouraged us to critically reflect on our 'pedagogy' (which I eventually looked up in the dictionary). During that year I absorbed an amazing amount of creative ideas from Yvonne as well as from the other brilliant student teachers around me. Since then I have had the pleasure of working with some incredibly creative and effective teachers – Ros (my boss) and Tim (head of History) to name drop just a couple! I would like to think my strength lies in collating teaching ideas, adapting them, and applying them in my classroom. Think about how many great ideas we come across day to day but forget to use. This led me to produce a *Psychology Teacher's Toolkit* with the help of colleagues and Internet forums. Ultimately, it was this 'toolkit' that led to the publishers asking me to co-author this resource pack! Writing the resource has been an extremely enriching experience that I hope will help me in my next role as Course Leader of Psychology at St Bede's School, Redhill. In addition, I sincerely hope it will prove to be a useful 'companion' for you, your lessons and your students.

Ros Geillis

Ros Geillis: Firstly, I must say a big thank you to Mike for asking me to co-author both Teacher's Companions and for always being keen to discuss ideas, topics and help me when text boxes are not doing what I want them to. Sitting down to produce handouts for the second Teacher's Companion was daunting to begin with but I soon realised how lucky I am to work with colleagues from a range of different subjects who are more than willing to share their ideas and skills. I have now been teaching Psychology for eight years (which makes me feel rather old!) and while our class sizes and department have grown, I am still learning new ways to get students thinking. As mentioned in the AS Teacher's Companion, I have been lucky enough to meet wonderful people who not only exposed me to a range of teaching ideas but encouraged me to develop my own activities. From those people I learnt that one of the most valuable resources you have are your fellow teachers. The activities within this book are drawn from AS handouts, observations of other teachers, sharing good practice sessions and classroom tasks from across the key stages. They have been tweaked, altered, re-modelled or have sparked ideas for tasks to suit the content of the AQA(A) Psychology exam. As such, I hope you find that many of the handouts can be adapted to your chosen sections from PSYA3 and PSYA4. So please rummage through the pages and use the basic activity ideas, simply replacing the content with research relating to your chosen section. I hope you and your students enjoy the activities found within this companion and that they help to reduce time spent planning lessons.

Cara Flanagan

Cara Flanagan: My role in this excellent resource pack is a small one, as advisor and subject editor. I have a long history as a teacher, senior examiner and author, and hope that I have been able to use the associated knowledge to polish up the gems that Mike and Ros have produced. The pack owes some debt to the original A2 Teacher's Companion (co-authored by myself, Sara Berman and Adrian Frost) – lots of the ideas have formed the basis for new handouts and lesson plans but a great deal is new.

WHAT YOU GET!

The written materials start with a Table of Contents that will show you where to find everything. This is organised according to the sections of the specification, subdivided into topics. The pack itself is divided into three sections. Many of the activities designed and described in this book could be easily adapted and adjusted for other topics as you see appropriate. We have highlighted just a few of these for you and they are denoted with a small star in the contents pages.

Section 1: General topics

This covers topics such as how to facilitate self- and peer-assessment, how to encourage your students to elaborate their evaluative commentary, and how to approach the specification. Full details of the general topics are given in the Table of Contents.

Section 2: Lesson notes

Notes about the different activities, their rationale and how you might organise them. Links are given to handouts, and simple keys are used to highlight provision for different learning styles and ability differentiation.

Section 3: Handouts

Ready-to-run, photocopiable material.

TABLE OF CONTENTS

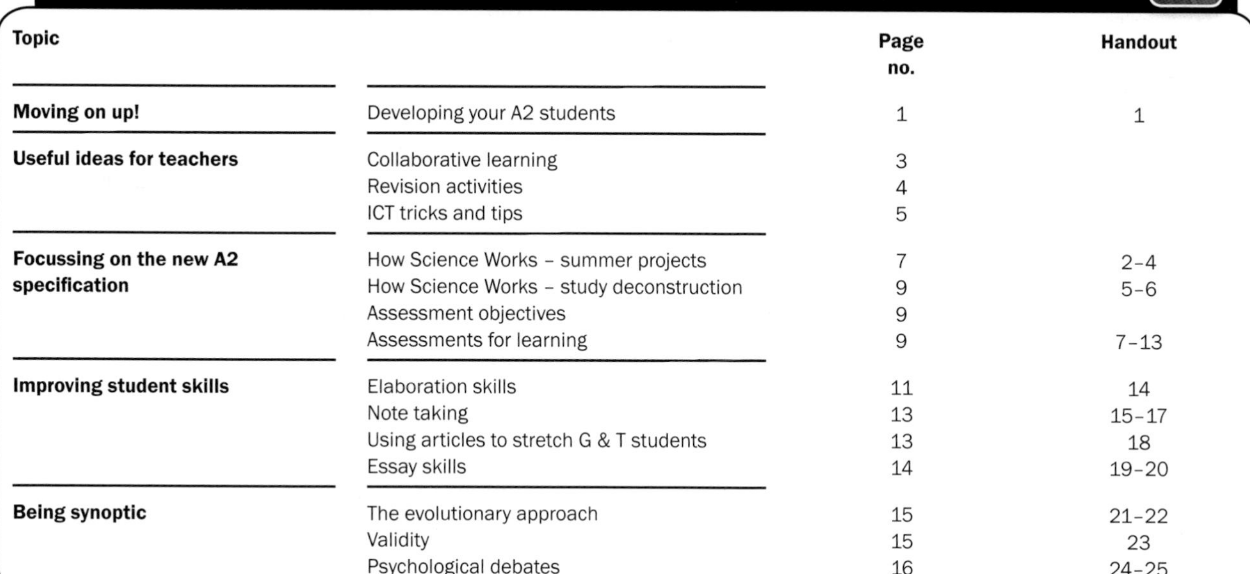

Section 1: General topics

Table of contents

Section 2: Lesson notes and Section 3: Handouts

Biological rhythms and sleep

Perception

Table of contents

Relationships

Aggression

Table of contents

Eating behaviour

Gender

Table of contents

Intelligence and learning

Cognition and development

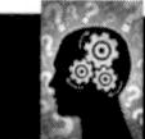

Table of contents

Schizophrenia

Depression

Phobic disorders

Table of contents

Table of contents

Anomalistic psychology

Psychological research and scientific method

SECTION 1

General topics

1 MOVING ON UP!

Essay skills

For me (RCG) one of the most noticeable differences between AS and A2 is the jump from extended writing questions at AS (12 marks) and the essay questions at A2 (25 marks). Initially my new A2 students underestimated the depth required in answering A2 questions and often their essay skills needed to be developed to enable them to make effective evaluations.

A second area my students said they found challenging was the way in which research studies were used at A2 compared to AS. They felt AS involved outlining a study in detail (APFC – refers to aim, procedure, findings, conclusions; AS key studies are often taught by splitting details of the investigation into these four areas.) then learning one or two evaluative points. However, A2 requires them to use studies as one aspect of a detailed evaluation of a concept or explanation. They found it hard to move away from producing a simple outline of a study or stating a vague evaluation point such as 'the study lacks ecological validity and so the findings may not occur in real life settings'.

The suggestions mentioned in the elaboration skills article (see page 11) and related handouts should help students develop the depth at which they evaluate and improve their ability to use research to build an effective commentary.

Vocabulary

Though students have already met a wide range of psychological terminology at AS, it may be helpful to encourage A2 students to keep a glossary specific to each topic of study. This will improve their essay writing skills and enable them to identify the requirements of each exam question. For example, the term 'clinical characteristic' = the symptoms displayed by sufferers of a specific mental illness, listed in DSM-IV as a way of diagnosing that illness. The exam could ask students to 'outline clinical characteristics of . . .' therefore they need to know the precise meaning of the term. Likewise the research methods section could ask students to identify the 'research design' or 'sampling technique'. Students need to know such terms to enable them to understand what the exam question is asking them. While more able students may quickly add new vocabulary to their psychological knowledge, less able students may benefit from having a handy reference in their notes.

Research methods

After the summer AS exams our (RCG/MWG) students undertook an individual research project, see How Science Works summer projects article on page 7 and related handout. This provided students with an opportunity to produce their own investigation into an area that interested them and built upon their understanding of the research process gained from AS study.

On returning in September we began teaching PSYA4 and developed their understanding of the research process by focussing immediately on the psychological research and scientific method section (question 7 in the exam).

Having experienced the research process themselves, we found students had a better understanding of the concepts involved in this section and were keen to plan further research projects.

It is possible the exam will ask students to devise a piece of research (for 10 or 12 marks). The more students are familiar with the various components that form a complete answer and are able to give justifications for methodological decisions, the better their attainment.

The completed student projects can be used in statistics lessons by giving students a peer's data and test value then asking them to identify the test they used and decide whether results were significant.

Projects can also be used to explain the peer review process, with students evaluating each other's work. It is possible to introduce other areas of the specification through the teaching of research methods and there are some examples of this in the handouts. This enables students to develop their understanding of research methods as well as familiarising them with research they will meet in other areas of PSYA4 and PSYA3.

If you have decided to teach PSYA3 first, students can focus on research related to the topic of study in a research activity, which will help them access later PSYA4 concepts. For example, if teaching eating behaviour, students could investigate the influence of nutritional information on food choice (see **Handouts 176–177** for a related research activity). This would introduce students to previous research into the area, providing a secure base for subsequent learning and hopefully improving retention of knowledge for the exam.

Focussing students

In the *AS Teacher Companion* a number of general handouts were included to help students organise their notes. We have included **Handout 1** this time to help students separate different sections of their folder by topic as well as remind them of relevant key terms and A2 skills.

At A2 we have continued to request students use the same content page (described on page 9) to ensure they have a complete set of notes and that work is in chronological order.

At AS each piece of work marked to exam standard showed student's mark, the grade obtained and the student's target grade. When grading student work we (RCG/MWG) based our boundaries on the UMS marks: 80% A, 70% B, 60% C, 50% D, 40% E.

It is important to say here though that these percentages are in actual fact often much higher than those required for each grade in the exam. This is because the students' raw marks (the total marks they achieve in the exam) are then converted in to uniformed and scaled marks (known as UMS). For example, in June 2009, 51 out of 72 (71%) was enough for an A grade (equal to 80 UMS marks) in PSYA2. Confused? Us too! A useful article explaining all this can be found at: http://www.qcda.gov.uk/libraryAssets/media/7183_factsheet_a_levels_gra.pdf

As the raw mark boundaries can change with each exam period (though in reality they change very little) staff would be required to find the current grade boundaries then calculate each grade based on the total of the assessment, for example, 12 marks.

Using the UMS boundaries results in higher boundaries but we feel it is much easier and reflects expectations for a high standard of work. Should you prefer to use raw mark grade boundaries, these can be found at: http://www.aqa.org.uk/over/stat.html.

The target grade that you give to your students could be based on ALIS, or an equivalent predictive grade based on GCSE scores or a grade negotiated between you and the student. Whatever method is used to form a target grade, it is important students understand it is a grade that should be aimed for and if possible surpassed, not a statement of fact.

For many students the start of A2 is a time for choosing university courses, training schemes or job opportunities. As such, many students are focussed on the grades they need in Psychology and their other A-levels. It may be helpful to record these in your mark book and remind students of their personal targets as necessary.

Reminding students

With the introduction of new topics, a deeper level of understanding and evaluation is required as well as a greater demand on application of knowledge rather than simple recall. This means that students may find the start of A2 daunting.

Students may sit their first exam, either PSYA3 or PSYA4, just over 3 months after starting A2. Therefore students need to adapt quickly to the demands of A2. Starting each topic with an extract of the specification that relates specifically to the topic of study, a guide to basic terms and essay writing reminders as well as the students' own glossary will assist this process.

2 USEFUL IDEAS FOR TEACHERS

2.1 COLLABORATIVE LEARNING

This section was included in the *AS Teacher's Companion* and is included again here due to the fact that many of the activities in Section 2 will make reference to **collaborative learning structures**.

Despite all the warnings and all the training, it did take me a long time to realise that group work in my lessons entailed the following: diligent students in the group doing most of the work, the drama students doing most of the feeding back to class, and many other students anonymous in the middle!

Whether we are using small groups for discussions, presentations, or more creative work, it can be difficult to ensure that *all* students are on task, and *all* students are learning as a result of the task set.

The trick to making sure group work is successful is by ensuring the tasks you devise are based on the following principles:

- Students are dependent on each other in order to complete the task successfully.
- Students are also individually accountable for the work they have done.
- Students participate equally.

With these aims in mind, here are some simple ideas for structuring your group work:

Random numbers – When setting a discussion question, ask the students to number themselves in their groups. Then make it clear that when you ask the group to feed back their answer, you will choose a number randomly and that person will have to feed back. This ensures that all group members are involved in the discussion and need to pay close attention to what is being said. In addition, it ensures that more gifted students will need to 'teach' their higher order arguments to the weaker students, so that they are able to feed back that idea.

Group statements – Set your students a discussion question. Individually, students should write their response to that question and elaborate their answers as fully as possible. Following this, students should share their statements with members of their group. Finally, the group should write a group statement that reflects the opinions, arguments and ideas of the group as a whole. This prevents the strongest and most confident students from taking over the activity and writing the statement without input from weaker/less confident students.

Snowballing – Ask students to individually write down three ideas in response to a question. For example, 'list three evaluation points for Bandura's Bobo doll study'. This works better if you give them a short time limit – say 2 minutes. After those 2 minutes are over, tell students to share their ideas with the person on their left and write down any new ideas they hadn't thought of – give them another 2 minutes to do this. Then repeat the process with students who sit across from them. Hopefully by the end of the activity they should have picked up different ideas from the students around them, as well as have the opportunity to share theirs.

Student dimension line – Display some sort of continuum on your PowerPoint or whiteboard. For example, Bandura's Bobo doll was ethical – strongly agree, to strongly disagree. Ask your students to stand along that line to indicate their opinion on this matter. As the teacher, you can now use this line to structure group work. For example, you could 'fold' the line so that the person who most 'strongly agrees' ends up facing the person who most 'strongly disagrees'. Students can then discuss their ideas with the students opposite them (e.g. use 'think, pair, share' – described below). Alternatively, you could use a 'systematic sample(!)' – go along the line giving students numbers and then asking them to sit in groups, ensuring that your groups are mixed by having people who 'strongly agree', 'agree', 'disagree' and 'strongly disagree' with the original statement. This idea works particularly well when the original question you set is something like: 'To what extent do you understand ethical issues?' Constructing a dimension line like this also means you can sort your students into differentiated or mixed-ability groups.

Think, pair, share – I am sure many people have heard of this technique already, it is perhaps the most well-known collaborative learning structure. Set your students some kind of discussion question and give them a few moments of thinking time to gather their thoughts individually. Then students should share their ideas with the person next to them. In the feed back phase of this activity, ask students to feed back their partner's ideas as opposed to their own. This encourages active listening and clear communication.

2.2 REVISION ACTIVITIES

Talking to my (RCG) students it seemed the favourite method employed to revise for exams was reading over notes and rewriting them using different coloured pens. It may be that some chose this method as it seemed the easiest option compared to practising exam questions, while others felt reading was enough to ensure recall. Many of them did not seem to understand they needed to actively engage with the material to improve their chances of remembering research in an exam setting. Furthermore, many students found comfort in revising work they understood and were familiar with and ignored areas they found difficult and harder to recall. However, a few students did use more engaging methods in their revision and the strategies they employed are included in this section. Working with my classes, we produced a list of revision activities. Students are set a topic to revise using one of the tasks from the list. This gives students a feeling of ownership as they can choose their mode of revision. However, once that activity had been used another must be employed for the next topic.

Activities that help organisation of material

- *Mindmaps* – Many students quickly come to enjoy the plotting of information on large A3 sheets using coloured branches and pictures to organise a topic into: theory, research for, research against, key words, synoptic links. However, some found this method posed more challenges than opportunities. They liked their maps to be balanced with all areas of the paper equally covered or disliked only recording key words or researcher names; they wanted to record chunks of text. There are many examples of mindmaps on the Internet that students could be directed to, to help learn the rules of mindmapping and experience examples of successful mapping. Mindmaps can help students build essays, as once all information is recorded, each branch can be numbered according to the order they wish to discuss each area in an exam response. A class activity could see mixed ability groups working to create a mindmap for an essay question. This is then photocopied and distributed to each group member. Individually students then use the map to answer the exam question.
- *Tables* – This method may not be suitable for all topics but could be helpful for revising AO1 summaries such as clinical characteristics of a mental illness.

  For example, in depression:

Name	Insomnia	Negative self-concept
Example	Difficulties in sleeping	Feelings of worthlessness
domain	physical	cognitive

  Tables are also useful for elaboration of AO2 points: State point, give example, provide an explanation.

- *Flow charts* – A number of the handouts found later in this book are based on the idea of flow charts, where each box is connected to the subsequent one, encouraging students to develop their discussion of a topic. This format can be used to guide revision of a theory or research study.

  Box 1 - outline of the research

  ↓

  Box 2 - identification of underlying approach

  ↓

  Box 3 - related supporting evidence

  ↓

  Box 4 - methodological issues for box 3

  ↓

  Box 5 - contradictory evidence

  ↓

  Box 6 - methodological issues for box 5

  ↓

  Box 7 - student's conclusion of box 1 research

Flow charts could be linear, travelling down the page, or circular with the final box ending next to the first box. Box headings could be altered to form a conversation: biological explanations would suggest. . . , yet, many feel this approach ignores. . . ; however, research evidence does seem to reflect a biological element. . . .

Activities that test recall of information

- *Question and answer cards* – These cards can be made in class and used by students with willing friends, relatives or guardians. Using postcard-sized pieces of paper, students write a question and answer on one side of the card. On the reverse students write one key word that will cue their recall of the answer. The students' helpful friend or relative holds the card and reads the question aloud. The students tries to provide the answer they have previously written on the card. Their only clue is the cue word they can see on the other side of the card. If needed the 'question master' could provide additional hints as well as the cue word displayed from the answer shown on the card. A number of sets could be made, one for each topics with a different coloured card being used for each one.
- *20 bullet points* – Students number 1 to 20 in the margin of their page, leaving a line between each number. They then fold their page in half lengthwise. Without using notes, students try to give 20 points about a specific topic. Once they have made 20 points or the allotted time is up students return to their notes and for each point made add additional information on the right-hand side.
- *Hear facts, list facts* – Working in small groups, one student is nominated as the speaker, the rest of the group are the listeners. The speaker identifies ten facts and reads each one out loud to the group. In a set time the listeners then record the ten facts they heard. Once completed the speaker re-reads the facts and listeners check their recall. Working as a whole group, students identify the facts that were hardest to recall and devise strategies to help recall.

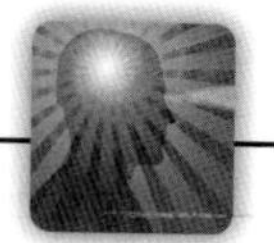

Activities that focus on exam practice

- *Create a question* – Students can produce their own exam questions to answer by following the 'rules of the game'. The 'rules of the game' are the rules used by principal examiners when setting exam questions, and students can use them too.

  NB these rules have been written in March 2010 and it is possible that they may change with successive exam seasons, so take care to check recent exam papers to see that the rules apply.

The rules of the game

1 In each question there must be 9 marks AO1 (description) and 16 marks AO2/AO3 (evaluation).
2 All questions must use the wording of the specification.
3 Description and evaluation are signalled by the use of injunctions:
AO1 injunctions – outline, describe, explain
AO2/AO3 injunctions – evaluate, consider, explain
AO1/AO2/AO3 injunctions – discuss, explain
4 Numbers may be used in questions. For example: 'Discuss **two** theories of xxx', or 'Describe **one or more** studies relating to …'. Numbers are used to help candidates focus on what is required.
If a word is in the plural, this means two or more. For example, 'Describe theories of xxx' means you are required to present at least two theories.
5 Questions may be parted, as shown below. In all examples the AO1 marks still add up to 9 and the AO2/AO3 marks add up to 16:

★ Part (a) might be all AO1 and part (b) all AO2
(a) Describe **two** theories of xxx. (*9 marks*)
(b) Evaluate **one** of the theories you described in part (a). (*16 marks*)

★ Part (a) might be all AO1 and part (b) is a mixture of AO1 and AO2/AO3. In such cases the mark division for the mixture is shown:
(a) Outline clinical characteristics of xxx. (*5 marks*)
(b) Discuss **two** biological explanations of xxx. (*4 marks + 16 marks*)

★ Parts (a) and (b) might both be a mixture of AO1 and AO2/AO3
(a) Explain the use of xxx. (*4 marks + 6 marks*)
(b) Outline and evaluate biological therapies of xxx. (*5 marks + 10 marks*)

★ There may be three parts to a question
(a) Explain the use of xxx. (*7 marks*)
(b) Outline and evaluate **one** biological explanation of xxx. (*4 marks + 4 marks*)
(c) Discuss **one** biological treatment for xxx. (*5 marks + 5 marks*)

- *Team work* – Once students have created their own questions the whole class can be set one question or, working in small groups, they can choose one question to answer. As a class (or small group), students create a list or mindmap of research that should be included in the answer. This acts as a guide during the team work task. Students write their name at the top of their paper and begin writing the essay. After a set time, maybe ten minutes, students rotate their essays and begin where the previous author finished, writing their name in the margin at the point they began writing. They should continue following the mindmap. Students should be advised to read what has already been written to avoid repeating points that have already been made. At the end of the task students should receive their original essay with a range of students' contributions.
- *Breaking down the response to the question* – Using the exam questions created, each student chooses one question and then writes a number of sub-tasks that would be required when answering the exam question. For example:

Outline and evaluate one or more explanations of depression. (25 marks)

Q1 = How would the biological approach explain depression?
Q2 = Give one piece of research that could be seen to support the role of neurotransmitters in depression.
Q3 = What factors may biological explanations ignore in their analysis of depression's cause?
Q4 = Is the explanation an example of the influence of nature or nurture on depression?

The sub-tasks could then be given to other students as a challenge to form a complete exam response.

2.3 ICT TRICKS AND TIPS

This is another section that we included in the AS version of this book. Several of the activities in Section 2 of this book (Lesson notes) refer to the ideas suggested here.

Rolling shows **–** These can be created using PowerPoint and essentially consist of a slideshow of images relevant to the lesson. They are very useful to use at the start of lessons when students are coming into the room. When played with relevant music, they create a good atmosphere and let students know that from the moment they walk into your classroom, they are in a learning environment.

Find a series of images related to the content of the lesson. Insert an image onto each slide of your PowerPoint. You could also insert questions for the students to read. When you have finished inserting your images/text, select <Slide Show> from the top menu bar, and then <Slide Transition> from the drop down menu – this should open a menu to the right-hand side of the window. Here you can select which animation you would like to be used to change from one slide to another – I find that 'fade' looks the most professional. Untick the option <On mouse click> and instead select the tick box <Automatically after> and then set the transition to every 5 seconds (or other). Make sure you click the <Apply to all slides> box beneath this. Lastly, select <Slide Show> once again from the top menu bar, and then <Set up show> from the drop down menu. Clicking the tick box for <Loop

continuously until 'ESC'> will ensure that your slideshow will cycle through the images until you want it to stop.

***Randomiser* –** This is another technique that can be used with PowerPoint and enables you to select students randomly – for example, to answer a question, or to sort them into groups. Enter your student's names into PowerPoint, with one name on each slide. When you have finished this, select <Slide Show> from the top menu bar, and then <Slide Transition> from the drop down menu – this should open a menu to the right-hand side of the window. Ensure that <No Transition> is selected at the top of this menu. Then, untick the option <On mouse click> and instead select the tick box <Automatically after> and then set the transition to every 0 seconds – this is important to make the process random as you will see later. Make sure you click the <Apply to all slides> box beneath this. Lastly, select <Slide Show> once again from the top menu bar, and then <Set up show> from the drop down menu. Clicking the tick box for <Loop continuously until 'ESC'> will ensure that your slideshow will cycle through the names until you want it to stop. To stop the slideshow on one of the names simply press 'S' on your keyboard, this will stop the slideshow. To select another name, simply press 'S' again to restart the slideshow.

Although I have suggested doing this with names, it can also be used to 'randomise' questions, key terms and even essay titles.

***Templates* –** Another PowerPoint idea. PowerPoints can often look dull and generic, and it is difficult to make them look more exciting without sacrificing your work–life balance! A simple way around this is to design one 'fancy' template that you use for all future PowerPoints. Spend some time designing a 'title' slide – for example, I include a lesson title, an image, an aim, and key words on mine. Then design a 'main body' slide with a title, text font, and background that are easy on the eye. Then save this design as a template – select <File> from the top menu bar, then <Save as…> from the drop down menu. In the <Save as type:> drop down box select <Design template>. When you open this design template you will find that all your design features remain, and you can just amend the text, titles, etc., for that lesson. It is impossible to save over the template meaning it can never be lost. I have a design template for each topic (i.e. social, developmental, etc.) and have also created a similar worksheet template in Word so that there is consistency across topics for my students. Using templates ensures you only put the hard design work in once, but are still able to make your presentations a little less dull!

***Bluetooth mouse* –** This idea requires a little investment but is extremely effective if you do not have an interactive whiteboard. Consider purchasing a Bluetooth mouse (search in Amazon, you can get them for around £30 at time of writing). They are essentially a wireless mouse but the signal is much more powerful. This means they can be used at the back of the classroom by your students! You can set up matching games, etc., in Publisher, Word or other software – and your students can play them from their seats! I like to call it the 'Lazy man's interactive whiteboard'. If your laptop or computer is slightly older, you may also need to purchase a 'Bluetooth dongle', perhaps ask your IT technicians about these.

***Vdownloader* –** Is YouTube blocked at your school? Want to download a YouTube video and save to your laptop for future use? Vdownloader is a piece of free software that downloads YouTube videos and converts them into a format that can be played using Windows Media Player. All you need to do is simply search for 'Vdownloader' on Google, and download the file from any number of websites. For example, www.vdownloader.es. Once downloaded and installed onto your computer, all you have to do is copy and paste the address of the video into the software, and the rest is done for you! There are a number of other websites that do this too, e.g. 'zamzar' and 'keepvid'.

***Windows Movie Maker* –** This is a free programme that is installed on every Windows machine (unless the over zealous IT technicians at your school have removed it!). It is an extremely easy programme to use and allows you to edit videos and insert text on top. This is useful to edit videos you have downloaded (e.g. using Vdownloader) or videos you have recorded on a digital camera (e.g. a re-enacted student version of Milgram!). There are plenty of tutorials for using this programme on the Internet, simply search for 'Windows Movie Maker tutorial' on the Internet. Alternatively, I wrote a beginners guide for a staff INSET last year, which I can email on request. Feel free to email bigmacca23@googlemail.com and I will do my best to send you a copy.

***MonkeyJam* –** This free software is also relatively easy to use and allows students to make animations, with drawings, themselves, or plasticine. The process takes a while but is ideal for extended projects or after school clubs. Again, there are many tutorials available on the internet. A video camera or good webcam is required.

***Crosswords, word searches, and cartoon strips* –** It is possible to find loads of websites that will create free resources for you. All you need to do is find the right combination of words to search Google with. For example, try 'create your own crossword', 'play millionaire', etc.

3 FOCUSSING ON THE NEW A2 SPECIFICATION

3.1a HOW SCIENCE WORKS – SUMMER PROJECTS

After students had completed their AS exams in May, we (RCG, MWG) decided to run an individual research project until students left in July (a mark scheme for you to use/adapt is included on **Handouts 2-4**). This was mentioned briefly in the previous *AS Teacher's Companion* along with other options for the remainder of Year 12 before the summer holidays. Students completed each section of the project in draft, collected data and analysed findings during lesson time then used the summer holiday to produce the final version of their investigation, if they decided to remain on the course. Some students who did not stay on to A2 still wanted their projects marked, and discussed the skills they had employed in their UCAS personal statement.

Should your school/college offer students the opportunity to undertake the extended project qualification, their summer project could be submitted for accreditation (the required taught element is the AS research methods content).

We decided to run the project as a means to strengthen students' individual research skills, allow them to produce a piece of work that relates to an area of their particular interest and develop their appreciation of the psychological research process.

- By completing a review of previous studies and theories, students are developing their research skills and encouraged to apply the information found to a specific topic.
- In devising their own research method, students are relying upon their ability to work independently. They have to make decisions about samples, methodology and analyse their own data. The summer projects handouts can be used as a guide to help students build each section of the project and act as a checklist to ensure all areas are included.
- The area of focus can be related to an area of interest for the student. Those who do not wish to continue to A2 may choose to study an aspect of Unit 1 or 2 to assist any re-sit revision that may be needed. Students who are applying for degree courses in other areas could select a topic that would strengthen their UCAS application. For example, a student interested in journalism may wish to study the impact of advertising slogans on recall of products. Students considering studying at A2 may wish to focus on an area they will meet in PSYA3 or PSYA4.
- The results section will help students understand the use of statistics to assess the probability of data being a result of the independent variable (if conducting an experiment), rather than chance. It will also introduce students to the notion of choosing a suitable test, an aspect of the PSYA4, AQA ('A') scientific method section.
- By producing a discussion of their project, students are developing their evaluation skills through identification of methodological issues and application of findings to previous research.

What topics could be investigated?

Our students were allowed to choose any topic they wished, even if it did not relate to the specification, so long as the sample would not involve under 16 year olds (to remove issue of parental consent) and the subject matter and procedure would not raise any ethical concerns. For example, a few students had to be discouraged from investigating participants' attitude to eating and their own body size. In these cases it was suggested students remove the focus from perception of self onto society's perception of ideal body size.

In keeping with the research process, students were expected to begin by reviewing past research, from which they then developed a hypothesis. Many students will want to start with a hypothesis and then look for relevant research studies. To discourage this, students could be asked to select a broad area of interest and outline three relevant studies or theories. Working in small groups, students could present their findings and the group discuss possible research ideas from which one is selected and a hypothesis is developed.

Before selecting a topic, students were asked to research their area of interest to ensure they would be able to gather enough research for their introduction section. Immediately students wanted to use the Internet, despite a well-stocked bookshelf in each psychology room. Ground rules were set so students used textbooks and articles first before turning to the Internet to access university sites to ensure credibility of research (the British Psychological Society site proved very useful).

A selection of topics our students investigated were:

- Gender differences in perception of ideal female body size.
- Whether a difference in score on an aggression questionnaire can be seen between those who played a combat computer game and those who played a puzzle game.
- Investigation into the relationship between fear of an animal and how disgusting that animal is deemed to be.
- Is recall of words easier then recall of images?
- Differences in view of ideal female figure between students who previously viewed celebrity magazines and students who viewed non-celebrity magazines.
- Whether the gender of a dreamer can be correctly identified by reading a report of their dream.
- Do pet owners score lower on a stress questionnaire than those without a pet?

Students found it helpful to see examples of old coursework to help understand what was expected of them.

What does the project entail?

Many of you will have experience of the old AQA ('A') coursework upon which this project is based. However, newly qualified staff or those new to teaching Psychology may not have had this experience.

- Abstract

The first section of the project. A 150-word paragraph written at the end of the project that acts as a summary of the investigation. Students briefly mention the aim,

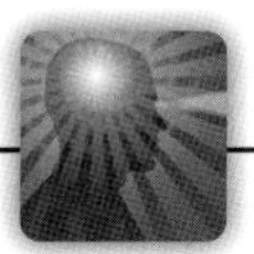

hypothesis, sample and method, findings (including test value and critical value), stating significance and hypothesis accepted, conclusion reached. There should be an emphasis on a concise and coherent writing style.

- Introduction

We set our students a target of three research items (theories or studies), though some students may wish to include more. This section forms a funnel; moving from a general introduction to a specific aim.

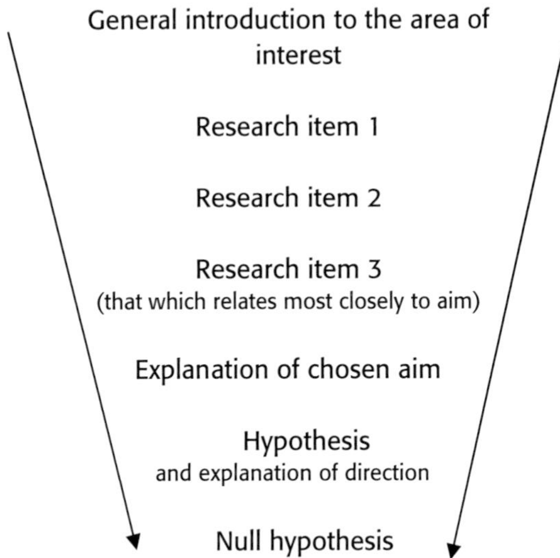

- Method

In order to plan their method, students may wish to make use of the study deconstruction sheet on **Handouts 5 and 6**.

When writing the method, students could split this into mini sections, each with a sub-heading, to help with the organisation of information.

Design – Explain the research design used. Clearly state the IV and DV or other variables. Identify whether the research is looking for a difference or a relationship between variables.

Participants – Explain the sample method used and reasons for choice. Record the amount of participants and how they were assigned to groups, if necessary. Note any relevant demographics such as age, gender.

Material and apparatus – Any materials used should be listed here and copies placed in an appendix. For example, standardised instructions, debrief, questionnaires, word lists, record sheets. If film clips used, time or scene should be listed.

Procedure – The procedure of the investigation should be recorded in step-by-step detail to allow full replication. Time limits for each task should be noted. Ethical considerations should be seen here.

- Results

Once data is collected, students should record their findings in a suitable, fully labelled graph. They then need to decide upon the correct statistics test to analyse their findings.

Looking for a difference	***Unrelated data***	***Related data***
Nominal level	Chi squared	
Ordinal level	Mann Whitney	Wilcoxon *T* test

Looking for a relationship	
Ordinal level	Spearman's Rho

Students should record the test value achieved, the critical value, Probability level, N or degrees of freedom and the hypothesis accepted. Any trends or anomalies in the data could also be explained.

- Discussion

This section is divided into four sub-sections. Although this should be written as continuous prose, weaker students may find the use of subheadings helpful. Each section asks students to reflect on their investigation. **Handout 3** explains what needs to be included in each of the four areas: review of findings, relating findings to background research, limitations and modifications, implications and future research.

- References, project style, student input and design decisions

All research mentioned should be referenced correctly following BPS guidelines. Informal spellings such as 'didn't', 'couldn't' should be discouraged. Student input refers to the amount of help, guidance (or nagging!) needed from the teacher. Finally design decision refers to the planning of a successful investigation that tests the IV and minimises extraneous variables.

3.1b HOW SCIENCE WORKS – STUDY DECONSTRUCTION

Sometimes the mistake we make is to teach the content and forget to provide opportunities for our students to apply their knowledge.

For example, you may spend weeks helping students learn different statistical tests, sampling techniques and experimental designs, but place less emphasis on deconstructing actual scientific studies – and 'how they work'.

Handouts 5 and 6 are designed to be used with almost any psychological study that you are looking at in class. They require students to research and 'deconstruct' the studies into 'how they work'. It may also be very useful for students to use these sheets when planning their own study – particularly the summer project described in the previous section.

You may wish to use these in particular when teaching PSYA4. The section C element of the exam paper requires students to use very similar skills.

3.2 ASSESSMENT OBJECTIVES

The essays are marked using three assessment objectives:

* AO1 Knowledge and understanding of psychology.
* AO2 Analysis and evaluation of knowledge and processes.
* AO3 How science works in psychology.

AO1 is assessed using one set of marking criteria (see page vii of the *A2 Complete Companion*).

AO2 and AO3 are marked together using a second set of marking criteria (see page vii of the *A2 Complete Companion*).

IMPORTANT NOTE The mark scheme states that, in each A2 question, there are 12 AO2 marks and 4 AO3 marks but these AO3 marks are not assessed separately *unless* there is a part of a question that specifically relates to research methods. It is assumed that good evaluation will contain some reference to 'how science works' (AO3).

The mark schemes do not make any reference to how much 'how science works' must be included but they do suggest that candidates who fail to make more than superficial reference to issues, debates and approaches in their answer may not receive marks above 'basic' (i.e. 8 out of 16 AO2/AO3 marks).

3.3 ASSESSMENTS FOR LEARNING

Where am I? Where do I want to be? How can I get there?

These three questions seem to underlie the reason teachers seem to spend a large part of their free time hunched over reams of lined paper with a white knuckle grip on a red pen. Of course students need to experience exam questions as a form of assessment but how do we help them track their progress and remind them of their personal targets. The following topic is designed to provide you with a few ideas.

You might also like to read pp. 4–5 of AS *Teacher's Companion*, which also details a different variety of ideas of AFL (assessment for learning).

- *Smileys* – At the start of each lesson we ask students to write down the title and the aim of the lesson on an index page – see **Handouts 7 and 8**. At the end of the lesson students then have to indicate to what extent they feel they achieved that aim – with a happy face, a neutral face, or an unhappy face. The benefit of these index pages is that they also help students, particularly the lads, to organise their folders.

- *Progress checkers* – We have recently changed the way we record and organise students' assignments. It used to be that they handed them in, we handed them back with feedback, and then 50% of the students lost the essays and/or feedback! This obviously defeats the purpose of feedback, which is to provide students with ideas to improve their work skills. They cannot do this if they no longer have the advice. So, now we keep all their assignments and assessments in their own personal wallets (which we keep). At the front of those wallets is a sheet similar to **Handouts 9 and 10**. Here the students can reflect on their targets and progress more systematically (and with reference to their target grade). Obviously students can request their wallet at any time and you may wish to show them to students before setting an assignment so they can remind themselves of their targets. We also give the wallets back to the students some time before exams so they can revise from their work.
- *Self-evaluation form* – Unfortunately, students often do not check through their essays! We make students hand in their essays with a self-assessment form – see **Handout 11**. This forces students to consider the success of their essay by asking them to rate certain criteria between 1 (strongly agree) and 3 (disagree). This handout could also be used for peer assessment. We included a very similar sheet in the AS version of this book but have updated it to reflect A2 skills and mark schemes.

- *Teacher feedback form* – This is another handout we have updated from the AS version to reflect A2 mark schemes. We use **Handout 12** by highlighting the statements we feel most closely reflect their work and justify this with brief notes, and ideas for improvement.

- *Hitting targets* – Alternatively you might like to use the feedback form included on **Handout 13**. Again, we would use this by highlighting the targets we feel the students had achieved in their essays. The nice thing about this sheet is that it gives students an idea about how you arrived at their actual grade and also shows them that they could have achieved a grade A skill in one area, but are only achieving grade D in another. The different shaped targets try to demarcate the AO1 and AO2/AO3 skills required in order to do well in essay assessments. In the past we have given back these forms and then given students 20 minutes to achieve a couple more targets by adding to or amending their work. This is 'real' assessment for learning because the feedback you provide is then used to make tangible improvements and 'there-and-then' development. We have found this to be extremely effective – more so than just expecting students to improve in the next essay.

4 IMPROVING STUDENT SKILLS

4.1 ELABORATION SKILLS

One of the most noticeable differences between AS and A2 for our students (RCG/MWG) is the way in which research evidence is used. Students found the move from APFC key study format (aims, procedure, findings, conclusion) to briefer summaries in the context of evaluation challenging. By building on the PEE structure to form methodological evaluations (see *AS Teacher's Companion*, which contains handouts that introduce PEE structure to help students develop their evaluative comments), it is hoped students can apply this format to produce evaluations based upon research evidence. When faced with a psychology essay, many students panic and basic English skills seem forgotten in a flurry of lesson notes and numerous crossings out. Paragraphs are omitted and in a few cases even full stops seem a distant memory! Often the result is a reasonable outline of a relevant explanation or concept followed by a list of underdeveloped evaluation points that only vaguely relate to the essay title.

Within the *AS Teacher's Companion* a number of handouts can be found that focus on creating effective evaluations and this theme is continued into A2. The basic structure of each evaluative comment is derived from a technique used in English teaching to help students develop the content of paragraphs in their written work.

P = State the **point** of the paragraph.
E = Give the **evidence** relating to the point.
E = **Expand**: how does evidence relate to the point?

Handout 14 is provided for you to photocopy and give to your students as a guide.

Many of the activities you will find in this *Teacher's Companion* target students' essay writing, in particular the notion of producing one complete paragraph per comment to encourage the expansion of one point rather than creating a block of writing that simply lists criticisms. From experience it seems students quickly come to understand the idea of PEE and adopt this style in their essays. However, while P (point) and E (evidence) are done well, the final part of the paragraph (E = expansion) is a harder skill to acquire and for many remains a single statement unless they have teacher support and modelling of how to construct comments in lesson time. Students may find **Handout 14** useful to help them begin the point and expansion sections that sandwich the evidence. Working as a class to model one or two paragraphs will guide students and develop their confidence in attempting their own expansions. The following PEE examples are offered to illustrate the different methods of expanding upon a piece of research evidence.

Depression

Point	The Biological approach in explaining depression at a chemical level seems to have some support.
Evidence	McNeal and Cimbolic's (1986) findings support a link between low synaptic serotonin levels and depression. The cerebrospinal fluid of depressed and especially suicidal patients contained reduced amounts of a major serotonin by-product.
Expansion	This finding can be seen as an indication of reduced levels of serotonin in the brain itself.
Further expansion	However, McNeal and Cimbolic's data is correlational, meaning we are unsure whether low levels of serotonin by-product are the cause of a depressed mood or simply another symptom.
Further expansion	For example, it could be the presence of faulty thinking or inaccurate information processing that lead to a reduction in serotonin and therefore less by-product can be found.

Biorhythms

Point	Free running cycle studies seem to suggest we have an internal pacemaker that expands to about 25 hours in the absence of zeitgebers.
Evidence	Aschoff and Wever (1976) placed participants in an underground World War II bunker in the absence of environmental and social time cues. They found most people displayed circadian rhythms between 24 and 25 hours, though some rhythms were as long as 29 hours.
Expansion	Initially this seems strong evidence for an internal mechanism. However, subsequent research suggests artificial light can act as a zeitgeber. Czeisler *et al.* (1999) found it is possible to alter circadian rhythms down to 22 hours and up to 28 hours simply by using dim artificial lighting.
Further expansion	However, the fact a number of researchers have found 22 hours seems the lowest point they can reduce the circadian rhythm to suggests that there is an internal mechanism in action that can only be altered within a two- or three-hour time frame.

The depth to which students develop their comments may be related to ability and so students could be challenged to provide one, two or three expansion points.

Expansion points are an important opportunity for students to comment on issues, debates and approaches as well as allowing methodological comments to be made.

Activities to encourage PEE

- Question cobwebs (e.g. **Handout 122**). Students could be encouraged to make their own cobwebs for another topic once this task is completed.
- Cut and paste activities (e.g. **Handout 120**) in which students choose one 'rudimentary' comment to pair with a 'basic' comment then develop further by adding a 'reasonable' and final 'effective' comment. Again once students are used to the process, they could develop their own cut and paste activity or use a table format:

Rudimentary	Basic	Reasonable	Effective

- Once an essay has been completed, students could be asked to label each paragraph 'P', 'Ev', 'Ex' to highlight to themselves (and the teacher) that they have used PEE and attempted to expand each comment made.
- A development of the above task would be to ask students to swap their work with a peer for them to annotate each paragraph; P, Ev, Ex. More able students could be paired with a peer who finds the work more challenging and asked to produce an example PEE for their partner or to pick one paragraph and complete the expansion.
- Whole class modelling is a useful activity to complete before asking students to work individually at the PEE handouts in this book.
- Ladders (e.g. **Handout 139**) may provide a visual structure to help students understand how to really develop their comments:

Therefore ...

If internal validity can be questioned then...

However, a confounding variable may be...

The research evidence implies...

Questions students could ask to encourage expansion:

- How does the research study provide support for the explanation/concept/therapy?
- Why do the research findings cast doubt on the explanation/concept/therapy?
- Can the research be applied to the general population (population validity) or was the sample limited?
- Could anomalies have affected the data due to a small sample size?
- Were there any methodological issues that could impact on the internal validity of the study? For example:
  - Issues with measurement tool used?
  - Risk of demand characteristics?
  - Risk of social desirability?
  - Order effects present if repeated measures design is employed?
- Could the findings be explained differently?
- Can cause and effect be assured or have researchers only investigated the possibility of a relationship?
- If the study was not longitudinal, can we be sure behaviour will continue in the same form as shown in the investigation?
- Does the method ignore qualitative aspects of behaviour? For example, sufferers' views of their symptoms or drug therapy.
- Are there ethical issues surrounding the research; either methodology or socially sensitive topics?
- If the research is reductionist, what other factors that may contribute to the behaviour in question have been overlooked?
- Does the research take a nature/nurture or interactionist approach? What are the (dis)advantages of taking this view?
- Has the research ignored the role of free will? Why might this be important?
- How can research be used to improve daily life?
- Would you be able to apply the findings to other cultures?
- If only male participants were used, can the conclusions drawn also explain female behaviour?
- Could the research be specific to the era in which it was conducted and so unable to translate to today's society?

References

Aschoff , J. & Wever, R. (1976). Human circadian rhythms: a multiple oscillatory system. *Federation proceedings*, 35, 2326–32.

Czeisler, C.A. *et al.* (1999). Stability, precision and near 24-hour period of the human circadian pacemaker. *Science*, 284, 2177–81.

McNeal, C.T. & Cimbolic, P. (1986). Antidepressants and biochemical theories of depression. *Psychological Bulletin*, 99, 361–74.

4.2 NOTE TAKING

It often concerns me (MWG) that in order to achieve the best exam results, we end up 'spoon-feeding' our students. For example, cutting out the relevant parts of the textbook you feel the students need to learn and just photocopying *that* part – and leaving out the rest. We do this because we know that textbooks always contain much more information than they actually need.

Of course, by doing this we are 'note-taking', summarising information and writing synopses for our students and denying them the chance to develop this skill themselves.

I think we do this most of the time because we know we will do a better job! But, we have to remember that an overwhelming majority of A2 students will be going to university. When the lecturer gives them a reading list, they will not know what the hell to do with it! In my experience, the reading list for one lecture would be more books than I'd ever read in my life. So, if we do everything for our students, they will inevitably suffer in the long run. (By the way, how many of your students can use the index and glossary in a textbook?)

You might consider using some of the following activities with your students, which aim to help them develop 'selectivity' in their note-making:

- *Filtration* – In this activity you give your students a piece of text. This could be the description of a theory, study or newspaper article that you have found that is relevant to the topic you are studying. On **Handout 15**, students write down what they think are the key points, words, studies, etc. You could give them a limit, for example 10 key words. They then compare with the class or small group and arrive at a decision about which are the most important. Here, for example, you could ask them to further 'filter' their key words from 10 to 5. Following this, students then write a summary of the article at the bottom of the sheet.
- *Treasure or Trash?* – **Handout 16** is a similar exercise to above but more active and kinaesthetic. Give students a text relevant to the lesson. Then students have to decide which of the text to 'treasure' (i.e. keep) and which of the text to 'trash' (i.e. discard). They could do this either by simply writing fragments of the text onto the handout or actually cutting the text up and sticking the various fragments into the appropriate areas on the handout.
- *'Brief summaries'* – This is a superb idea from Jo Gotts at www.psychexchange.co.uk (used with her kind permission). Essentially the activity involves students summarising information and as such, choosing the most important to retain in the synopsis. **Handout 17** provides three briefs in which to write 'brief summaries' (Do you see what Jo did?) of whatever text you give them. The briefs are intentionally small so that the students only provide the most important details. We have described on page 37 how this activity might be used in a specific lesson.

4.3 USING ARTICLES TO STRETCH G & T STUDENTS

A simple extension task to give your gifted and talented students is to give them an extra article to read that is related to the lesson content. However, even the gifted and talented students can find it difficult to structure their reading, and draw relevant links.

We use a standard extension proforma (**Handout 18**) that students can use with any extra reading you give them, which asks them to deconstruct the article, assess the relevance to the lesson's learning objectives, and attempt to use a higher order thinking skill.

Again, this also helps students prepare for life at university, where independent reading is the essential ingredient for degree-level success.

4.4 ESSAY SKILLS

At A2 students will really need to hone their essay skills in order to succeed. On the old AS specification students would have been more used to extended writing; however, the new AS specification has changed in style and means that in our opinion, the step up to A2 essays is harder. In addition, students need twice as much AO2 as AO1 and therefore really need to develop these skills.

Here are a couple of ideas to help your students come to terms with A2-standard writing.

- *Golden nuggets* – For top AO2 marks candidates must have demonstrated coherent elaboration. For example, it is not enough to say that a study lacked ecological validity but the candidate must give evidence to support this claim and should also say why this is a criticism. Indeed, this links in to the idea of a PEE structure to commentary. The exact length and form of an elaboration statement depends on the criticism/ comment but you can be sure that simple one-liners have not been elaborated. **Handout 19** provides students with some 'golden nuggets' that can be used in a whole range of essays as long as they remember to make them directly relevant to the essay in hand.
- *Useful phrases and connectives* – For me (MWG), a good essay can be transformed into an excellent essay sometimes simply through good use of connectives. By this I mean that sometimes a student has included some excellent analysis and commentary, but somehow the essay doesn't flow or fit together and this makes the thinking behind the essay seem disjointed. I always say to my students, I should know within 0.5 seconds of reading each paragraph where they are going. For example, if they simply start the paragraph with 'However', I know they are going to provide an argument against the previous paragraph(s). If they start the paragraph with 'These findings imply', I know that they are going to write some sort of conclusion. This helps orientate the reader to the narrative of the essay and helps the essay contain a 'clear line of argument' (required for the higher grades in A2 essays). **Handout 20** provides students with some connectives and phrases that could help them do this.

References

Crowne, D. P. & Marlowe, D. (1960). A new scale of social desirability independent of psychopathology. *Journal of Consulting Psychology,* 24, 349–54.

Orne, M. T. (1962). On the social psychology of the psychological experiment: With particular reference to demand characteristics and their implications. *American Psychologist*, 17, 776–83.

Rosenthal, R. (1966). *Experimenter effects in behavioral research.* New York, Appleton-Century-Crofts.

Rosenthal, R. & Fode, K. L. (1963). Psychology of the scientist: V. Three experiments in experimenter bias. *Psychological Reports,* 12, 491–511.

Roethlisberger, F. J. & Dickson, W. J. (1939). *Management and the Worker.* Cambridge, Mass: Harvard University Press.

Sears, D. O. (1986). College Sophomores in the laboratory: Influences of a narrow data base on social psychology's view of human nature. *Journal of Personality and Social Psychology,* 51(3), 515–30.

5 BEING SYNOPTIC

In order to obtain good marks for evaluation (AO2/AO3) students must make reference to issues, debates and/or approaches in their evaluations. These can be referred to as 'IDA' or 'synopticity' (providing a general view of the whole of psychology).

IT IS VERY IMPORTANT to include effective reference to issues, debates and approaches BUT students must not overdo this. It is only one component of the AO2/AO3 mark and the main focus must be on the essay topic.

In an essay that contains 16 marks for evaluation, a student will be restricted to 8 marks or less if the synoptic content of their answer is just superficial. To gain more marks the synoptic material must be effective:

Examples of superficial reference
This is an example of a determinist approach.
Nature-nurture is an issue in this kind of research.

Examples of effective use
This is an example of a determinist approach because the biochemical explanation suggests that we have no control over our own behaviour, it is determined by our brain biochemistry. One difficulty with this approach is that people who are depressed think that taking a drug will magically change this because depression is determined by biochemicals.

In the remainder of this section you will hopefully find some ideas and activities you could use for 'recurring themes' such as the evolutionary approach, validity and psychological debates.

5.1 THE EVOLUTIONARY APPROACH

As a result of writing this *A2 Teacher's Companion*, it seems clear to us that the evolutionary approach is much more prominent. Almost every section contains an explanation of behaviour rooted in this approach.

Although the evolutionary approach seems quite straightforward, many students do struggle to get their heads around the different terms and how they relate to modern-day behaviour.

Handout 21 describes a really effective student activity designed to help them understand concepts such as the EEA (environment of evolutionary adaptation), genome lag, natural selection, etc. It requires them to explain how one of the 'monsters' evolved to fit in with the current environment, and why some of its features might be maladaptive to the current environment.

When using this activity you should emphasise how environments can change overnight, but how evolution is an extremely slow process.

The activity can be used as a building block to understanding specific explanations of human behaviour.

When evaluating evolutionary explanations of human behaviour, certain strengths and weaknesses are common to many theories rooted in this paradigm.

Handout 22 describes some 'classic' AO2 points that students can customise depending on the particular theory they are evaluating.

Reference

Davison, G. & Neale, J. (1990). *Abnormal Psychology* (5th edn). New York: Wiley.

5.2 VALIDITY

I've (MWG) never quite been able to work out why, but the following activity, which I use with students to help them learn about the different types of validity, has consistently improved their understanding, which has always been reflected in the quality of their study evaluations.

It is actually a very simple activity. **Handout 23** contains a simple validity diagram that outlines the main types and their definitions. I usually display this diagram on a PowerPoint and outline it slowly to the students. I then ask them to repeat the diagram from memory, Over a series of 3 to 4 lessons, I keep making them do this until they do it perfectly.

With a few exceptions, students report that this helps them to organise in their minds the types of validity and is a useful 'visual' reference point when asked to evaluate studies on their own as they can simply work through the diagram in their heads.

5.3 PSYCHOLOGICAL DEBATES

Handout 24 is an activity related to the free will vs. determinism debate.

The handout actually outlines quite a difficult task and students may not get it without heavy prompting, but it should at least facilitate discussion.

One way to get a grip on it might be something like the following diagram. Once the positions have been laid out, different psychological approaches can be mapped on to the diagram and the implications of each position discussed.

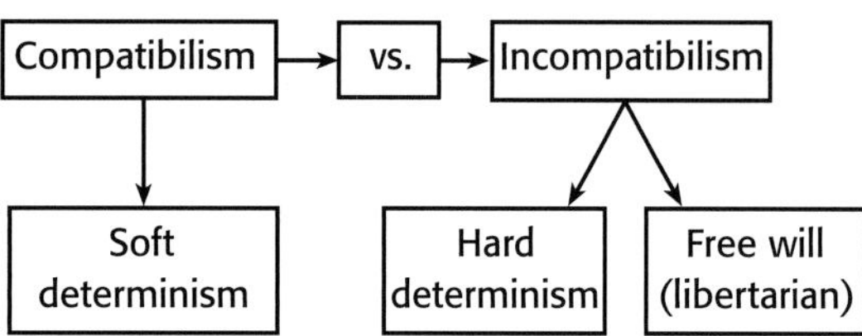

Handout 25, on the other hand, is an exercise that can help students write paragraphs on reductionism for theories that you and they feel are appropriate. In particular, it can be used as an AO2 discussion topic.

Some practice examples are provided at the bottom of the sheet.

SECTION 2

Lesson notes

YOUR LESSON NOTES SECTION

This section has been written with some specific objectives in mind:

1) To provide teachers with plenty of ideas for teaching the A2 AQA 'A' Psychology specification.

2) To provide teachers of psychology with a 'toolkit' that helps to alleviate workload, specifically in the planning and creation of resources.

3) To assist teachers in identifying opportunities for differentiation in their lessons and catering for different 'learning styles'.

'PLENTY OF IDEAS'

Within this section we hope you will find plenty of ideas that you might consider using when delivering the A2 AQA 'A' Psychology specification.

We have tried to structure this section in a way that mirrors the AQA 'A' course so that you can easily identify how the ideas and resources fit in with your delivery of the specification. As a result, those of you who have purchased *The A2 Complete Companion* will find that our structure is borrowed from the chapter breakdown used in the textbook.

The lesson notes include ideas for starters, plenaries, main activities and study replications. We have decided not to include detailed lesson plans, as there is rarely a one-size-fits-all approach to teaching – it is often more effective for teachers to adapt ideas to suit their own teaching techniques.

'CREATION OF RESOURCES'

For many of the ideas and activities included in this section, there are accompanying photocopiable handouts that can be used in lessons.

We hope that these handouts will ease some of your workload and bring you closer to that elusive work–life balance!

These handouts can be found on pages 91–274. They are numbered so that you can find them easily.

DIFFERENTIATION

Undoubtedly one of the most challenging responsibilities for a teacher is planning opportunities for differentiation in lessons. In our own experience of the classroom, we have taught students predicted A's, alongside other students who are predicted U's (yes I know, hard to believe isn't it?).

Much of the time we are differentiating without even thinking about it. However, if you are anything like us, you may start to panic when asked to identify 'strategies for differentiation' on lesson plans! To a certain extent, the skill is in identifying what we are already doing, as opposed to reinventing the wheel.

Consequently, we have tried to identify how the lesson ideas in this section may provide opportunities to stretch the gifted and talented, while supporting the weaker students, so that you can highlight these on your lesson plans and schemes of work.

The Lesson notes section will use the following key:

H **Higher order thinking skills**
One of the best ways to stretch gifted and talented students is to provide opportunities to use the higher order thinking skills. We often provide these opportunities without specific thought for differentiation. Indeed, the new A2 AQA 'A' specification requires us to consider higher skills such as evaluation, analysis, application and hypothesising.

O **Outcome**
This is where students undertake the same activity but the outcome is different according to their ability. The task is designed in such a way that students can complete that task at their own level of understanding.

R **Resource**
Handouts and resources can be designed to give weaker students writing frames to help them structure their work, without stifling the output from more gifted students.

G **Grouping**
Many tasks outlined in this pack lend themselves to mixed ability group work and the use of collaborative learning techniques (see page 3). Using mixed ability groups in a collaborative fashion allows gifted students to consolidate and 'teach' their understanding, while weaker students learn topics in a more student-friendly way from their peers.

T **Task**
This is when students are set specific tasks according to their ability. The difficulty, level of guidance, or structure can all be manipulated to achieve differentiated materials. This might also include the creation of extension tasks/worksheets to stretch the most gifted students.

S **Support**
Lengthier activities give teachers the time to target students identified as needing extra support. This could be, for example, because the task involves extended writing, or the use of mathematical concepts. These individuals can be highlighted on lesson plans alongside information from IEPs (Individual Education Plans), which may provide strategies for supporting a student with dyslexia.

'LEARNING STYLES'

One thing I (MWG) have noticed about education is how training providers often present ideas that have been 'scientifically proven'. Of course in reality, they rarely present that 'evidence', but the majority of people seem to be convinced by the mere mention of these words.

Did you know, for example, that if students cover their left nostril and then inhale through the other, they are sending oxygen to right side of their brain, thereby increasing their creativity? This was an idea presented to me at one training meeting. I thought it prudent to point out that the oxygen was far more likely to travel to the lungs!

My brother (also a teacher) was once told that his students should not write in yellow on their mindmaps and must write above the branches, otherwise the information would 'fall out of their brains'! I must confess I am not aware of this dubious 'scientific' research.

As psychologists, you may have your own opinion on the reliability and validity of 'learning styles', or perhaps you haven't given them much thought.

The research evidence I have read, for example, is not complimentary. Kavale and Forness's (1987) meta-analysis of studies matching teaching to learning styles found absolutely no effect on student achievement. Snider's (1992) review highlighted the unreliability of classifying individuals to learning styles. Indeed, there is little empirical evidence that learning styles even exist. Coffield *et al.*'s (2004) review concluded that the matching of teaching and learning styles was 'highly questionable'.

The popularity of learning styles might be likened to the Forer effect (1949); people tend to accept vague personality descriptions as unique to themselves, when they are in fact general enough to apply to anyone.

That said, the popularity of learning styles and the way in which teachers now cater for them, has almost undoubtedly improved the variety of teaching within lessons, and the quality of teaching overall. Teaching now rarely includes the monotonous reading of textbooks, followed by comprehension questions. Although that isn't to say that this is not a good learning strategy for students in moderation. However, by including different ways to teach topics, be they visual, auditory or kinaesthetic, we are surely giving our students different opportunities to understand and access the topics we teach them.

As such, while 'learning styles' may be psychologically dubious, it is still incredibly useful for teachers to consider the different ways in which our students might be able to access psychology, and the ways in which we might be able to help them to understand it. Crucially, though, we should **not** be 'matching' teaching styles to individual 'learning styles'.

Nevertheless, the undeniable truth is that educational leaders, OFSTED and your line managers will all be looking for evidence that you are catering for 'learning styles' in your lesson plans, so we have tried to identify where our lesson ideas might fit in with this.

In the Lesson notes section we will use the following key. Ironically, perhaps, we have used a tick box approach!

V = *Visual*. Resources or activities that have a written or visually descriptive format.

A = *Auditory*. Activities that entail hearing and/or discussing information, ideas and arguments.

K = *Kinaesthetic*. Resources or activities that involve movement and/or arrangement of ideas, concepts, or arguments.

References

Coffield, F., Mosely, D., Hall, E. & Ecclestone, K. (2004). *Should we be using learning styles?* London: Learning and Skills Development Agency. Retrieved from: http://www.lsda. org. uk/files/PDF/1540.pdf

Forer, B. R. (1949). The fallacy of personal validation: A classroom demonstration of gullibility. *Journal of Abnormal and Social Psychology*, 44, 118–23.

Kavale, K. A. & Forness, S. R. (1987). Substance over style: Assessing the efficacy of modality testing and teaching. *Exceptional Children,* 54, 228–39.

Snider, V. E. (1992). Learning styles and learning to read. *Remedial and Special Education,* 13, 6–18.

V A✓K ★OGS HANDOUT 26

TOPIC: Biological rhythms: The circadian rhythm

CURIOUS COLIN'S CIRCADIAN STUDY

This handout can be used across a number of lessons to create a mini scheme of work for circadian sleep-wake studies. After learning about the circadian cycle, students are asked to complete a 'little literature' review into free-running cycle studies. Students could be directed to textbooks or Internet research and assigned the task of finding one study which they then present to the class using PowerPoint. The class records each group's research on their handout. Using previous research as a guide and the questions on the handout, students work in pairs to design their own study into the free-running circadian cycle. These pairs could be mixed ability to allow more able students to develop their understanding as they guide another student through the process and model to less able students the detail needed when justifying decisions. I (RCG) feel the task will help prepare students for PSYA4 scientific methods or can be used as an activity that introduces an area of PSYA3 to be studied after their PSYA4 exam.

V✓A✓K ★OS HANDOUT 27

TOPIC: Infradian and ultradian rhythms

ULTRADIAN UPDATE: SLEEP SUMMARY

Students use their textbook to research the different stages and cycles of sleep. They then take 10 minutes to rehearse the information by either talking to a friend about what they have learnt or producing a mindmap. Following this, textbooks are closed and mindmaps hidden. Students try to complete the summary table on the handout by filling in the table and circling the correct answers shown below the table. To conclude, students check their recall by reopening their textbook and looking back at their mindmap. They tick the appropriate evaluation on the clip board and set themselves one 'to-do' to help improve recall of sleep stages and cycles. These targets can be used as an individual starter activity for the following lesson.

TOPIC: Endogenous pacemakers, exogenous zeitgebers

CUT AND PASTE PACEMAKERS AND ZEITGEBERS

The first section of the handout illustrates what the exam board requires students to know and breaks down the terms endogenous pacemaker and exogenous zeitgeber to help students' understanding. Before beginning the task students are to rate their confidence level towards this topic by circling one of the smiley faces. This can be developed into an extended activity by asking students to find another student with the same rating or a different one and discuss the questions shown in this area of the handout. As a teacher you could use the ratings to match students to work in pairs for the following task.

Students are provided with the challenge card from **Handout 29**. They use this to create a flow diagram of the interaction between exogenous zeitgebers and the endogenous pacemaker SCN. Images contained on the handout are to be cut out and pasted onto paper to produce this diagram. The challenge card does not explain the process in a direct order yet many students' initial attempts will simply represent the images in the order they appear on the challenge card. Students should be encouraged to think about what they are reading to create an accurate diagram. Less able students could use the check card instead of the challenge card, while the more able can be given the check card to assess the accuracy of their completed diagram.

V A✓K HOT HANDOUT 30

TOPIC: Endogenous pacemakers, exogenous zeitgebers

CUNNING COMMENTARY

When evaluating the role of endogenous pacemakers it is not enough just to state evidence for their existence, students need to use the research to address exam questions. They should be encouraged to analyse research, consider implications of findings and look at wider psychological issues. The boxes on the left-hand side of the handout contain outlines of research into the SCN and circadian rhythms. All students must attempt two bold-edged question boxes that ask students to simply identify aspects of the research. Most should also attempt to complete two dashed question boxes that require a higher level of thinking. Finally a few could consider a further two questions from the starred boxes. Completing these tasks results in all students considering at least two research studies at a basic level.

References

DeCoursey, P. J., Walker, J. K. & Smith, S. A. (2000). A circadian pacemaker in free-living chipmunks: essential for survival? *Journal of Comparative Physiology*, 186, 169–80.

Folkard, S. (1996). Bags of time to play. *Daily Express*, 28 September.

Morgan, E. (1995). Measuring time with a biological clock. *Biological Sciences Review*, 7, 2–5.

Sackett, G. & Korner, A. (1993). Sleep-waking states in conjoined twin neonates. *Sleep*, 16, 414–27.

V✓A✓K HGT HANDOUT 31

TOPIC: Consequences of disrupting biological rhythms

DETERMINING DISRUPTION

The handout introduces Lennie, who has been assigned the task of conducting a survey into the effects of shift work. Using the question strips as a guide, students should work in small groups (this could be mixed ability or ability based) to produce a questionnaire Lennie could distribute to workers. The question strips address a range of higher order thinking skills and not all may be considered. You could mark on each group's handout which question strips they should focus on. Question strips assess students' knowledge of the topic, understanding of questionnaires and validity. Therefore, this activity can also be used as a scientific method activity. Once questionnaires have been produced students are asked to write a short speech to encourage workers to complete the survey. These speeches will hopefully highlight the importance of conducting such research to improve workers' productivity and individual health: a useful AO2 comment when discussing shift work research.

This task takes the form of an ICT lesson with questionnaires emailed to local businesses, if such contacts exist, or posted on the school intranet with a request for parents/guardians to complete. Should students wish to develop this activity they could collate any data gathered and produce a qualitative summary of the findings.

V A✓K OS HANDOUT 32

TOPIC: The nature of sleep and lifespan changes

GUESS WHO?

The statements of five sleepers are presented for students to identify the life stage of each sleeper. To add a level of competition, students could mark at which point of each description they realised the age of the author. The class could compare their markings to find the person who identified the life stage at the earliest point. Following this, students use the statements and research in their textbook to complete the statements shown at the bottom of the handout. As a homework task students can use their work on this handout to answer the question, 'Outline, in about 200–300 words, the lifespan changes in patterns of sleep' (AO1). Alternatively the handout could help students produce the 9-mark AO1 section of the essay 'Describe and evaluate lifespan changes in sleep (9 marks + 16 marks)'.

V A✓K ★ O S HANDOUT 33

TOPIC: Functions of sleep: Restoration theory

BRAIN BOX

Using information from their textbook students fill each box on the handout with information. These headings aim to guide students in their reading so they approach a task with a reason for reading the text; they know what they are looking for. The statement refers to the point they wish to make, for example slow wave sleep seems particularly important during childhood as growth hormone is secreted during this time. The theory behind the statement refers to the psychological or biological approach, which may be evaluated in turn, providing synoptic links (issues, debates, approaches) (the box below). For example, biological knowledge has advanced greatly since initial theories developed due to advances in brain imagery techniques. Supporting evidence needs to be identified that relates to the point made in the top box and beneath that the strength of this research is considered, such as forms of validity and reliability.

I (RCG) find the boxes stack together to produce one part of an answer to the exam question 'outline and evaluate restoration theory as an explanation of the function of sleep (25 marks)'.

As an extension students try to think of other statements that could be built upon in the same way to produce a complete essay.

V A✓K ★ O S HANDOUT 34

TOPIC: Functions of sleep: Evolutionary explanations

SLEEPY SPECIES

Students are asked to explain the different amounts of sleep for the animals on the handout. As a starter to this activity, a PowerPoint quiz could be made where each slide displays an animal and students guess the amount of sleep; or play higher and lower, where the class decides whether the animal has more or less sleep than the previous one, students who guess incorrectly drop out and the game continues until one winner is left.

Sleep times for a wide range of animals can be found at www.bu.edu/phylogeny/. This starter could develop into a discussion of reasons why some animals may sleep more than others, with contributing factors being listed on the board. Ideas generated will help students complete the first task of the handout by providing a basis for their textbook reading. The three columns at the bottom form an AO2 commentary on the evolutionary explanation of sleep.

V A✓K ★ O G T HANDOUT 35

TOPIC: Sleep disorders: Explanations for insomnia

INVESTIGATING INSOMNIA

My (RCG) fictional case studies of two insomniacs are presented to students. Using the questions as a guide, students take on the role of a psychologist and diagnose and treat their sleep disorder. Feeding back the diagnosis could take a number of forms: written report, PowerPoint, role play between client and doctor. The form taken could act as differentiation.

V A✓K ★ O G T HANDOUT 36

TOPIC: Other sleep disorders

RATING THE REASONS

Once students have stated an explanation for the cause of narcolepsy they need to be able to consider the usefulness of that suggestion. One way to do this is to identify supporting research. However, while research may seem to add weight to an explanation, can we confidently accept the research findings? For each explanation students record a supporting study gathered from their textbook or individual research. They then need to rate each study in regards to degree to which the research offers support to the explanation. The further towards the right on the rating scale, the more useful the research is deemed to be. In explaining how they reached this rating the following questions could be considered: Was the sample size suitable? Can we apply animal research to humans? Could the measurement tool be improved? Is the study taking a reductionist approach? Has a nature or nurture stance been adopted? Does the study provide full support for the explanation?

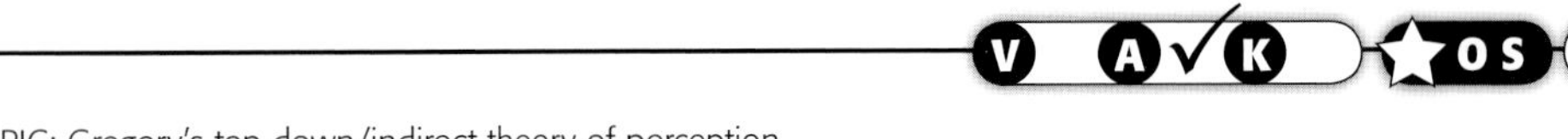

TOPIC: Gregory's top-down/indirect theory of perception

TOP-DOWN TAG LINES

A tag line is a simple sentence or slogan that summarises an event or story. You often see them accompanying film trailers, for example Shrek (2001) 'The Greatest fairy tale never told'. This activity requires a tag line to be created for each word shown relating to Gregory's top-down theory of perception. For example, 'construction' = perception created from combining direct observation with stored knowledge. Creating tag lines ensures students understand the key terms within the explanation and encourages concise writing style. As an extension, students then use the tag lines to create a 300-word summary of Gregory's theory.

I (RCG) feel this handout can be used for any topic, just change the words shown in the boxes.

Reference

Gregory, R. L. (1974). *Concepts and Mechanisms of Perception*. London. Duckworth.

TOPIC: Gibson's bottom-up/direct theory of perception

BOTTOM-UP MATCH-UP

A simple activity to help students read their textbook on the bottom-up explanation of perception. The task involves matching key terms to their definitions. This could be done via colour coding or cutting and sticking onto a new sheet of paper. The activity can take a number of forms; as an individual using text to complete the task; in pairs hypothesising which word belongs to which definition, then checking ideas using a textbook; or as a revision tool nearer exam time.

Reference

Gibson, J. J. (1979). *The Ecological Approach to Visual Perception*. Boston, Houghton Mifflin.

TOPIC: Perceptual development: Infant studies

INFANT EYES

The handout asks students to consider the question, 'What perceptual ability is a child born with (nature) and how much is a result of environmental experience (nurture)?'. Before reading about the debate, students are to record their ideas in the first box on the handout and mark along the continuum the degree of nature and nurture involved in perceptual ability.

The second section of the handout requires reading of research into infant perception to produce an outline of at least two studies into infant perception. Each outline should be approximately 100 words. You may wish students to create a balanced record by including one study that suggests infants are born with sophisticated perceptual ability (nature) and another that suggests some abilities develop as the infant interacts with their environment (nurture).

Provided on the handout is a list of points that less able students could use as subheadings to structure their writing. More able students could be directed to make methodological evaluations. For each study give one difficulty of using infants in perception research and one criticism relating directly to the method used or conclusions drawn. Once research has been considered, students form a second opinion on the contribution nature and nurture make in infant perception based on their newfound knowledge.

As a plenary I (RCG) would project two continuums onto the board. On the first students mark their initial position and on the second their informed position. Has anyone drastically changed their viewpoint? This task could be transformed to a kinaesthetic activity where students stand along a line representing initial then informed viewpoints.

TOPIC: Perceptual development: Cross-cultural studies

CROSS-CULTURAL CRITIQUE

The handout presents brief outlines of four cross-cultural studies. Students initially have to identify which area of perception the study relates to. This first task could take the form of a class vote. Following reading of these studies students are to form a summary statement relating to the nature vs. nurture debate based on the research evidence. Less able students may benefit from the support mixed ability pairing offers. The final section involves evaluation of research methodology. Once completed, this handout can be used to help students form PEE paragraphs for essay writing. For example, Point = there seems to be an environmental influence on perceptual ability, Evidence = outline Segall *et al.* (1963), Expansion = however, such studies may suffer from methodological problems that impact on validity. (See page 11 for an explanation of PEE.)

References

Allport, G. W. & Pettigrew, T. F. (1957). Cultural influence on the perception of movement: the trapezoidal illusion among Zulus. *Journal of Abnormal and Social Psychology*, 55, 441–85.

Hudson, W. (1960). Pictorial depth perception in subcultural groups in Africa. *Journal of Social Psychology*, 52, 183–208.

Segall, M. H., Campbell, D. T. & Herskovits, M. J. (1963). Cultural differences in the perception of geometric illusions. *Science*, 139, 769–71.

Turnbull, C. (1963). *The Forest People*. London, Reprint Society.

TOPIC: Perception and the nature-nurture debate

SORTING STATEMENTS

Cut out each statement on the handout and sort them into two groups: statements supporting nature's influence on the development of perceptual ability, and statements supporting nurture's influence on the development of perceptual ability. These can then be used to create an outline of each position. Less able students may focus on simply sorting statements, while the more able may wish to stick statements in a logical order to produce a reasoned line of argument in each group. An alternative could be to colour code statements as nature or nurture then stick them in two columns to form a debate between the two positions. Students may wish to add their own linking statements or development of arguments.

References

Banks, M. S., Aslin, R. N. & Letson, R. D. (1975). Sensitive period for the development of human binocular vision. *Science*, 190, 675–7.

Blakemore, C. & Cooper, G. F. (1970). Development of the brain depends on the visual environment. *Nature*, 228, 477–8.

Gibson, J. J. (1979). *The Ecological Approach to Visual Perception*. Boston, Houghton Mifflin.

Gregory, R. L. (1974). *Concepts and Mechanisms of Perception*. London, Duckworth.

Hubel, D. H. & Wiesel, T. N. (1970). The period of susceptibility to the physiological effects of unilateral eye closure in kittens. *Journal of Physiology*, 206, 419–36.

Slater, A., Mattock, A. & Brown, E. (1990). Size consistency at birth: newborn infants' responses to retinal and real size. *Journal of Experimental Psychology*, 49, 314–22.

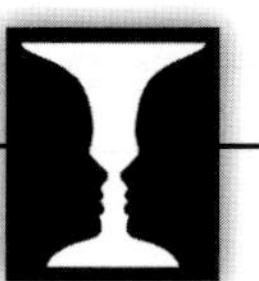

TOPIC: Bruce and Young's theory of face recognition

RESEARCHING FACE RECOGNITION AND RESOURCES

These two handouts form the instructions and resources to allow students to carry out their own investigation into face recognition. Either in groups or as a class, students divide into two groups; one collects data using 'Set 1' resources, the other using 'Set 2'. The handout contains questions to guide sample choice that can be addressed within groups and as a whole. On completion of the study students can attempt questions that relate to PSYA4 scientific method. This activity can be used as part of the perception scheme of work or be included in the PSYA4 scheme of work.

Bruce and Young's (1986) model of face recognition sets out the process as a series of stages accessed one after the other. One path through the model explains the process of recognising familiar faces.

Face recognition units (FRUs) contain information about faces you know. If the encoded information has a reasonable match with this information, then the FRU is activated and triggers the next node, the personal identity node (PIN). PIN contains information about a person's identity, such as their occupation. Once the person's identity is established, the next stage is to retrieve their name recognition unit (NRU). Owing to the serial nature of the model, names are only accessed after identity has been established: there is no link from face to name.

In the handout activity this model would suggest participant recall for face and name only condition (Set 2) would be poorer than the recall from face, name and information condition (Set 1). However, Stanhope and Cohen (1993) found that the participants could retrieve the names for faces despite having no information about the PIN.

References

Bruce, V. & Young, A. W. (1986). Understanding face recognition. *British Journal of Psychology*, 77, 305–27.
Stanhope, N. & Cohen, G. (1993). Retrieval of proper names: testing the models. *British Journal of Psychology*, 84, 51–65.

TOPIC: Visual agnosias

AGNOSIA ANALYSIS

The handout acts as a visual record of research into agnosia. By providing the handout at the time of reading information, students are given a purpose for their reading and can approach the task with questions that need to be answered. Students may prefer to work individually and share findings with a peer later or work in a small group, assigning each member a section to complete then teach each other.

V ✓ A K ✓ HOTS HANDOUT 45

TOPIC: The formation of romantic relationships

STATEMENT SORTING

This activity could either be used as a starter or plenary for a lesson on explanations of the formation of romantic relationships.

Each of the statements on **Handout 45** relates to either the *Reward/Need Satisfaction Theory*, or the *Similarity* hypothesis for the formation of romantic relationships.

To use as a starter, simply ask the students to cut out the statements and arrange them into two groups. In order to do this they will need to read the statements carefully and try and think about how some of them might be linked. For lower ability students, you might consider giving them the titles of the two explanations (and possibly a one-sentence summary) beforehand in order to guide their reading. For higher ability students you could leave them to their own devices in order to stretch their higher order thinking skills.

Following this, you could go through the answers in order to make sure each student has the correct statements in the correct groups, and then ask them to write a summary for each theory using the statements to guide them.

Alternatively, you could use this type of activity as a plenary in order to assess students' knowledge and understanding of the explanations once you have already gone through them.

Answers

Reward/Need Satisfaction Theory – Statements 2, 3, 5, 7, 8, 9, 10, 11, 15.
Similarity – Statements 1, 4, 6, 12, 13, 14.

V A K ✓ HORTS HANDOUT 46

TOPIC: The formation of romantic relationships

MORE TO IT THAN CUPID...!

Anyone who has read or seen Bloom's Taxonomy will know that knowledge and understanding are actually two of the lowest order thinking skills.

In order to stretch our students and facilitate 'deep learning' (this year's fashionable buzz word at our school) it is a good idea to get our students *applying* their knowledge and understanding in order to *analyse* unseen situations. In fact, it seems that the new AQA course has very much incorporated that idea into the assessment of students.

As such, **Handout 46** provides students with an opportunity to use their knowledge of relationship formation explanations in order to explain three fictional romantic case studies. In order to focus their efforts, key words they may wish to use, have been provided as well. This should also help lower ability students who may find it hard to know where to start their analysis.

References

Byrne, D. & Clore, G. L. (1970). A reinforcement model of evaluative responses. *Personality: An International Journal,* 1, 103–28.
Byrne, D., Clore, G. L. & Smeaton, G. (1986). The attraction hypothesis: do similar attitudes affect anything? *Journal of Personality and Social Psychology,* 51, 1167–70.

TOPIC: The maintenance of romantic relationships

MAINTENANCE STRATEGIES QUESTIONNAIRE

This activity could be used as an excellent research activity in general. Dindia and Baxter (1987) used a questionnaire to find out what strategies were used by married couples to maintain their relationship. The questionnaire consisted of just two questions (given on **Handout 47**).

To collect their data, Dindia and Baxter asked 50 students to each find a married couple who they knew personally and give the questions to each partner to answer independently. They analysed the answers by searching for identifiable categories. The 12 categories below are also given on the handout.

In the original study Dindia and Baxter coded the answers separately – each of them read through one participant's responses to questions 1 and 2 and decided which categories were represented in the strategies listed. They then compared their codings for each participant and found 82% agreement in their coding, quite high agreement.

You could try and replicate this study with your students and analyse their findings. They could use married couples, or co-habitees, or friends who have been in long-term relationships. The analysis provides an opportunity to practise content analysis.

In conducting this study students should take special care to safeguard the confidentiality of the participants.

The findings from the original study are included in the table below.

Reference

Dindia, K. & Baxter, L. A. (1987). Maintenance and repair strategies in marital relationships. *Journal of Social and Personal Relationships*, 4, 143–58.

Categories for analysis	Number of statements provided by participants	
	Maintenance	Repair
1 Change external environment	1	1
2 Increase communication with partner (e.g. talk to partner, have symbolic contact, share feelings)	53	30
3 Metacommunication (talk about the problem)	21	47
4 Avoid talking about problem, hoping it will pass	6	3
5 Antisocial behaviour (coercive attempts to change partner, e.g. insolence, sullenness, hyper-critical behaviour, refusal to compromise, breaking contact, acting cold)	1	5
6 Prosocial behaviour (friendliness and refraining from criticism when partner is being difficult, talking about future plans [engagement, marriage, children, buying a house], being warm)	77	51
7 Ritualistic behaviour (celebrating anniversaries, birthdays, giving gifts)	58	39
8 Trying new things	12	1
9 Spending more time together	63	26
10 Spending more time in independent activities	7	5
11 Seeking outside assistance	19	10
12 Other	50	38

V A ✓ K HOG

TOPIC: The maintenance of romantic relationships

GROUP STATEMENTS – GENDER DIFFERENCES

In A2 Psychology, a much larger emphasis is placed on the students providing commentary, evaluation and analysis as opposed to simply learning the commentary and analysis (as is often the case at AS). Indeed in PSYA4, in particular, exam questions may ask students to simply use their knowledge of certain theories to comment on factional studies. As such, it is important we try and give them opportunities to practise these skills.

One way to do this is to simply show students a study, and then ask them to jot down analysis. For example….

Steil and Weltman (1991) found that, among married working couples, husbands who earned more than their wives rated their own careers as more important than their wives' careers. In such couples, the women generally also rated their husbands' careers as more important than their own. However, in couples where the woman's income exceeded the man's, neither partner rated their career as more important. (Extract from *A2 Complete Companion*, p. 45.)

In order to help your students comment on this study, write some of the following questions on the board. What could we conclude from this study? How could the results be explained? How do they link to theories/explanations we have covered in class? Can this study be evaluated?

This type of activity works particularly well when asking the students to work collaboratively, for example using the **Group statements** technique (see page 3).

TOPIC: The breakdown of relationships

ETHICS IN BREAKDOWN OF RELATIONSHIPS RESEARCH

The handout describes various studies on the breakdown of relationships and asks students to draw on their knowledge of ethical issues and the BPS guidelines from AS studies to consider some of the problems inherent in this kind of research.

This is useful because the mark schemes require students to show evidence of synoptic commentary throughout A2.

This activity provides students with an opportunity to prepare material in order to gain these marks.

For the higher ability students, **Handout 48** also provides them with the opportunity to consider the tension and sometimes mutual exclusivity between ethical guidelines and scientific validity.

References

Boekhout, B., Hendrick, S. & Hendrick, C. (1999). Relationship infidelity: a loss perspective. *Journal of Personality and Interpersonal Loss,* 4, 97–123.

Cina, A., Bodenmann, G. & Blattner, D. (2003). *The effect of the CCET in enhancing parenting skills.* Paper presented at the 2nd Family Congress, Munich, Germany.

Tashiro, T. & Frazier, P. (2003). 'I'll never be in a relationship like that again.' Personal growth following romantic relationship break-ups. *Personal Relationships,* 10, 113–28.

V A K ✓ HOS HANDOUT 49

TOPIC: The breakdown of relationships

REPORT: RELATIONSHIP BREAKDOWN

Encouraging students to apply their knowledge and understanding in order to analyse different situations and case studies is an excellent way to develop A2 Psychology students and steer them away from simple rote learning.

Handout 49 asks students to produce a psychological report into a relationship breakdown – from a film, soap, celebrity, etc. It will obviously be important here that students analyse a fictional relationship or high profile relationship as opposed to a private and personal relationship. Inevitably students may start to apply some of the theories to situations close to their own lives but this subject matter would obviously not be suitable for an explicit classroom activity.

Ensure that the students include all the factors listed on the report brief and encourage them to maintain a psychological focus rather than drifting into more anecdotal speculation.

Reference

Rollie, S. S. & Duck, S. W. (2006). Stage theories in marital breakdown. In J. H. Harvey and M. A. Fine (eds.) *Handbook of Divorce and Dissolution of Romantic Relationships.* Mahwah, NJ: Lawrence Erlbaum Associates, 176–93.

TOPIC: Sexual selection

CONTENT ANALYSIS: LONELY HEARTS ADS

A number of studies have investigated evolutionary explanations of interpersonal attraction using 'lonely hearts' ads in newspapers. The idea used to be a popular one for coursework but could be done on a small scale as a classroom activity to enable a deeper discussion of sexual selection.

Waynforth and Dunbar (1995) found that 42% of men sought a youthful mate compared to 25% of females; 44% of males sought a physically attractive partner compared with 22% of women.

In another variation, the focus has been on caring – as times have changed and women are more financially independent, they may seek for a partner who is willing to offer support in terms of being caring rather than in terms of resources.

For example, Bereczkei *et al.* (1997) found that females advertised for men who were family-orientated as well as financially sound.

In a slightly different type of study, Buss (1989) explored what males and females looked for in a marriage partner. Among the results were that women more than men desired mates who had 'good financial prospects', e.g. ambition, and qualities linked to resource acquisition.

Handouts 50 and **51** provide you with some ads to work with in the classroom (these are taken from a variety of papers). **Handout 52** provides you with possible hypotheses and a guide for scoring the ads (this handout is adapted from http://instruct1.cit.cornell.edu/courses/taresources/221HM.PDF accessed March 2007).

You could perhaps have different members of the class researching different hypotheses and then feeding back their results to class at the end.

Try and encourage your students to relate their findings back to previous research (such as those discussed here), the concepts and logic of sexual selection, and whether their findings support or undermine the hypotheses.

References

Bereczkei, T., Vorgos, S., Gal, A. & Bernath, L. (1997). Resources, attractiveness, family commitment; reproductive decisions in human mate choice. *Ethology. ALQ*, 103, 681–99.

Buss, D. M. (1989). Sex differences in human mate preferences: Evolutionary hypotheses tested in 37 cultures. *Behavioral and Brain Sciences,* 12, 1–49.

Dunbar, R. (1995). Are you lonesome tonight? *New Scientist*, 145 (February), 26–31.

Waynforth, D. & Dunbar, R. I. M. (1995). Conditional mate choice strategies in humans: Evidence from lonely hearts advertisements. *Behaviour*, 132, 755–79.

V A ✓ K HO

TOPIC: Sexual selection

REGISTER QUESTIONS

Another way to introduce the topic of sexual selection is via a simple 'register questions starter technique'.

Rather than asking your students to say 'Yes Sir' or 'Yes Miss' (or grunting) in response to your register, ask the males to say what they think females find attractive in males, and the females what they think males find attractive in females!

Ask one of the students to write a list on the board and introduce the rule that there can be no repeats!

After the register is completed, ask students to try and explain the results. Why are there gender differences. Students are likely to point out more immediate social differences, so after a while, try and provoke more evolutionary explanations by asking questions such as: 'What might this have to do with humans one million years ago?'

TOPIC: Parental investment

WHAT DO MUMS AND DADS DO? PARENTAL INVESTMENT

This is a discussion activity designed to kick-start a consideration of differences in parental investment. Students have to use the table on **Handout 53** to record their answers. The one on the handout is blank. The version below has some discussion prompts for you. The final entry always generates loads of discussions!

.	Mum's contribution	Dad's contribution
Hours of sleep lost in first three years of child's life	Students can attempt to quantify from their own experience or that of others	Students can attempt to quantify from their own experience or that of others
Money contributed to upkeep of child in first three years of life	ditto	ditto
Amount of bodily material contributed to conception, to 'making a baby'	Ova is hundred times larger than a sperm. Female will only produce a few hundred – males produce millions of sperm	
Bodily resources devoted to foetus during pregnancy	Mother supplies all nutrients from her own supply	None
Bodily resources devoted to child during breastfeeding	Mother supplies all nutrients from her own supply	None
Risks taken during childbirth	Many – dangers of injury, complications or even death	None
Time devoted to childcare during first year of life	Students can attempt to quantify from their own experience or that of others	Students can attempt to quantify from their own experience or that of others

	Mum	Dad
How many children could each have in a lifetime ?	The record (69) is held by a Russian mother	A 16th century Sultan of Morocco was reputed to have 888 offspring

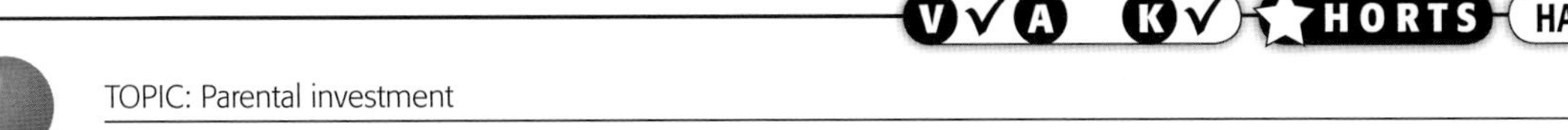

TOPIC: Parental investment

TRIVERS' PREDICTIONS

Handout 54 is designed not only to help your students evaluate Trivers' ideas on parent-offspring conflict, but also to reinforce the relationship between hypotheses, evidence and the scientific process, which is so integral to the new AQA course (AO3).

The handout essentially provides students with a writing frame with which to articulate an evaluation of Trivers' predictions.

It requires them to explain the logic of Trivers' predictions in an evolutionary sense and then to find evidence to support or contradict those predictions.

Higher ability students may wish to provide extra commentary on the validity of the evidence used to evaluate Trivers' ideas.

Reference

Trivers, R. L. (1974). Parent-offspring conflict. *American Zoologist,* 14, 249–64.

V ✓ A K ✓ HOS

TOPIC: Parental investment

EVOLUTIONARY GUIDE TO PARENTING

Using their knowledge and information from their textbooks, you could ask your students to write: 'An evolutionary guide to parenting'.

As always, it would be a good idea to give your students specific instructions as to what to include in the guide – with reference to what you have been studying.

For example, you could ask them to write a guide on maternal investment and its consequences, issues of male investment (e.g. cuckoldry and sexual jealousy). In addition, you could ask them to write a guide on sibling rivalry, parent-offspring conflict before birth, and parent-offspring conflict after birth.

The focus of the evolutionary parenting guide could be to maximise evolutionary success (i.e. amount of genes passed on into future generations).

You should also ensure that the guide contains plenty of scientific evidence.

V ✓ A ✓ K ✓ HOS HANDOUT 55

TOPIC: The influence of childhood and adolescent experiences on adult relationships

WHAT'S GOING ON?

Handout 55 describes a fictitious longitudinal study which correlated infant attachment with adult attachment.

The study links to concepts studied at AS such as secure attachment, insecure attachment, internal working model, and continuity hypothesis.

The questions at the bottom of the sheet ask students to link the results of the study to their knowledge of AS developmental psychology, whilst also encouraging them to analyse the study using their knowledge of 'How Science Works' (AO3).

This handout would be a good way to introduce and discuss the topic of the influence of childhood and adolescent experiences on adult relationships.

V A K ✓ ★ O S HANDOUT 56

TOPIC: The influence of childhood and adolescent experiences on adult relationships

LOVE QUIZ

This research activity links nicely to this topic, since Hazan and Shaver's (1987) study investigated the idea that childhood attachment style was related to adult romantic attachment style.

Closely linked is Bowlby's theory of attachment, which suggests that the infant's relationships with their caregiver forms the basis of the child's internal working model of relationships. This will affect the child's expectations about what relationships (including romantic ones) will be like. Therefore, we would expect a link between early attachments, attitudes about romantic relationships and actual romantic relationships. This is called the *continuity hypothesis*.

Hazen and Shaver's study

Hazan and Shaver (1987) tested Bowlby's hypothesis with their 'love quiz'. The quiz, which contained nearly 100 questions, was published in the *Rocky Mountain News*. They received 620 replies to their questionnaire and drew the following conclusions:

Securely attached adults:

- had certain beliefs about relationships (love is enduring)
- reported certain experiences in relationships (e.g. mutual trust)
- were less likely to have been divorced.

Insecurely attached adults:

- felt true love was rare, and fell in and out of love easily
- found relationships less easy
- were more likely to be divorced.

(See table below)

	Secure adults	Resistant (anxious) adults	Avoidant adults
Different love experiences	Relationships are positive	Preoccupied by love	Fearful of closeness
Adults' views of relationships	Trust others and believe in enduring love	Fall in love easily but have trouble finding *true* love	Love is not durable nor necessary for happiness
Memories of the mother–child relationship	Positive image of mother as dependable and caring	Conflicting memories of mother being positive *and* rejecting	Remember mothers as cold and rejecting

Analysis of the data revealed that infant attachment style predicted attitudes towards love (internal working model) and experience of love (continuity hypothesis).

Handout 56 has a shortened version of the quiz. The questions make assessments as follows:

- Q 1, 2 and 3 assess attachment history.
- Q 4, 5 and 6 assess adult attachment type.
- Q 7, 8 and 9 assess mental models of relationships.

Ethics briefing

This study involves questions that may be related to sensitive information about an individual's early life experience and which may suggest problematic adult relationships. When replicating this study, always seek informed consent beforehand, where possible, or offer a thorough debriefing, including the right to withhold individual data.

It should also be emphasised that the suggested association between early experience and later relationships is not 100% – there are many individuals who overcome early unfavourable circumstances. In addition this correlation is not proven.

A further point to make is that the original survey involved nearly 100 questions, whereas this shorter version involves just nine. Therefore, the reliability and validity of this exercise will be low, so little can be read into the results.

That said, it is a useful exercise to undertake to understand how Hazan and Shaver collected the evidence that is often used to support Bowlby's hypothesis.

To work out scores use the table on page 32.

Reference

Hazan, C. & Shaver, P. R. (1987). Romantic love conceptualised as an attachment process. *Journal of Personality and Social Psychology*, 52, 511–24.

Question	a	b	c
1	secure	insecure avoidant	insecure resistant
2	secure	insecure resistant	insecure avoidant
3	insecure resistant	secure	insecure avoidant
Score for part A (the dominant category chosen: secure, insecure-avoidant or insecure-resistant) =			
4	insecure resistant	insecure avoidant	secure
5	secure	insecure resistant	insecure avoidant
6	insecure avoidant	secure	insecure resistant
Score for part B (the dominant category chosen: secure, insecure-avoidant or insecure-resistant) =			
7	insecure avoidant	insecure resistant	secure
8	insecure avoidant	secure	insecure resistant
9	insecure resistant	secure	insecure avoidant
Score for part C (the dominant category chosen: secure, insecure-avoidant or insecure-resistant) =			

V✓A✓K HOS

TOPIC: The influence of childhood and adolescent experiences on adult relationships

FILM REPORT – GOOD WILL HUNTING

Good Will Hunting is a film starring Robin Williams, Matt Damon and Ben Affleck. In my (MWG) opinion it is a superb portrayal of reactive attachment disorder and a fantastic way to illustrate to pupils how early experiences can affect romantic relationships later in life.

As a boy, Will Hunting is abused and sent from foster home to foster home. The film explores how this impacts on him later as a man.

Consider watching this film or part of this film with your students and ask them to think about the following questions:

- What is revealed about Will's background as a child?
- According to Bowlby, what might this mean for his development?
- When sitting on the bench in the park, what point is the therapist (Robin Williams) trying to make?
- Why do you think Will is so scared about leaving for California with his girlfriend and saying that he loves her? Why is he pushing her away?
- What does the therapist mean by a 'defence mechanism'? Why doesn't Will trust anybody?

V✓ A✓ K✓ ★ O G S

TOPIC: Relationships in different cultures

CULTURE – STUDENT DIMENSION LINE

Having taught similar topics to this before, I (MWG) know that it is easy to assume that students know what culture is and therefore spend little time reflecting on what the term actually means. In fact often students are not comfortable with what the term means, or think they are, but when questioned they cannot articulate their understanding.

A good way to start this topic would be to use the **student dimension line** (see page 3) collaborative learning structure.

Pose the question, 'Can you define the term culture?' Then ask students to indicate their confidence in their ability to do that using the dimension line.

Fold the line or differentiation (see page 3) and then ask the small groups to come up with their own definition of culture – you could perhaps use **random numbers** (see page 3) here to ensure interdependence and accountability for the entire small group.

V✓ A K✓ ★ O S HANDOUT 57

TOPIC: Relationships in different cultures

SPOT THE CULTURAL DIFFERENCE!

This activity could be used in conjunction with any textbook.

Students must illustrate any cultural difference they can find between individualist and collectivist cultures.

In order to do that you can encourage them to draw silly images with stick-people, thought bubbles and speech bubbles.

I (MWG) personally could not stand art or drawing when I was at school, so be sure to reassure your students that the end results will not be entered into any competitions and that you are more concerned with the process of the activity as opposed to the end result!

Students will also need to explain their drawings and provide evidence for the drawings using their textbooks.

V A K✓ HORS

TOPIC: Social learning theory

DESIGN A STUDY!

Social learning theory is an excellent area of psychology to practise some of the 'How Science Works' concepts, particularly in preparation for PSYA4, where students may be asked to design a study in detail during the research methods section of the exam paper.

Social learning theory contains some simple hypotheses that you could ask your student to design a study for. For example:

- Children are more likely to imitate aggressive behaviour if they observe it.
- Children are more likely to imitate aggressive behaviour if they have observed it from a model they identify with.
- Children are more likely to imitate aggressive behaviour if vicarious reinforcement occurs.

Using these as guidance, your students could design an in-depth study to test any of these hypotheses (although they should focus on just one).

To do this they should work out the IV, DV, how they will operationalise the variables, the operationalised hypothesis, the sample, ethical considerations, what stats test they would use to analyse the data, etc.

You could give them **Handout 163** to help them structure this.

TOPIC: Social learning theory

SOCIAL LEARNING THEORY BINGO

Bingo is an excellent way to review key terms for any theory or topic that you have been covering.

Give students one of the 3 x 3 bingo grids provided on **Handouts 58–59**. Alternatively, you could make your own.

Read your students various definitions, questions, or descriptions of the terms in those grids. Students can then mark them off if they think one of the terms on their grid corresponds to your definition/question.

Once they have crossed off all their squares they call 'bingo' and they have won the game! As long as they haven't made any mistakes!

Guidance for the terms on the handouts is provided in the table below.

Specifics of aggressive behaviour	These are learnt as a result of observation, e.g. the form it takes, how often it is enacted, the targets towards which it is directed.
Vicarious reinforcement	When children learn about the consequences of aggressive behaviour by watching others being reinforced or punished.
Mental representation	This must occur in order for social learning to take place. It involves the child imagining themselves performing the aggressive behaviour they have observed.
Direct reinforcement	This occurs if a child is rewarded for a behaviour, e.g. gets what they want. It leads to them being more likely to repeat that behaviour in future.
Self-efficacy	Refers to the confidence a child has in their ability to carry out aggressive actions. Their confidence is higher if the behaviour has been successful in the past.
Imitation of behaviour	A child is more likely to do this if they have seen the behaviour vicariously reinforced.
Bobo doll	An inflatable toy that children observed someone being aggressive towards in Bandura's study.
Bandura et al. *(1961): Independent variable*	Whether or not the children saw an adult being aggressive towards the Bobo doll.
Bandura et al. *(1961): Dependent variable*	Whether or not the children were aggressive towards the Bobo doll.
Demand characteristics	Noble criticised the Bobo doll study because the children already seemed to know what behaviour was expected of them before they took part. This criticism is related to….
Ecological validity	Some have argued the results from Bandura's study cannot be generalised to performance of aggression against humans, since a Bobo doll is only inflatable and does not fight back. This criticism is related to…
Bandura and Walters (1963): Independent variable	Whether the adult being observed by children being aggressive (to the Bobo doll) was rewarded or punished.

Bandura and Walters (1963): Dependent variable	Whether or not the children were aggressive towards the Bobo doll.
Bandura et al. *(1961)*	This study supported the idea that the specifics of aggressive behaviour are learnt through observation of adult models.
Bandura and Walters (1963)	This study supported the idea that vicarious reinforcement makes the performance of aggressive behaviours more likely.
Phillips (1983)	This study indicated that social learning theory can explain adult behaviour since daily homicide rates in the US almost always increase in the week following a major boxing match.
Nurture	Social learning theory supports the idea of _________, i.e. that the environment shapes our behaviour.
Context-dependent learning	One of the strengths of social learning theory is that it can explain why people respond differently in different situations because they have observed that aggression is rewarded in some situations but not others. This is called . . . .

References

Bandura, A., Ross, D. & Ross, S. A. (1961). Transmission of aggression through imitation of aggressive models. *Journal of Abnormal Social Psychology*, 63, 575–82.

Bandura, A. & Walters, R. H. (1963). *Social Learning and Personality Development.* New York: Holt, Rinehart and Winston.

Phillips, D. P. (1983). The impact of mass media violence on U.S. homicides. *American Sociological Review*, 48, 560–8.

HANDOUT 60

TOPIC: Social learning theory

LINKS – TURNING STUDY EVALUATION INTO THEORY EVALUATION

Imagine that the following essay question comes up on the PSYA3 exam:

*Outline and evaluate **two** social psychological explanations of human aggression. (25 marks)*

In this particular exam question, students may opt to outline and evaluate social learning theory and deindividuation.

Students would need to find 9 AO1 marks, 16 AO2/AO3 marks.

In order to gain the AO2/AO3 marks it is useful to include *'methodological evaluation of studies used to support or challenge explanations of human aggression'.*

From past experience with my (MWG) students, this skill is harder than it sounds. On the face of it, all students have to do is evaluate studies they have used to support or undermine the explanations. For example, they could evaluate Bandura's Bobo doll studies, which they probably used to support Social learning theory.

However, owing to the emphasis on study evaluation at AS, I find that students forget that they are actually supposed to be evaluating Social learning theory, and instead spend most of their time 'vomiting' out their evaluations of the study (that is a phrase I use in the classroom I am afraid to say!). As such, their essay loses focus and they forget to evaluate the theories with the studies.

This 'links' activity aims to try and get students thinking about how they can turn their study evaluations into evaluations of the theory – rather than just blindly evaluating the study without any reference to the essay demands.

It includes a four-step process for doing this successfully as well as one completed example.

TOPIC: Deindividuation

SITUATIONAL FACTORS IN AGGRESSION

This activity is a good way to introduce the concept of deindividuation. I (MWG) would ask students to complete this activity before introducing the term and its meaning.

Handout 61 contains six images that could be said to relate to the deindividuation explanation of human aggression.

Give students the handout and ask them to explain how each image could increase the likelihood of aggression.

As an extension activity for the higher ability, you could ask them to explain how they think the images are linked.

Alternatively, you could give 1 or 2 of the images to small groups and ask them to feed back to the group using a collaborative learning structure (described on page 3).

Some likely answers:

A – Anonymity. 007 has no identifiable name.

B – Group pressure, anonymity, conformity.

C – 'Hoodie' obscures face, anonymity.

D – Uniform gives legitimacy. Uniform makes people feel more part of a unit rather than themselves.

E – Feeling part of a big group, anonymity, conformity.

F – Anonymity, legitimacy.

V A K ✓ HOS HANDOUT 62

TOPIC: Deindividuation

GETTING SHIRTY

Should football shirts be banned? Are they the cause of deindividuation and aggression on the terraces?

Handout 62 provides students with a fictional news report describing the plans for an introduction of a new policy that bans football shirts.

It asks students to take a strong view against and to use evidence to construct their arguments.

TOPIC: Deindividuation

DESIGN AN OUTFIT

This activity could be used shortly after introducing some of the concepts of deindividuation.

Simply ask students to design an outfit that maximises the potential for aggression in the person wearing it. However, ban the outfit from containing any weaponry.

As such, students will need to think about the process of deindividuation and elements that would encourage it to occur.

You could then show them clips from the Stanford Prison experiment (can be found on YouTube) or show them examples of army uniform. You could even link these two ideas together and show them footage or images from the Abu Ghraib scandal in Iraq (again, images can be found on the Internet – but be careful to choose only those appropriate to show within the context of the classroom).

V ✓ A K OS

TOPIC: Institutional aggression

ROLLING SHOW

Rolling shows are a great idea to start lessons. Details on how to create a rolling show using PowerPoint are described on page 5.

There are many different examples and images of institutional aggression that you could include on the rolling show that would help orientate the students towards the content of the lesson and hopefully capture their interest.

Here are some examples you could search the Internet for, but again, be careful which images you select to show your students:

- Private Andrei Sychev's brutal beating by older soldiers at the Chelyabinsk Military School.
- Zimbardo's prison experiment.
- Abuse of Iraqi prisoners at Abu Ghraib.
- Rwandan genocide.
- The Holocaust.
- Bradford and Birmingham race riots.

VA K HORS HANDOUT 63

TOPIC: Institutional aggression

WHY, WHY, WHY?

The activity described on **Handout 63** asks students to try and explain why institutional aggression occurs with reference to a particular example they have studied in class.

The main aim of the handout is to try and encourage students to delve a little deeper.

Often when I (MWG) ask students to try and explain something they will identify an excellent point and then almost always I will ask them to elaborate. It annoys the hell out of them!

So, I thought I'd design a handout to do it for me! Once they have identified a reason why they think it happened or happens, they then have to delve deeper by keep asking themselves why. Ideally, at some point they will dig deep enough and provide some excellent psychological analysis.

TOPIC: Neural and hormonal mechanisms in aggression

MODELLING NEURAL NETWORKS

There really is little point talking to students about the role of neurotransmitters, synapses and neural pathways in aggression unless they have a basic grasp of biological mechanisms in the brain.

Unless all of your students study A level Biology, this is somewhat unlikely!

So, why not give your students some materials to make and model their own neural pathways or synapses. You could give them cardboard, glue, pipe cleaners, plasticine – anything!

My (MWG) students found the whole topic much easier once they had modelled the biological mechanisms themselves and could make reference to them when trying to apply them to different types of behaviour.

VA K ORS HANDOUT 64

TOPIC: Neural and hormonal mechanisms in aggression

'BRIEF' SUMMARIES

This is a fantastic idea stolen (with permission!) from Jo Gotts at www.psychexchange.co.uk.

Essentially the activity involves students summarising information and as such, choosing the most important bits to retain in the synopsis.

Handout 64 therefore provides four briefs in which to write 'brief summaries' (Do you see what Jo did?) of the roles of serotonin, dopamine, testosterone and cortisol.

Beneath each 'brief' are some key words/studies that students should aim to include in their summary. You could change or adapt this sheet to suit your needs.

Reference

Mann, L. (1981). The baiting crowd in episodes of threatened suicide. *Journal of Personality and Social Psychology,* 41, 703–9.

V✓A K✓ ★OS HANDOUT 65

TOPIC: Genetic factors in aggression

UNDERSTANDING TWIN STUDIES

Investigating the genetic basis of any behaviour usually involves the use of twin studies – aggression is no different.

Students sometimes find the logic of twin studies and the interpretation of the results very difficult and therefore it is good to give them an opportunity to try and work through the design of the study in order to understand how and why twin studies support or challenge the concept of a genetic basis for behaviour.

Suggested answers to **Handout 65.**

Two types of Twin

Identical twins share 100% of their genes and are also known as monozygotic twins (MZ). Non-identical twins are likely to share 50% of their genes and are also known as dizygotic twins (DZ).

Assuming aggressive behaviour is completely genetic, what are the chances of Dave's identical twin Arnold developing the disorder?

If you assume that aggressive behaviour is completely genetic, the chances of Arnold developing the disorder is 100%. This is because Dave and Arnold are genetically identical, so the gene(s) determining Dave's disorder will also be present in Arnold.

Arnold does NOT suffer from an aggressive behaviour disorder. Are Dave and Arnold concordant?

No, they are not concordant. Concordant would mean they BOTH have the disorder.

What is a concordance rate?

This is measured by researchers when they wish to find out the influence that genetics have on behaviour. It refers to the percentage of twins that share a particular trait. If a behaviour is completely genetic, the percentage in MZ twins should be 100%, and in DZ twins it should be somewhere around 50%.

TOPIC: Genetic factors in aggression

INTERPRETING TWIN STUDIES

Once your students have completed **Handout 65** and understand the basic design of twin studies, it would be a good idea to give them an opportunity to apply their knowledge to interpret a twin study in relation to aggression.

Put the results of a twin study on aggression on the whiteboard.

For example, *a twin study is conducted into an aggressive behavioural disorder and it is found that there is a 50% MZ concordance rate, and a 25% DZ concordance rate. What could you conclude from this study?*

It would be useful for differentiation here if you used a collaborative learning structure such as **Random numbers** or **Group statements** (see page 3) so that the weaker students are given every opportunity to help develop their understanding as well as the higher ability given the opportunity to articulate their understanding to others.

V✓A K✓ ★HOS HANDOUT 66

TOPIC: Genetic factors in aggression

NATURE VS. NURTURE

Covering the idea of a genetic basis of aggression provides students with a perfect opportunity to include synoptic commentary by linking the evidence to the nature vs. nuture debate. In the AQA A2 specification and exam marks schemes, there is strong emphasis on students being synoptic.

Handout 66 is designed to encourage students to consider the nature vs. nurture synoptic debate.

All they have to do is choose three colours for the key and then shade in the evidence depending on which side of the debate it supports. Students should then try and articulate how and why.

References

Caspi, A., McClay, J., Moffitt, T. E., Mill, J., Martin, J. & Craig, I. W. (2002). Role of genotype in the cycle of violence in maltreated children. *Science,* 297, 851–4.

Coccaro, E. F., Bergman, C. S., Kavoussi, R. J. & Seroczynski, A. D. (1997). Heritability of aggression and irritability: a twin study of Buss-Durkee Aggression Scales in adult male subjects. *Biological Psychiatry,* 41, 273–84.

Hutchings, B. & Mednick, S. A. (1975). Registered criminality in the adoptive and biological parents of registered male criminal adoptees. In R. R. Fieve, D. Rosenthal & H. Brill (eds.) *Genetic research in psychiatry.* Baltimore, MD: Johns Hopkins University Press, 106–22.

Plomin, R., Foch, T. T. & Rowe, D. C. (1981). Bobo clown aggression in childhood: environment, not genes. *Journal of Research in Personality,* 15, 331–42.

V✓ A K✓ ★ HORS

TOPIC: Evolutionary explanations of human aggression

EVOLUTIONARY MONSTERS!

Students will understand the evolutionary theories of aggression in much more depth if they first get to grips with the principles of evolutionary explanations of behaviour.

The **evolutionary monsters** activity is a fantastic way to help students with this (see page 15 for a full description and link to **Handout 21**).

V A K✓ ★ HORS HANDOUT 67

TOPIC: Evolutionary explanations of human aggression

EVOLUTIONARY EXPLANATIONS OF BEHAVIOUR

This activity follows on really well from the previous activity.

Once students have a decent grasp of the evolutionary approach and its major principles, they can then start to consider how it might be applied to human aggression.

Handout 67 describes a variety of different situations that lead to human aggression.

Using their textbooks, students need to describe why that behaviour is happening according to the evolutionary approach.

In order to encourage them to use key terms and guide their answers, ask your students to ensure that they include all the terms provided underneath each situation.

V✓ A✓ K ★ HOS

TOPIC: Explanations of group display in humans

JERRY SPRINGER PLENARY

This group display topic can contain many harrowing examples of how group membership can result in extremely immoral acts of aggression. As such, it is good to get students thinking about what they have learnt in a broader way.

In the past, I've (MWG) found that a Jerry Springer style plenary can work well.

Explain that at the end of Jerry Springer's shows, he always does a summing up. It usually starts with the phrase 'So… what have we learnt here today? We have learnt that….'

Ask the students to complete their Jerry Springer summing up of the topic. It may help to display the lesson objectives in order to focus their efforts and you could also encourage a moral/citizenship dimension to their summaries.

You could get some of your students to read out their ideas at the end of the lesson.

Alternatively, you could create a rolling show (see page 5) with each slide showing a student's summary and play it at the start of the next lesson. This provides a wonderful start to the lesson and a good opportunity to link previous learning to a new topic.

V✓ A K✓ ★ HORS HANDOUT 68

TOPIC: Explanations of group display in humans

REDUCTIONISM

In order to get the highest marks in A2 Psychology, students must now include synoptic commentary (appropriate links to issues, debates and approaches).

One way in which they can do this is to link their knowledge and analysis of a topic to a **psychological debate**.

One debate centres on **reductionism** – breaking down a complex phenomenon into simple components. Psychologists often use reductionism because it helps us understand behaviour on a simpler level. However, taken too far, reductionism can be counter-productive.

Handout 68 provides students with a writing frame in which to discuss whether the explanations of group display in humans, and evolutionary explanations in particular, are too reductionist.

TOPIC: Attitudes to food and eating behaviour

READING BETWEEN THE (HEAD)LINES

For each headline, students rate the truthfulness of each story: 1 = false, no element of truth, 10 = truthful statement. To encourage informed decision making, students need to include at least one piece of research evidence to support their judgement. Judgements could be informed by methodological issues such as sample size, procedure employed and external validity. Less able students may find this task easier if they are provided with sufficient information to complete PEE paragraphs (where P = the headline, E = research study identified and E = the reasons for their judgement on the truthfulness (validity) of the headline; PEE is explained on page 11). More able students may wish to take one headline and develop this into a complete news article through their own research into that particular area of eating behaviour.

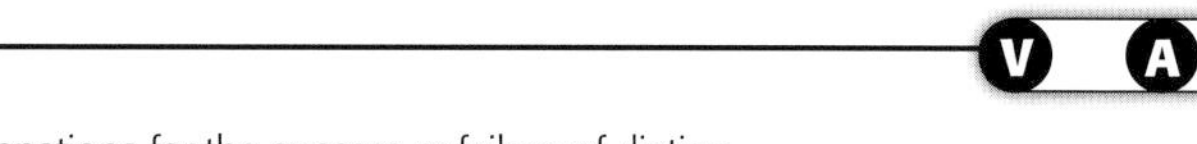

TOPIC: Explanations for the success or failure of dieting

DAISY'S DIET CLUB

Students are introduced to Daisy, who has produced a leaflet to help her diet club members stick to their eating regimes. I (RCG) based each tip on psychological research into the success and failure of dieting. Students are asked to identify the psychology behind each strategy. Every student must choose one statement, most should attempt two statements and include research evidence in their explanation, while a few could choose three or more. As an extension to the task, students can employ higher order thinking skills, evaluation, by ordering Daisy's diet tips from most to least successful, giving reasons for the choices made.

TOPIC: Neural mechanisms controlling eating and satiation

SWITCHING EATING ON AND OFF

The handout contains two tasks to develop students' understanding of the mechanisms involved in switching eating on and off and helping them write about this process in depth. First, students cut out the strips and decide whether they are related to turning eating on (creating hungry feeling), or are responsible for switching eating off (feeling full). They then stick them in order to represent the control of hunger, using the arrow images to help represent this mechanism.

The second task instructs students to give two critical points for the control of eating and satiation mechanism they have just built. Each criticism should be about 50 words in length. An example is given as a guide to help students give a fully elaborated response.

Reference

Lutter, M., Sakata, I., Osborne-Lawrence, S., Rovinsky, S. A., Anderson, J. G., Jung, S., Birnbaum, S., Yanagisawa, M. Elmquist, J. K., Nestler, E. J. & Zigman, J. M. (2008). The orexigenic hormone ghrelin defends against depressive symptoms of stress. *Nature Neuroscience*, 11, 752–3.

V A K O G HANDOUT 72

TOPIC: Evolutionary explanations for food preference

OUTLINING EVOLUTIONARY EXPLANATIONS

Two tasks are presented on the handout that students could attempt in any order. Each task shows an example of what needs to be done in the other task. The 'Preference for meat' task on the left side of the handout gives examples of key words deemed central to the explanation, while the task on the right-hand side asks for key words to be identified from the explanation given below.

The 'Taste aversion' task can be used as a model for students when completing the 'Preference for meat' task. Less able students may find it difficult to produce a detailed outline so may wish to attempt the key word task on the left first. They may also benefit from working in a small group of mixed ability students in which more able students can support their understanding. As a form of peer assessment for 'Preference for meat', students can swap handouts and highlight the key words used in each other's explanations; have any students managed to include all key words shown?

To assess understanding of 'Taste aversion' you could play class bingo. The teacher (or a confident student) calls out key words and students highlight each word on the handout grid. Prizes could be awarded for completed rows, columns or a full house.

Reference

Sandell, M. A. & Breslin, P. A. S. (2006). Variability in a taste-receptor gene determines whether we taste toxins in food. *Current Biology*, 16(18), R792–4.

TOPIC: Evolutionary explanations for food preference

EVOLUTIONARY MONSTERS!

Students will understand the evolutionary explanations in much more depth if they first get to grips with the principles of evolutionary explanations of behaviour.

The **evolutionary monsters** activity is a fantastic way to help students with this (see page 15 for a full description and link to **Handout 21**).

TOPIC: Evolutionary explanations for food preference

EVOLVING FOOD PREFERENCES

Why is it the food we enjoy the most is always bad for us?

This is a question I often pose my students when teaching evolutionary explanations of anything. It helps them to understand and relate to how our behaviour today is affected by the environment of yesterday – well, thousands of years ago in the environment of evolutionary adaptation (EEA) to be exact.

One simple evolutionary explanation is that in the EEA, calories required for energy were not as plentiful as they are today, so it makes sense that animals and humans evolved a distinct preference for foods rich in calories.

Despite the fact that the environment has changed (development of technology has meant a huge improvement in the availability of calories!) but genome lag means that we still crave 'calorific' food.

Use **Handout 73** with your students to encourage them to explain how evolution may have shaped their food preferences and to develop their use of evolutionary terms and principles.

TOPIC: Evolutionary explanations for food preference

ON THE ONE HAND... ON THE OTHER

This is a simple activity that could be used for almost any topic really.

Ask your students to draw around both their hands and fingers on an A3 sheet of paper.

They should include the title: 'On the one hand, on the other hand – Evolution has shaped our food preferences'.

Using their textbook to help them, on each finger of their left hand they should write an argument or explain evidence that supports the idea that evolution has shaped our food preferences.

They should do exactly the same for each finger of their right hand.

NB. When I say, 'on each finger', I of course mean the fingers they have drawn as opposed to their actual fingers. This may well be worth mentioning to those of your students lacking common sense!

TOPIC: Evolutionary explanations for food preference

DEBATE

An engaging way to introduce this topic is to provide time within your scheme of work to allow a debate on the challenging topic of whether the media is to blame for eating disorders in girls.

Allow students time to research arguments for and against this proposition and then time in lesson to express their views.

If your students are lacking in independence, be sure to prescribe them specific roles and ensure accountability.

TOPIC: Psychological explanations for anorexia nervosa

HAS BODY IMAGE CHANGED? … EVIDENCE FROM MISS AMERICA PAGEANT WINNERS

Garner *et al.* (1980) conducted a kind of cross-cultural study in that they compared desirable female bodies from different historical periods as well as considering changes in attitudes towards dieting. Their study revealed changing sociocultural pressures on eating disorders in Western society in the last 20 years; ideal female body shape and attitudes towards dieting had changed.

They used a form of indirect observation by using photographs of women taken during a 20-year period – centrefolds from *Playboy* magazine and contestants and winners of the Miss America pageant in the years from 1959 to 1978. They also looked at articles about dieting in six popular women's magazines.

The photographs show that there has been a gradual but definite change in the preferred shape for women toward a more angular and thinner physique. In addition to weight changes, bust and hip measurements became smaller. According to this data, 69 per cent of *Playboy* centrefolds and 60 per cent of Miss America participants from 1959 to 1978 had weights 15 per cent or less of the average weights for their age and height.

Moreover, in the 1970s those women who won the pageants weighed less than the other contestants. Meanwhile, actuarial statistics published in 1979 showed that the average female weight for the population had increased during that 20-year period. During that same period, they also found an increase in the number of diet articles in six popular women's magazines.

This suggests a growing disparity between actual body sizes and the cultural standard, and a parallel increase in the culture's interest in and attention to dieting, thinness and appearance in women.

Garner *et al.* concluded that this changing sociocultural pressure has had an enormous impact on women and this, together with family expectations and individual characteristics, determines the causes of eating disorders.

Procedure

You could conduct a similar study using the data on Miss America pageant winners provided on **Handouts 74** and **75**.

References

Garner, D. M., Garfinkel, P. E., Schwartz, D. & Thompson, M. (1980). Cultural expectations of thinness in women. *Psychological Reports*, 47, 483–91.

Rubenstein, S. & Caballero, B. (2000). Is Miss America an undernourished role model? *JAMA,* 283 (12), 1569.

TOPIC: Psychological explanations for anorexia nervosa

COLLECTIVE MEMORY

One of the studies often cited as support for the influence of the media on eating habits (and by implication eating disorders) is Becker *et al.*'s (2002) study of adolescent Fijian girls following the introduction of television for the first time in 1995. Surveys of the girls revealed that after being exposed to Western media, the girls were stating a desire to lose weight and become more like the models on the television. These results could be explained by learning theory and the association between body shape and success.

Handout 76 is a pictorial representation of this study.' Collective memory can be a fun activity at the start of the lesson. Assign class members to small groups and assign a number for each person in that small group.

When the activity begins, allow the 'number 1s' to come to the front of the room and study **Handout 76** for 30 seconds. Then they have to go back to their place and reproduce as much of the drawing as they can. Meanwhile, the 'number 2s' are allowed to come and study the handout for 30 seconds… and so on.

At the end of the activity you can award a prize for the group who have reproduced the handout most accurately.

You could also conduct a short quiz with the groups to see who can interpret the picture the best.

Eventually, this can stimulate good discussion among the students about the study. Students generally also report remembering the details of the study in good depth as a result of the activity.

Reference

Becker, A. E., Burwell, R. A., Gilman, S. E., Herzog, D. B. & Hamburg, P. (2002). Eating behaviours and attitudes following prolonged exposure to television among ethnic Fijian adolescent girls. *British Journal of Psychiatry*, 180, 509–14.

V √ A K √ HORS HANDOUT 77

TOPIC: Biological explanations for anorexia nervosa

AFFH CONNECTIONS

Handout 77 aims to help students understand the 'adapted to flee' hypothesis (AFFH).

Students have to fill in the boxes on the left- and right-hand sides by explaining the term or phrase given.

In the middle of the boxes (between the dashed arrows) the students must explained how these terms are connected.

This should help students develop their understanding of the hypothesis and help them to see the 'bigger picture' and how certain concepts link together.

TOPIC: Psychological explanations for bulimia nervosa

BULIMIA – A VICIOUS COGNITIVE CIRCLE

Cooper *et al.*'s (2004) cognitive model of bulimia nervosa (BN) explains the maintenance of the eating disorder as a 'vicious circle' of thoughts, e.g. an individual with BN may believe that binge-eating will make them feel better, or that they are unable to control their eating. These kinds of thoughts trigger a binge, which might continue until thoughts such as 'I will get fat' take over. This then triggers the purge phase of BN, and the individual may then begin vomiting to reduce the harm done by the binge-eating. This then leads to feelings of worthlessness, which may be (temporarily) reduced by eating, then purging, and so the whole process repeats itself.

Handout 78 provides a diagrammatic representation of this process. The tasks at the bottom invite students to explain the process in their own words as well as using key terminology.

Reference

Cooper, P. J., Whelan, E., Woolgar, M., Morrell, J. & Murray, L. (2004). Association between childhood feeding problems and maternal eating disorder: role of the family environment. *The British Journal of Psychiatry*, 184(3), 210–15.

V √ A K √ OS

TOPIC: Biological explanations for bulimia nervosa

MODELLING NEURAL NETWORKS

Like many areas of psychology, there really is little point talking to students about the role of neurotransmitters, synapses and neural pathways in bulimia nervosa unless they have a basic grasp of biological mechanisms in the brain! This modelling activity is described earlier on page 37.

TOPIC: Biological explanations for bulimia nervosa

TRANSLATION

Many of the weaker students are intimidated by the complex language that textbooks sometimes use, particularly when describing biological explanations of behaviour, which can involve unfamiliar terminology.

One way to turn this to your advantage is to ask students to translate passages of text into more familiar language. This is actually a very worthwhile learning activity, as the students will have to process and understand the passage in order to do this. In turn, hopefully this will allow them to develop their confidence in reading, understanding and interpreting the information for themselves.

In **Handout 79,** instructions for this type of activity are included and students are asked to translate the neural explanation of bulimia nervosa for a 12-year-old sufferer so that she can understand one of the possible explanations of her disorder.

Reference

Kaye, W. H., Nagata, T., Weltzin, T. E., Hsua, L. K. G., Sokol, M. S., McConaha, C., Plotnikov, K. H., Weise, J. & Deep, D. (2001). Double-blind placebo-controlled administration of fluoxetine in restricting- and restricting-purging-type anorexia nervosa. *Biological Psychiatry,* 49, 644.

V A K ✓ ★ HORS HANDOUT 80

TOPIC: Biological explanations for bulimia nervosa

BURGER EVALUATIONS

This technique can be used with your students to develop their ability to evaluate *theories* with studies. I (MWG) often find that students struggle with the structure of using research evidence to evaluate a theory. What students forget to do is illustrate that they understand how and why the evidence undermines or supports a theory. Instead, they simply describe a relevant study and expect the reader to draw their own conclusions!

The burger technique asks students to 'sandwich' their study descriptions with evaluative commentary (AO2). You will see from **Handout 80** that students are first encouraged to outline whether the evidence 'supports' or 'undermines' the theory at the top of the burger. Then, in the middle of the burger they outline that evidence – ensuring that they only outline the relevant information of that study, and not every detail. Lastly, and most importantly, at the bottom of the burger they must explain how that study undermines or supports the theory.

In order to evaluate the neural explanation of bulimia nervosa, descriptions of two studies are provided (Walsh *et al.*, 2000; Frank *et al.*, 2002).

References

Frank, G., Kaye, W. H., Meltzer, C. C., Price, J. C., Greer, P., McConaha, C. & Skovira, K. (2002). Reduced 5-HT2A receptor binding after recovery from anorexia nervosa. *Biological Psychiatry*, 52, 896–906.

Walsh, B. T., Wilson, G. T., Loeb, K. L., Devlin, M. J., Pike, K. M., Roose, S. P., Fleiss, J. & Waternaux, C. (2000). Medication and psychotherapy in the treatment of bulimia nervosa. *American Journal Psychiatry,* 154, 523–31.

TOPIC: The role of genes and hormones

PERSONALITY CHARACTERISTICS QUESTIONNAIRE

I (MWG) often find that a good way to start a topic on personality is with some sort of psychometric-style questionnaire. It often generates discussion and then leads in nicely to an introduction to the ideas we will cover in the next few weeks.

Many people believe that males and females differ in a number of their personality traits. (Such beliefs are labelled 'gender stereotypes'.) Like all stereotypes, they may accurately describe some people, but often are exaggerations. When people of both sexes report on their own traits, do they in fact reflect the stereotype? The Personal characteristics questionnaire was designed to find out. See **Handout 81** (scoring instructions on **Handout 82**).

The handout lists 24 statements about socially desirable personality characteristics that have been shown to be gender stereotyped. That is, males are commonly believed to exhibit some of them to a greater degree than females. For others, the reverse is true: females are commonly believed to exhibit them to a greater degree than males.

Possible discussion points

- Compare total scores for males and females in your group on masculinity and femininity scales, as well as masculine–feminine scales.
- What can we conclude about gender stereotypes?
- Are all the males quite similar in what they report about themselves or are they quite variable? What about the females?
- Possible extension for the higher ability: What evaluations could you make of this self-report technique?

References

Spence, J. T. & Helmreich, R. L. (1978). *Masculinity and Femininity: Their Psychological Dimensions, Correlates and Antecedents*. Austin, TX: University of Texas Press.

Spence, J. T., Helmreich, R. L. & Stapp, J. (1973). The Personal Attributes Questionnaire: A measure of sex-role stereotypes and masculinity-femininity. *JSAS Catalog of Selected Documents in Psychology*, 4, 43–44 (Ms. 617).

TOPIC: The role of genes and hormones

MEN ARE FROM MARS, WOMEN FROM VENUS

A good alternative for introducing this topic might be to play a class game of 'Men are from Mars, Women are from Venus'. The board game contains some excellent questions that tease out gender stereotypes. Just search for the board game online. Or perhaps consider buying the CD-Rom version to show on the digital projector. At the time of writing these were available on Amazon for less than £5.

V A K ✓ OS HANDOUT 83

TOPIC: The role of genes and hormones

SPOT THE DELIBERATE MISTAKES

Once you have taught your students the role of genes and hormones in gender development, you could test your students' knowledge and understanding by asking them to spot the 10 deliberate mistakes on **Handout 83**. This can be a good activity to consolidate key terms or key principles, as well as build their confidence about biological mechanisms.

Answers

Correct version: words in bold replace wrong ones on the handout.

Each person has **23** pairs of chromosomes (in each cell of the body). Each of these chromosomes carries hundreds of genes containing instructions about physical and behavioural characteristics such as eye colour and predisposition to certain mental illnesses.

One pair of chromosomes is called the sex chromosomes because they determine an individual's **sex**. In the case of a **female** this pair is called XX because both chromosomes are shaped like Xs. The **male** chromosome pair is described as XY. The Y chromosome carries very little genetic material, although it does determine the sex of a child.

There is usually a direct link between an individual's chromosomal sex (XX and XY) and their **external** genitalia (vagina or penis) and **internal** genitalia (ovaries or testes). During prenatal development all individuals start out the same – a few weeks after conception both male and female embryos have external genitalia that look essentially **feminine**. When the foetus is about three months old, if it is to develop as a male, the testes normally produce the male hormone **testosterone**, which causes male external genitalia to develop.

Genetic transmission explains how individuals acquire their sex. It may also explain some aspects of gender (a person's sense of whether they are male or

female), because of the link between genes, genitalia and hormones.

Chromosomes determine a person's sex but most gender development is actually governed by hormones. These are produced prenatally (e.g. testosterone as described above) and in **adolescence** (a surge of hormones in puberty leads to **secondary** sexual characteristics such as pubic hair). Hormones influence the development of genitalia and/or affect the development of the brain, both of which influence gender development.

V✓A K✓ HORS

TOPIC: Evolutionary explanations of gender roles

EVOLUTIONARY MONSTERS!

Students will understand the evolutionary explanations in much more depth if they first get to grips with the principles of evolutionary explanations of behaviour.

The **evolutionary monsters** activity is a fantastic way to help students with this (see page 15 for a full description and links to **Handout 21**).

V A✓K✓ HOS HANDOUT 84

TOPIC: Evolutionary explanations of gender roles

EVOLVING GENDER ROLES

This activity would follow on particularly well from the 'evolutionary monsters' activity (see above).

Once your students have a basic grasp of evolutionary principles, they can try and apply some of those ideas to gender roles.

Handout 84 describes some of the differences between men and women (stereotyped). Ask your students to hypothesise as to why those differences might have evolved and encourage them to use key words.

Afterwards you can go through some of the psychological theories and compare with your students' ideas.

V✓A✓K HORS HANDOUTS 85-86

TOPIC: The biosocial approach to gender development

THE BOY WHO WAS RAISED A GIRL

One of the classic pieces of gender research concerned twin boys involved in an accidental castration, providing Dr John Money with the perfect opportunity to test the nature vs. nurture explanations of gender identity. In recent years the true facts of this case became known (see John Colapinto's book, *As Nature Made Him*, published by Quartet Books, 2000). In November 2004 the BBC's *Horizon* programme provided a further update of this case after the tragic suicide of 'David Reimer' (see http://www.bbc.co.uk/sn/tvradio/programmes/horizon/dr_money_prog_summary.shtml).

Students never fail to be fascinated by this extreme case study and it is definitely worth reviewing the story in more detail. **Handouts 85 and 86** contain a series of questions for students to answer.

The best way for students to find the answers is to watch the BBC Horizon documentary on the case called 'Dr Money and the Boy with no penis'. At the time of writing this video was available to view at http://www.youtube.com/watch?v=6HRuig46Y8w (then follow the links on the left to parts 2, 3, 4 and 5).

The alternative is to set this as an independent study activity, with students seeking information from a variety of sources: the Internet, textbooks, the library, etc.

References

Curtiss, S. (1977). *Genie: A psycholinguistic study of a modern day 'wild child'*. London: Academic Press.

Rymer, R. (1993). *Genie: Escape from a silent childhood.* London: Michael Joseph.

TOPIC: The biosocial approach to gender development

YOU SAY, WE PAY

Many students feel less confident about any area of psychology that touches on anything biological! This is partly due to the fact that when they pick psychology, despite many warnings, they fail to understand that it contains a lot of biology!

As such, it is wise to spend a healthy amount of time in lessons helping students develop their confidence in key terms and understanding in this area.

An activity my (MWG) students like to play is 'You Say, We Pay' which is basically a variation of a game Richard and Judy used to play on their Channel 4 programme!

Arrange students into groups of three or four. One of the students in each group should be sat on their chair facing away from the front so that they cannot see the whiteboard.

The rest of the group should be positioned so that they can see the whiteboard.

As teacher, you then display key words, phrases or study names one by one on the whiteboard. Those students who can see what you have shown/written need to explain to the student who cannot see what it is. The first team to do this successfully win a point.

If you are a fan of gimmicks (which I clearly am) you can set this up as a race. Superimpose your face onto a stereotypical man's or woman's body (depending on which you think is funnier!) and print as many copies as you have groups. Place them with blue-tack on the left-hand side of the board and whenever a group wins a round, their figure gets moved to the left until they reach the right-hand side of the board and win the race!

Some terms, phrases, etc., you might consider using for this activity are listed below.

- Biosocial
- Testosterone
- Intersex
- Evolution
- Sex difference
- Social role
- Division of labour
- Mate choice
- Social constructionist
- Socialisation
- Selective pressures
- Cultural differences

TOPIC: Cognitive development theory

GENDER CONSTANCY THEORY

On **Handout 87** students must illustrate the limitations children have in their gender thinking at each stage according to their theory. They should use their textbooks to help.

You can encourage them to draw silly images with stick-people, thought bubbles and speech bubbles. I (MWG) personally could not stand drawing when I was at school, so be sure to reassure your students that the end results will not be entered into any competitions and that you are more concerned with the process of the activity as opposed to the end result!

Simple activities like these help students process the information in their textbooks, make the theory relevant in terms of concrete examples, and help the students revise the topics with visual aids.

Reference

Kohlberg, L. (1966). A cognitive-developmental analysis of children's sex-role concepts and attitudes. In E. E. Maccoby (ed.) *The Development of Sex Differences*. Stanford, CA: Stanford University Press.

TOPIC: Cognitive development theory

QUESTION RAFFLE

This is a simple plenary idea that could be used for any topic really where all the students do the work! Definitely a plenary to keep in your armoury when ideas or planning time have dried up!

Give all your students a slip of paper and ask them to write down one question that will test students' knowledge of cognitive development theory. For example, 'Describe stage 2 of gender constancy theory'. The students then each pick a question to answer.

I (MWG) would usually include some question stems on the board to help them.

For example:

- Identify…
- Describe…
- Explain…
- What…
- Who…
- Define…
- Why…

HANDOUTS 88-89

TOPIC: Psychological androgyny and gender dysphoria

THE STORY OF X

Handouts 88 and **89** have a summarised version of the story by Lois Gould 'X', from *Ms.* magazine, May 1980. It links in nicely to some of the issues surrounding psychological androgyny and gender dysphoria.

You could read the story to the students, they could take it in turns to read it out loud, or they could read it on their own. Occasionally if I (MWG) have time, I will illustrate the story on a PowerPoint slide with images, etc.

Possible discussion points

- Could it happen today?
- Why or why not?
- What might the consequences be – to the individual child and its peers?
- How would society have to change (e.g. shops, media, marketing, etc.)?
- How does this study relate to theories of gender?
- How might this study relate to psychological androgyny and gender dysphoria?

TOPIC: Social influences on gender roles

CONTENT ANALYSIS OF ADVERTISEMENTS

This is an excellent idea that was included in the previous version of the *A2 Teacher's Companion*. In the days when students had to do a non-experimental piece of coursework, a popular choice was to conduct a content analysis of advertisements on TV related to gender stereotypes. The importance of ads is that they affirm existing gender stereotypes, which lead us to have different expectations for female and male behaviour, which then has a profound influence on how we behave. Research has not just focussed on TV ads but also looked at ads in magazines.

There is a variety of research on this topic. The following summary is adapted from: Copyright [1981] by Psi Chi, the National Honor Society in Psychology [www.psichi.org]. Reprinted with permission. All rights reserved.

- **Women are underrepresented.**

Sommers-Flanagan *et al.* (1993) found that music videos feature roughly twice as many males as females. Women are not seen much, but they are heard even less. You can simply count the gender of the person doing voiceovers on ads or gender representation in music videos.

- **Women's and men's bodies are represented differently.**

In magazine advertisements women are much more likely than men to serve a decorative function. Women recline in seductive clothing, caressing a liquor bottle, or they drape themselves coyly on the nearest male. They bend their bodies at a ludicrous angle, or they look as helpless as six year olds. They also may be painfully thin. In contrast, men stand up, they look competent, and they look purposeful (Jones, 1991).

- **Women and men are shown doing different activities.**

In magazine advertisements, men are rarely portrayed doing housework. Instead, men are more likely than women to be shown working outside the home. The world of paid employment is not emphasised for women. For example, an analysis of the articles in *Seventeen* magazine demonstrated that only 7% of the contents concerned career planning, independence, and other self-development topics. In contrast, 46% of the contents concerned appearance (Peirce, 1990). In magazine advertisements, men are rarely portrayed doing housework. Basically, the media world often represents men and women as living in separate spheres.

- **Women are cast in a dependent role.**

One of the classic studies of TV advertising was conducted by Manstead and McCulloch (1981). They analysed 170 ads (they started with about 300 observed over a one-week period on British TV but ignored those that contained only children and animals). The adult central figure in each ad was identified and classified on a number of criteria. Women were found to be more likely to be portrayed as product users, to be cast in a dependent role, to produce no arguments in favour of the product and to be shown at home.

Similar results were produced in a later study by Harris and Stobart (1986), which also compared daytime versus evening ads. Harris and Stobart analysed eight aspects of the central figures' behaviour: credibility basis, role, argument, product type, location of central character, type of reward provided by the product for central character, gender of the background figures and humour. These categories could form the basis of a detailed content analysis.

Possible activities

- Ask students to bring in teen magazines and analyse the gender stereotyping in the ads in terms of central character, how male/female bodies are represented, what men and women are portrayed doing.
- Ask students to watch music videos and compare male and female vocalists in terms of what they are portrayed doing.
- Ask each student to observe TV ads. For each ad they should record the product being advertised, and the programme that was being shown either side of it (e.g. children's programme, male-interest, female-interest, family-interest). For each central character they should record gender and what that person is doing in the ad (were they the user or the authority or other role?).

You could compare daytime and evening advertising, or compare advertising during 'male' type programmes and 'female' type programmes.

References

Harris, P. R. & Stobart, J. (1986). Sex-role stereotyping in television advertisements. *British Journal of Social Psychology*, 25, 155–64.

Jones, M. (1991). Gender stereotyping in advertisements. *Teaching of Psychology,* 18, 231–3.

Manstead, A. & McCulloch, C. (1981). Sex-role stereotyping in British television advertisements. *British Journal of Social Psychology*, 20, 171–80.

Peirce, K. (1990). A feminist theoretical perspective on the socialization of teenage girls through *Seventeen* magazine. *Sex Roles*, 23, 491–500.

Sommers-Flanagan, R., Sommers-Flanagan, J. & Davis, B. (1993). What's happening on music television? A gender role content analysis. *Sex Roles*, 28, 745–53.

HANDOUT 90

TOPIC: Social influences on gender roles

DO TV SHOWS MAKE TEENAGERS SEXIST?

Handout 90 describes a recent study on the influence of the media on gender roles.

Rivadeneyra and Lebo (2008) investigated the relationship between TV use and gender role attitudes and behaviour in dating. In this study, they make reference to many TV shows that your students may be aware of, for example 'The OC'.

There are a series of questions at the bottom of the handout for students to answer or discuss in groups (e.g. using techniques such as **Random numbers** – see page 3), which encourage them to consider what we learn from the study as well as apply knowledge of 'How Science Works' (AO3).

This type of activity is increasingly important during A2 Psychology as students are expected to be much more independent in their commentary and analysis.

Moreover, we should always remember that many of them will be at university in less than a year's time and they won't have us to hold their hands!

References

Rivadeneyra, R. & Lebo, M. J. (2008). The association between television-viewing behaviours and adolescent dating role attitudes and behaviours. *Journal of Adolescence,* 31, 291–305.

Rivadeneyra, R. & Ward, L.M. (2005). From Ally McBeal to Sabado Gigante: Contributions of television viewing to the gender role attitudes of Latino adolescents. *Journal of Adolescent Research,* 20(4), 453–75.

TOPIC: Cross-cultural studies of gender role

COLLABORATIVE CONCLUSIONS

To start the cross-cultural studies topic, consider affording your students the opportunity to reflect on the relevance of this topic.

Set them a starter question such as: 'If gender roles were the same in every culture – what would this suggest?'

Ask students to consider this question using a collaborative learning structure such as **Random numbers** or **Group statements** (see page 3).

During the feedback session hopefully some of the groups will draw on the idea that the implication of the statement is that biology must determine gender role.

V A✓K✓ HOGS HANDOUT 91

TOPIC: Cross-cultural studies of gender role

STUDY DECONSTRUCTION

One of the most famous cross-cultural studies of gender differences is Buss' (1989) study of 37 cultures.

Handout 91 provides students with a study deconstruction sheet. In PSYA4 students may be expected to be able to analyse an unseen study in terms of 'How Science Works'. In addition, students are required to provide synoptic commentary throughout A2 Psychology. As such, it is wise to give your students opportunities to practise these skills and develop their confidence.

Ask them to use their textbooks or the Internet to research the study and complete this handout.

Reference

Buss, D. M. (1989). Sex differences in human mate preferences: evolutionary hypotheses tested in 37 cultures. *Behavioral and Brain Sciences*, 12, 1–49.

V A K✓ ★HOS

TOPIC: Cross-cultural studies of gender role

QUICK SENTENCE PLENARY

Another quick and simple plenary idea.

Ask your students to pick a number between 25 and 40 (alternatively you could use the ICT 'Randomiser' technique described on page 6).

Then ask them to summarise the topic (cross-cultural studies of gender role) in exactly that amount of words.

Encourage them not to make bland or vague statements but rather to pinpoint exactly what we learn from the topic in terms of gender.

This activity develops their summary skills analysis and allows them to reflect on what they have covered in lessons and the overall point.

V √ A √ K OGS HANDOUT 92

TOPIC: The psychometric approach

PSYCHOMETRIC WORD WALL

Three psychometric approaches are represented in the word wall at the top of the handout. Students are to colour code each brick in the wall according to the approach they relate to. Following this, students choose two theories to outline.

Before beginning this task, the sections below the word wall should be completed to encourage students to reflect on their knowledge and understanding.

Once students have decided which two theories they wish to outline, they could work in pairs to complete the 100-word summary, then form a new pairing to complete the 200-word summary. One method to speed up marking is to ask students to produce one piece of writing between them, then after marking that one piece, photocopy the work so both students receive a marked piece of work.

To ensure both students in the pair contribute, you could set a rule that each student must write one summary or, if using ICT, take it in turns to type. Grouping students could be based on ability, allowing the teacher to spend more time with students who may struggle with the task, or mixed ability pairings so more able students can take on the role of teacher.

References

Cattell, R. B. (1943). The measurement of adult intelligence. *Psychological Bulletin*, 40, 153–93.
Guildford, J. P. (1977). *Way beyond the IQ*. Amherst, MA: Creative Education Foundation.
Spearman, C. (1927). *The abilities of man, their nature, and measurement*. London: Macmillan Publishing.

V √ A √ K HS HANDOUT 93

TOPIC: The information-processing approach

EXPLODING THE EVALUATION: TRIARCHIC THEORY OF INTELLIGENCE

Three pieces of research relating to triarchic theory are displayed on the handout. Students are asked to apply their knowledge and understanding to this evidence, accessing AO1, AO2 and AO3 skills. Labelled text boxes are provided on the handout for students to explain words, apply their knowledge to real-life examples and evaluate the research outlined on the handout. Once completed, this work could form part of a writing frame for an essay on information processing, helping students to develop their evaluative points. For example, 'Discuss the information-processing approach to intelligence' (9 marks + 16 marks).

References

Berg, C. A. & Sternberg, R. J. (1985). A triarchic theory of intellectual development during adulthood. *Developmental Review*, 5, 334–70.
Cunningham, W. R. & Tomer, A. (1991). Intellectual abilities and age: Concepts, theories, and analysis. In E. Lovelace (ed.) *Aging and cognition: Mental processes, self-awareness and interventions*. Amsterdam: North Holland, 379–406.
Gottfredson, L. (2003). Dissecting practical intelligence theory: its claims and its evidence. *Intelligence,* 31, 343–97.
Spearman, C. (1927). *The abilities of man, their nature, and measurement*. London: Macmillan Publishing.
Sternberg, R. J., Grigorenko, E. L., Ferrari, M. & Clinkenbeard, P. (1999). The triarchic model applied to gifted identification, instruction and assessment. In N. Colangelo & S. G. Assouline (eds) *Talented development III: Proceedings from the Henry B and Jocelyn Wallace National Research Symposium on Talent development*. Scottsdale, AZ: Gifted and Talented Psychological Press, 71–80.
Williams, W. M., Blythe, T., White, N., Li, J., Gardner, H. & Sternberg, R. J. (2002). Practical intelligence for school: developing metacognitive sources of achievement in adolescence. *Developmental Review,* 22, 162–210.

V √ A √ K √ HOT HANDOUT 94

TOPIC: Gardner's theory of multiple intelligences

MULTIPLE INTELLIGENCE MIX UP AND MASTERMIND

A quick and easy task that can be used as a starter, introduction to multiple intelligences or as a revision activity. Students simply match the description of each intelligence to the relevant term. Matching could be by colour coding or cutting and sticking onto a fresh piece of paper. I (RCG) think a simple extension could involve students predicting which intelligence they feel they rely on the most, then test these predictions by completing a multiple intelligence questionnaire on line at: http://surfaquarium.com/MI/.

The second activity, Mastermind, employs higher order thinking. Students should try to answer as many questions as possible in the time set and challenge themselves by choosing at least one question they find difficult to answer. To differentiate the task, students could be assigned certain questions to address.

Reference

Gardner, H. (1983). *Frames of mind: the theory of multiple intelligences*. New York: Basic Books.

V A✓ K✓ OT HANDOUT 95

TOPIC: Classical conditioning

SEA LION TRAINING

To complete the first activity students need to apply their knowledge of behaviourist principles to explain the process of sea lion training. Students who complete this task quickly can be directed to the phenomena listed on the handout and asked to explain how they will deal with them in the course of the training. The remainder of the task focusses on reinforcement schedules, again asking students to apply their understanding of behaviourism to the process. Brave students could be encouraged to role play their training for the rest of the class, explaining the psychology behind their actions.

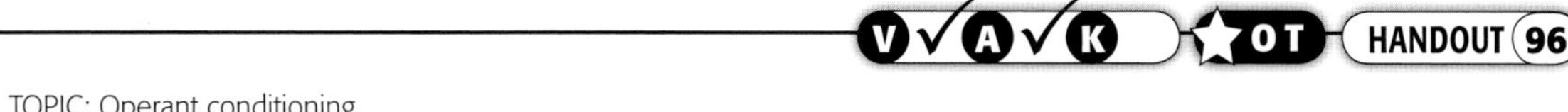

V✓ A✓ K OT HANDOUT 96

TOPIC: Operant conditioning

HELPING HANDS

This handout is split into AO1 and AO2 sections and can act as a writing frame for students writing essays on conditioning. The first two hands ask students to summarise classical and operant conditioning using five points for each. Students could draw round their own hands and write one point along each digit with the type of conditioning displayed on the palm.

The sections that follow allow students to practise their evaluation skills in asking them to identify research evidence that supports the points made on the handout. Should students complete this task and wish to deepen their understanding, they could be directed to the extension activity in which they consider the advantages and disadvantages of taking a reductionist approach.

V A✓ K HT HANDOUT 97

TOPIC: Conditioning and the behaviour of animals

MAKING PREDICTIONS

Students are challenged to apply their understanding of conditioning to the behaviour of animals by addressing the prediction questions on the handout. More able students may enjoy attempting this task before reading about the subject to extend their experience and then checking their ideas in their textbook. Less able students may find the activity more accessible if introduced to it after reading about animal training.

Reference

Clay, A. W., Bloomsmith, M. A., Marr, M. J. & Mapel, T. L. (2009). Habituation and desensitization as methods for reducing fearful behaviour in singly housed rhesus macaques. *American Journal of Primatology*, 71 (1), 30–9.

V✓ A✓ K OT HANDOUT 98

TOPIC: Intelligence in non-human animals

CARTOON CRITTERS

Students should read about self-awareness and then create a cartoon showing one research study into self-recognition in animals. In the handout I (RCG) gave the example of elephants but any animal study would be sufficient. These cartoons could be used to form a classroom display. You could encourage a little competition for the best cartoon as judged by another member of staff or class vote. Students who would benefit from developing the depth of their understanding could be directed to the extension question at the bottom of the handout and consider the validity of the research they have drawn. The handout refers to the elephant study but this can be easily changed to the animal they have researched.

Reference

Plotnik, J. M., de Waal, F. B. M. & Reiss, D. (2006). Self-recognition in an Asian elephant. *Proceedings of the National Academy of Sciences, USA,* 103(45), 17053–7.

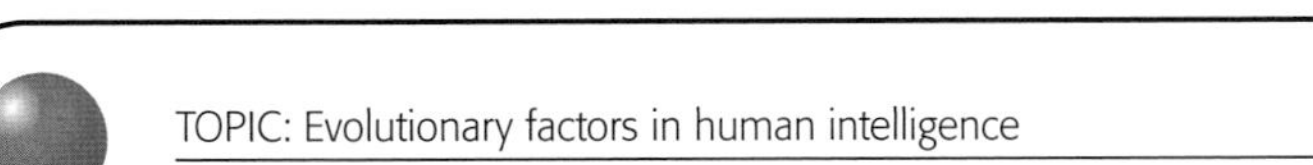

TOPIC: Evolutionary factors in human intelligence

COLOUR CODING

The initial colour coding task simply assesses AO1 understanding of the meat sharing hypothesis and Machiavellian intelligence. These statements could then be used for guide writing of a 100-word summary of each explanation.

The second task targets AO2 skills. Students read each evaluative comment and make a judgement: does it provide strong support for the theory (green light), does it only give reasonable support (amber) or does the comment only provide weak commentary (red light). Once a decision has been made students explain the judgements made and which explanation the comments relate to. It may help students to model the first study as a class to guide their judgement making, so they strive to produce a good level of detail.

References

Cosmides, L. (1989). The logic of social exchange: has natural selection shaped how humans reason? Studies with the Watson selection task. *Cognition,* 31, 187–276.

Hill, K. & Kaplan, K. (1988). Tradeoffs in male and female reproductive strategies among the Ache. In L. Betzig, M. Borgerhoff Mulder and P. Turke (eds) *Human Reproductive Behaviour: A Darwinian Perspective*. Cambridge, Cambridge University Press.

Mitani, J. & Watts, D. (2001). Why do chimpanzees hunt and share meat? *Animal Behaviour,* 61, 915–24.

Stanford, C. B. (1999). *The Hunting Apes: Meat-eating and the Origins of Human Behaviour*. Princeton, NJ, Princeton University Press.

Whitten, A. & Byrne, R. W. (1988). Tactical deception in primates. *Behavioural and Brain Sciences,* 11, 233–44.

Wrangham, R. W. (1975). The behavioural ecology of chimps in Gombe National Park, Tanzania. PhD thesis, University of Cambridge.

TOPIC: Genetic factors in intelligence-test performance

GUT REACTIONS

The gut reaction aspect of this handout could form the basis of small group discussions where students can discuss any aspect of each research study. This gut reaction could relate to any aspect and suggested topics are shown in the box below the two studies. Working in mixed ability groups may help generate a wider range of ideas that students can then feed back to the class. Individually students then record one gut reaction on their handout.

Again working as a group or alone, if preferred, students use their textbook to find one research study related to the comment and develop this into a PEE paragraph (see page 11 for details). Less able students may find the expansion section difficult and will benefit from teacher or peer support.

References

Bouchard, T. J. & McGue, M. (1981). Familial studies of intelligence: a review. *Science,* 212, 1055–9.

Hill, L., Craig, I. W., Chorney, M. J., Chorney, K. & Plomin, R. (1999). IGF2R and cognitive ability in children. *Molecular Psychiatry*, 4 (Suppl. 108).

TOPIC: Environmental factors in intelligence-test performance

ORGANISING INFORMATION

Ideally this handout should be photocopied onto A3 paper to provide enough space to record details for each section. Each section relates to a different environmental factor in intelligence-test performance. In the middle section record any key words relating to the factor, in the next band summarise the main ideas relating to each factor, the third band provides space to record research evidence, while for the final band students are asked to make a comment on the evidence. This comment could take the form of a methodological evaluation or noting additional support from another study or contradictory evidence. This outer band could be an option for some students but a requirement for those who are more confident in this topic. Reading for each section could be placed on different tables around the room and students move to each area to complete one section before moving on.

V A✓K✓ OG HANDOUT 102

TOPIC: Piaget's theory of cognitive development

PIAGET'S POSTCARDS

On receiving the handout I (RCG) ask students to cut out the two cards and stick them back to back to form a double-sided postcard. On the section headed 'Sender ______' students write their name and beneath explain one point or area they understand about Piaget's theory. On the facing side students are given the opportunity to nominate another classmate and ask them a question concerning an aspect of the theory they are unsure of. To ensure all students receive a post card the teacher could write a name on the 'To_____' header. This would allow differentiation to occur as students could receive a card from a peer of similar ability. Once cards have been received an answer to the query is recorded on the reverse of the card. However, in returning the card to the sender it becomes lost in the post and another student is asked to add further information on the top. To ensure random selection all completed postcards could be put in a box (representing a postman's sack) and students select a new card or a few students could be nominated as postmen/women and deliver the mail.

Reference

Piaget, J. (1954). *The Construction of Reality in the Child.* New York: Basic Books.

V A✓K✓ S

TOPIC: Piaget's theory of cognitive development

PIAGET'S POST-ITS

As a lesson starter the class may enjoy playing Piaget's Post-its. Write stages and key words from each stage, one on each Post-it until you have one for each student. Without looking at the word, students stick the note onto their forehead. Students have to work out what is written on their Post-it (stuck on their head) by only asking Yes or No questions. To extend this activity, once students have worked out their word, challenge the class to form groups of all relevant words and stages. First complete group wins.

V✓A✓K HS HANDOUT 103

TOPIC: Vygotsky's theory of cognitive development

READING FOR MEANING

This task encourages students to read a piece of text for meaning, i.e. to read to gather specific information. Below the passage students are given space to record in the magnifying glass any key words that should be a focus in any AO1 outline. The eraser provides a section to note words that may add to meaning but could be excluded in a briefer outline. Students are asked to represent the information in pictorial form on the note pad, this may be suited to a diagram of the zone of proximal development. To help revision, students record three points to remember on the memory pad in the left-hand corner of the handout.

This handout can be easily modified for use in other exam areas by simply changing the topic of the passage.

As a development of this handout students could be set a homework to write a letter to a Psychological Journal as if they were Vygotsky commenting on Piaget's ideas OR write a letter as Piaget as a reaction to reading Vygotsky's work in 1958 after it has been translated into English.

References

Piaget, J. (1954). *The Construction of Reality in the Child.* New York: Basic Books.

Vygotsky, L. S. (1934, reprinted 1962). *Thought and Language.* Cambridge, MA, MIT Press.

TOPIC: Bruner's theory of cognitive development

BRUNER WORD WEB

My (RCG) students find this is a challenging task involving higher order thinking to see connections between individual words. Students could be given a minimum amount of connections to complete either based on amount of two-word links or measured by length; for example, make a four-word connection. Working in a pair or small mixed ability group may help students see the links between words.

For example: enactive ----------early childhood------------ action-based skills.

An extension to this could involve choosing at least one of the word webs created and use it to produce an outline of one aspect of Bruner's theory of cognitive development.

References

Bower, G. H., Clark, M., Lesgold, A. & Winzenz, D. (1969). Hierarchical retrieval schemes, in recall categorised word lists. *Journal of Verbal Learning and Verbal Behaviour*, 8, 323–43.

Bruner, J. S. (1966). *Towards a theory of instruction.* Cambridge, MA: Harvard University Press.

TOPIC: Bruner's theory of cognitive development

20 QUESTIONS

Other activities you may wish to play are the 20 questions game used by Mosher & Hornsby (1966), who looked at the strategies used by children aged 6 to 12 in the game of 20 questions, to ascertain why a car went off the road. Older children used constraint-locating questions (Was it night-time?) whereas younger children asked direct hypothesis-testing questions.

Record the questions asked as you play to allow students to identify which questions are constraint-located and which are hypothesis-testing.

Alternatively, a starter based on Bower *et al.* (1969) would involve giving half the class key words randomly from the word web (before doing word web handout) while the other half of class have key words organised in lists (for each skill set, etc.). Students are given one minute to learn words then remove lists and set immediate recall challenge. Who does better?

References

Bower, G. H., Clark, M., Lesgold, A. & Winzenz, D. (1969). Hierarchical retrieval schemes, in recall categorised word lists. *Journal of Verbal Learning and Verbal Behaviour*, 8, 323–43.

Mosher, F. A. & Hornsby, J. R. (1966). On asking questions. In J. S. Bruner, R. R. Olver & P. M. Greenfield (eds) *Studies in cognitive growth.* New York: Wiley.

TOPIC: Applications of these theories to education

SAVE OR STEAL?

I (RCG) find this activity works well when students are placed in matched ability pairs. Initially working alone, students record two basic points relating to the application of each theory to education. Next, ideas are shared with a peer and recorded on the second section of the handout. A variation of this could see students moving around the class to find basic points from a range of different people rather than just one neighbour. Alone once again, students read the four points gathered for each theorist. They can only choose two points per theorist so have to decide whether to save their points or steal a neighbour's ideas by highlighting the comments they wish to keep. This requires students to consider the value of their own and others' comments and make a judgement on the work.

The remainder of the handout focuses on AO2 skills in evaluating each theorist.

References

Bruner, J. S. (1966). *Towards a theory of instruction.* Cambridge, MA: Harvard University Press.

Piaget, J. (1954). *The Construction of Reality in the Child.* New York: Basic Books.

Vygotsky, L. S. (1934, reprinted 1962). *Thought and Language*. Cambridge, MA: MIT Press.

Wood, D. J., Bruner, J. S. & Ross, G. (1976). The role of tutoring in problem-solving. *Journal of Child Psychology and Psychiatry,* 17, 89–100.

TOPIC: Applications of these theories to education

CLASS VOTE

You could consider holding a class vote regarding views of Wood *et al.* (1976): which of the six stages identified do students feel best promotes learning? Students tick or place their initials in a chart then explain their choice. Further to this, provide students with a copy of your school/college's lesson plan. Ask your students to create a lesson using activities influenced by one (or more) theory.

You could give them a psychology topic and ask them to teach the lesson.

Reference

Wood, D. J., Bruner, J. S. & Ross, G. (1976). The role of tutoring in problem-solving. *Journal of Child Psychology and Psychiatry,* 17, 89–100.

TOPIC: Kohlberg's theory of moral understanding

SYNOPTIC-I-TREE

This handout is best presented photocopied onto an A3 sheet to allow space to add details as the lesson progresses. Starting with the branches on the left students record the problems they can identify from simply reading about Kohlberg's theory. Halfway through the lesson stop and allow time to add any new understanding or the problems Kohlberg's theory faces to the middle branches. As a plenary, work as a class to add any final knowledge gained to the branches on the right. Each leaf provides an area to record a brief point or key word. At the end of the activity students could record comments such as issues relating to gender and cultural bias. This could form the basis of a classroom display with each student creating one larger leaf to be stuck onto a tree.

References

Kohlberg, L. (1966). A cognitive-developmental analysis of children's sex-role concepts and attitudes. In E. E. Maccoby (ed.) *The Development of Sex Differences.* Stanford, CA: Stanford University Press.

Kohlberg, L. (1975). The cognitive developmental approach to moral education. *Phi Delta Kappan,* 46, 670–7.

V✓ A✓ K✓ ★ O S

TOPIC: Kohlberg's theory of moral understanding

MAKING A DECISION

A second task could see the teacher reading the Heinz moral dilemma to the class. Anonymously students record their decision on a Post-it note. Display each stage of moral development identified by Kohlberg on the board and allow students to stick their Post-it notes on the relevant stage.

This could be achieved by gathering all decisions in and assigning them randomly to small groups to allocate to each level, or reading decisions made out loud to class and asking the class to assign them to a level (suitable for smaller classes).

References

Kohlberg, L. (1966). A cognitive-developmental analysis of children's sex-role concepts and attitudes. In E. E. Maccoby (ed.) *The Development of Sex Differences.* Stanford, CA: Stanford University Press.

Kohlberg, L. (1975). The cognitive developmental approach to moral education. *Phi Delta Kappan,* 46, 670–7.

HANDOUT 107

TOPIC: Eisenberg's theory of prosocial reasoning

LEVELS OF PROSOCIAL REASONING

Students read the scenario based on Eisenberg's prosocial stories. For each speech bubble the age of the speaker and the level of their reasoning need to be identified.

As an extension to this first task, students could try to create their own prosocial stories and carry out a research study into responses given by different ages or genders. Create categorical data by giving participants one of five choices (each choice relates to one specific level identified by Eisenberg).

Working in ability-based groups and using textbook reading, students build an evaluation of Eisenberg's theory.

Reference

Eisenberg, N. (1982). The development of reasoning regarding prosocial behaviour. In N. Eisenberg (ed.) *The Development of Prosocial Behaviour*. New York: Academic Press.

V✓ A✓ K ★RS HANDOUT 108

TOPIC: Development of a child's sense of self

EVALUATION OF SENSE OF SELF STUDIES

To encourage students to develop their evaluative paragraphs, this handout models the PEE structure (Point, Evidence, Expansion). Less able students may benefit from working as a class to complete the first PEE then give a short time frame to attempt the second before feeding back and attempting the remaining paragraphs. You may wish to promote independent research for more able students by removing the evidence information and asking them to find their own studies.

References

Baron-Cohen, S. (1995). *Mind blindness: an essay on autism and theory of mind*. Cambridge, MA: MIT Press.

Borke, J., Eickhorst, A. & Keller, H. (2007). Father-infant interaction, parental ideas about early childcare, and the consequences for development of children's self recognition. *The Journal of Genetic Psychology*, 168(4), 365–79.

Mahler, M. S., Pine, F. & Bergman, A. (1973). *The psychological birth of the human infant*. New York: Basic Books.

Pipp, S., Easterbrooks, M. A. & Harmon, R. J. (1992). The relationship between attachment and knowledge of self and mother in one-to-three-year-old infants. *Child Development*, 63, 738–50.

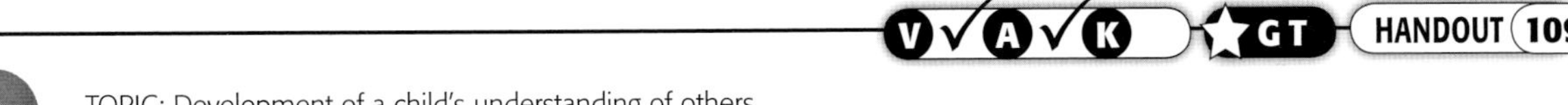

V✓ A✓ K ★GT HANDOUT 109

TOPIC: Development of a child's understanding of others

BUILDING BLOCKS

Using their textbook students read about research into children's understanding of others. From this they identify six key words from the passage and record them in the first set of blocks. Ask students to write some of the words on the board. From the class ideas students can then add any new words onto the second set of blocks. As a group, students decide which words are the most relevant and must be included in any description of research into children's understanding of others. Using these words the group creates a 300-word description of the development of a child's understanding of others, which each student records on the note page at the bottom of the handout.

One option to differentiate this task would be to colour code words: one colour for most words central to the topic, another for additional words that could be included. More able students have to include both sets of coloured blocks, less able just use the central words.

V✓ A✓ K✓ ★OT HANDOUT 110

TOPIC: Biological explanations of social cognition

STEPPING STONES

Students should move from the bottom of the page to the top of the page by answering the question in a stepping stone. The next stone chosen must be touching the stone they have just answered. Some stones may be easier than others, so students should be encouraged to challenge themselves. Stones cover AO1, AO2 and AO3 skills and students could be asked to colour code stones accordingly before or after completing the task. Student answers can be taken in to be marked or form the basis of a peer activity where students read their partner's answers to check they are accurate and detailed.

An alternative activity could involve giving students answers and asking them to decide which question the response relates to. To add a kinaesthetic element, stones could be reproduced, one stone on one A3 sheet and placed on the floor. Students have to physically move across the stones answering questions. This could form a race with three students (each one representing a small group) trying to cross the stones by answering questions in turn. Group members help their team mate by researching the answer to each stone and directing the player which stone to take. Only one player allowed on a stone at a time. An incorrect answer sends the player back one stone.

Reference

Slack, G. (2007). Source of human empathy found in brain. *New Scientist*, 12 November, 26–29.

V✓A K✓ OTS HANDOUT 111

TOPIC: Classification and diagnosis of schizophrenia

MATCHING CLINICAL KEY TERMS

The clinical diagnosis of schizophrenia, in particular, does seem to intimidate some students because it involves numerous unfamiliar terms.

A simple way to help students learn these or to recap their learning is a matching exercise (**Handout 111**).

Students can either cut out the boxes and rearrange, or they could simply draw lines from the term to the definition (although this can get messy).

An extension activity could be that students highlight the symptoms of schizophrenia in terms of positive symptoms (those that appear to excess or distort normal functions) and negative symptoms (those that reflect a loss of normal functions).

Not, as some students think, positive and negative symptoms in terms which are nice and which are bad (seriously, every year there is at least one despite my (MWG) explanations!).

V✓A✓K✓ HORS HANDOUTS 112-113

TOPIC: Classification and diagnosis of schizophrenia

IT IS NOT AS CLEAR CUT AS YOU THINK

Until now, many students will have probably considered schizophrenia an objective and absolute mental illness. They've heard about it on the TV and doctors talk about it.

However, as psychologists we know that to some extent schizophrenia is actually a social construction and merely a collective of symptoms bundled together and called 'schizophrenia' (I suppose this depends on your opinion).

In many ways it is difficult to open students' minds to the possibility that 'schizophrenia' as an objective and definitive illness doesn't actually exist (despite the fact that the symptoms do!).

A good starting point might be Rosenhan's (1973) 'On being sane in insane places' study, which opens the possibility that psychiatrists and their diagnoses might not be infallible. There are a number of good short video clips about this on YouTube.

Then consider using **Handouts 112** and **113** with your students.

They should use the list of symptoms in the box on **Handout 113** and place them in the Venn diagram on **Handout 112**. Then check their answers using their textbook or the Internet.

Hopefully, this activity will illustrate to students that diagnosis of schizophrenia is not 'clear cut' and that many of the symptoms used to diagnose schizophrenia are also used to diagnose depression and bipolar disorder. This would hopefully lead to a good discussion about the validity of the current clinical characteristics of diagnosis of this mental disorder.

For answers (according to my research!) see below.

Schizophrenia only:

- Disorganised speech
- Affective flattening
- Alogia (poverty of speech).

Schizophrenia and bipolar disorder:

- Delusions
- Halluncinations
- Psychomotor disturbances
- Subjective experience that thoughts are racing
- Inflated self-esteem and feelings/beliefs of grandiosity.

Bipolar disorder only:

- Periods of mania (elevated mood)
- Alternating moods between depression and mania
- Excessive involvement in pleasurable activities.

Bipolar disorder and depression:

- Depressed mood most of the day, nearly everyday
- Significant weight loss or weight gain
- Insomnia or hypersomnia
- Feelings of worthlessness
- Recurrent thoughts of suicide.

Depression only:

- Depressed mood most of the day, nearly every day without any periods of elevated mood (mania).

Depression, schizophrenia and bipolar disorder:

- Inability to do everyday tasks
- Difficulty concentrating.

Reference

Rosenhan, D. L. (1973). On being sane in insane places. *Science*, 179, 250–8.

TOPIC: Classification and diagnosis of schizophrenia

A BEAUTIFUL MIND

Schizophrenia can and has been extremely poorly portrayed in the media, with teenage soaps in particular being guilty. In fact, many students think that schizophrenia is more like split-personality disorder as a result of their viewing experiences.

One film which I (MWG) believe portrays schizophrenia in an excellent way is 'A Beautiful Mind', which stars Russell Crowe as John Nash, a famous academic who suffered from the disorder.

From what I am led to believe there are some fairly large inaccuracies in the film when compared to the experiences of John Nash (for example, he only ever suffered from auditory hallucinations, whereas in the film his hallucinations are visual, which I guess makes it a more watchable film!).

However, the film gives a much better sense of how a person can actually live a relatively normal life whilst suffering from the disorder when it is under control.

In addition, he does not kill anyone, bomb anyone, and the camera does not zoom in and out incessantly nor the focus blur when it is from his perspective in order to 'illustrate' his madness. Unfortunately all too many TV shows do depict schizophrenia in this way.

As such, to cut a long rant short, I (MWG) would advise your students to watch some clips from the film so they get a more rounded perspective! Perhaps even show the whole thing after school. Copies can be purchased on Amazon for as little as £3.

V A K O S

TOPIC: Biological explanations of schizophrenia

UNDERSTANDING TWIN STUDIES

The genetic and evolutionary explanations of schizophrenia often rest heavily on evidence from twin studies.

In the past, I (MWG) have found that many students struggle to understand and interpret the results of twin studies.

Consider using (and possibly adapting) **Handout 65** as a way of introducing the logic of twin studies. The activity was described earlier on page 38.

TOPIC: Biological explanations of schizophrenia

BEING SYNOPTIC – NATURE OR NUTURE?

Outlining and evaluating biological explanations provides students with a perfect opportunity to include synoptic commentary related to issues, debates and approaches and to gain extra AO2 marks.

Handout 114 provides students with a writing frame in which to practise this skill. They could use their textbook and notes to help them.

V A K H O S HANDOUT 115

TOPIC: Psychological explanations of schizophrenia

DOUBLE BINDS – NO WIN SITUATION!

Bateson *et al.* (1956) suggest that children who frequently receive contradictory messages from their parents are more likely to develop schizophrenia. For example, if a mother tells her son that she loves him, yet at the same time turns her head away in disgust, the child receives two conflicting messages about their relationship on different communicative levels, one of affection on the verbal level and one of animosity on the non-verbal level.

According to the theory these interactions prevent the development of an internally coherent construction of reality, and in the long run, this manifests itself as schizophrenic symptoms.

Bateson *et al.* (1956) called these contradictory messages 'double binds'. **Handout 115** provides examples of some double binds to help your students put this in context.

Ask them to explain how and why these examples are double binds.

Reference

Bateson, G., Jackson, D. D., Haley, J. & Weakland, J. H. (1956). Towards a theory of schizophrenia. *Behavioural Science*, 1(4), 251–64.

V✓ A✓ K✓ ★HOGS

TOPIC: Psychological explanations of schizophrenia

BACK TO NATURE VS. NURTURE – STUDENT DIMENSION LINE

Having completed your teaching of both the biological and psychological explanations of schizophrenia, this is another ideal time to reflect on the nature vs. nurture debate and synoptic commentary.

Display a dimension line on the whiteboard (from nature to nurture). Give each student a Post-it note and ask them to place it on the dimension line to reflect how much they think schizophrenia is the result of nature or nurture.

There should be a focus on evidence and evaluation in this activity. As such, either ask them to articulate a justification of their position on their Post-it note with evidence, or 'fold' the student dimension line (see page 3) and then get students to discuss with each other their ideas and feed back to class.

You could even use this activity for the basis of a debate.

V✓ A K✓ ★HORS HANDOUT 116

TOPIC: Biological therapies for schizophrenia

CONNECT 4

Often students are fazed by the biological model and the associated therapies because of the 'long words'(!) and the interconnected nature of it. Therefore, it is important to help students deconstruct the model into its basic parts, and then to help them link it together. This is the aim of **Handout 116**.

In the grey shaded areas, students should articulate their understanding of the principles, i.e. nature vs. nurture, neurotransmitters, antipsychotic medication, etc.

In between the grey shaded areas, students should try and explain how the elements of the theory link together. For example, neurotransmitters are linked to antipsychotic medication because the drugs influence the effects of neurotransmitters such as dopamine by binding to receptors and blocking their action (and hence reducing high dopamine activity associated with hallucinations and delusions).

V A✓ K ★HORGS HANDOUT 117

TOPIC: Biological therapies for schizophrenia

STORYTIME: 'THE MAGIC SHOES'

Handout 117 describes the story of Dave, his poor dancing and the (fake) 'magic shoes' that he buys from a con man.

The story tells the tale of a man who hates dancing and has no confidence in his ability. That is, until a man sells him 'magic shoes', which transform his dancing moves and coordination. Dave's dancing vastly improves.

The twist in the tale is that the 'magic shoes' were actually fake, yet Dave's dancing improved anyway.

This sounds to me like the perfect tale to explain the **placebo effect,** which students need to understand in order to interpret the findings of studies that investigate the effectiveness of drug therapies for schizophrenia.

Thank you very much to Alana Clogan for writing this story (and others) for this book. We think they are excellent!

V✓ A K✓ ★HORS HANDOUT 118

TOPIC: Psychological therapies for schizophrenia

EVALUATION AND ELABORATION: CBT

Handout 118 is designed to illustrate to students the level of depth required to achieve top AO2 marks.

Students should start by reading the boxes on the far left-hand side of the page, which outline simple evaluation points. Ask them to highlight (or shade in) each of the boxes in that column with a different colour.

The students should then read the boxes in the next column. Each represents further explanation and elaboration of one of the evaluation points, but they are not in the same order. Students should highlight (or shade in) those boxes with the correct, corresponding colour.

They should repeat this until all boxes in all columns are shaded in. This will require some thought from the students.

Purpose

Explain to students that the more they can elaborate their original evaluation points (e.g. 'one problem with much of the research in this area is subject attrition'), the more AO2 marks they are likely to get. This is denoted at the top of the handout. The evaluation comments start at 'rudimentary', and then increase in marks the further they are elaborated, through 'basic', 'reasonable' and 'effective'. These are loosely based on the AQA essay mark schemes.

The correct answers are as follows:

'One strength is that CBT has been supported by empirical research.'

- For example, Gould *et al.* (2001) found that all seven studies in their meta-analysis reported a statistically significant decrease in the positive symptoms of schizophrenia post-treatment.
- However, most studies of the effectiveness of CBT have been conducted at the same time with antipsychotic medication.
- Therefore it is very difficult to assess the effectiveness of CBT independent of biological therapies and unpick the variables involved in the recovery of schizophrenic patients.

'Further support for CBT comes from studies that indicate patients receiving CBT recover to a greater extent than those taking medication alone.'

- For example, those receiving CBT as well as medication experience fewer hallucinations and delusions, a 25–50% reduction in recovery time (Drury *et al.* 1996), lower drop-out rates and greater patient satisfaction (Kuipers *et al.* 1997).
- This perhaps indicates that there is more to schizophrenia than abnormal levels of neurotransmitters, and that there is also a need to address psychological abnormalities in thinking.
- However, some could argue that the improved recovery measures are the result of a placebo effect, with patients improving because they expect to rather than through the actual action of CBT.

'A problem with much of the research in this area is subject attrition.'

- This refers to the problem of patients dropping out of the research sample or refusing to cooperate with the researcher midway through the study.
- This results in a biased sample, as it could be argued that researchers are most likely to lose data from the patients with the most severe expression of schizophrenia.
- As a result the outcome of CBT studies perhaps shows the therapy to be more effective than it actually is.

'Another problem with CBT is that is it not suitable for some types of patient.'

- In Kingdon and Kirschen's (2006) study of 142 schizophrenic patients they found that many of the patients were deemed unsuitable for CBT because psychiatrists believed they would not fully engage with the therapy.
- In particular they found that older patients were deemed less suitable than younger patients.
- This presents a problem for the cognitive approach, since it suggests that maladaptive thinking is the *cause* of schizophrenia. As such a cognitive therapy *should* be effective and suitable for *all* those suffering from maladaptive thinking, since it is the very origin of their problems.

References

Drury, V., Birchwood, M., Cochrane, R. & MacMillan, F. (1996). Cognitive therapy and recovery from acute psychosis: a controlled trial. *British Journal of Psychiatry*, 169, 593–601.

Gould, R. A., Mueser, K. T., Bolton, E., Mays, V. & Goff, D. (2001). Cognitive therapy for psychosis in schizophrenia: an effect size analysis. *Schizophrenia Research*, 48, 335–42.

Kingdon, D. G. & Kirschen, H. (2006). Who does not get cognitive theory behavioural therapy for schizophrenia when therapy is readily available? *Psychiatric Services*, 57, 1792–4.

Kuipers, E., Garety, P., Fowler, D., Dunn, G., Bebbington, P., Freeman, D. & Hadley, C. (1997). London-East Anglia randomised controlled trial of cognitive-behavioural therapy for psychosis. I: effects of the treatment phases. *British Journal of Psychiatry*, 171, 319–27.

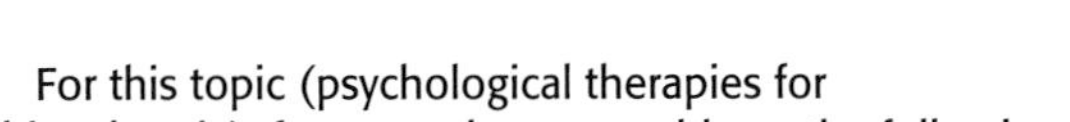

TOPIC: Psychological therapies for schizophrenia

ROLL UP!

This is a good key word and key concept game you could use at the start or end of any lesson.

Display the numbers 1 to 6 on your whiteboard with six corresponding key words, psychologists, theories or other. Ask individual students to roll a die and then say all they can about the topic that corresponds to the number they rolled. If you like your gimmicks (which I (MWG) unashamedly do!) then consider purchasing a large inflatable die for your classroom!

For this topic (psychological therapies for schizophrenia), for example, you could use the following:

1. CBT
2. Psychoanalysis
3. Maladaptive beliefs
4. Unconscious conflicts
5. Transference
6. Evaluation of CBT or psychoanalysis.

V✓A✓K ★OS HANDOUT 119

TOPIC: Diagnosis and classification of depression

DIAGNOSING DEPRESSION

The handout requires students to match each symptom to a likely statement a sufferer would make and identify the domain each symptom belongs to. Students are provided space to label each statement but could colour code the characteristics if desired.

AQA's 'A' Specification states students need to have an understanding of the clinical characteristics of depression. Following completion of this handout, students could use their work to help them complete the exam style question: 'Outline clinical characteristics of depression' (5 marks). My (RCG) students found they could peer assess each other's work using their own handout to check the author has included a detailed outline (i.e. named symptom, given an example such as the statements shown, and identified the domain).

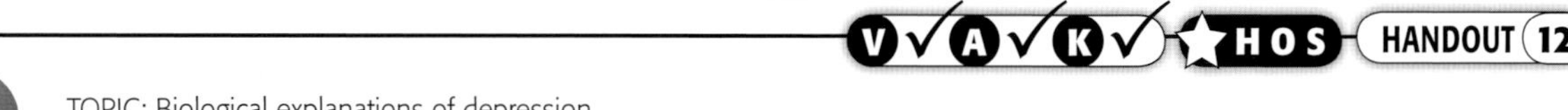

V✓A✓K✓ ★HOS HANDOUT 120

TOPIC: Biological explanations of depression

DEVELOPING DEPRESSION DISCUSSIONS: BIOCHEMISTRY

The PSYA4 essay is marked out of 25, 16 of which are for AO2.

The AO2 marks are determined as follows: Top band: Effective with coherent elaboration, Upper middle band: Reasonable elaboration, Lower middle band: Basic, only some evidence of elaboration, Bottom band: Rudimentary with material used ineffectually.

This handout asks students to build developed evaluations by matching four boxes. Students cut out all the 'rudimentary' boxes and stick them onto a sheet of paper (I would turn paper to landscape). They then cut out the four 'basic' and decide which box should follow each 'rudimentary' statement. Students complete this procedure with the remaining 'reasonable' and 'effective' boxes to build a line of four statements, that when taken together form a detailed paragraph.

As an extension you could challenge students to rewrite one of the lines in their own words, or for more able students ask them to create their own four boxes.

ANSWERS

'One problem is the effects of drugs are not immediate.'

- It normally takes several weeks before the effects of antidepressants on depression can be detected despite the fact that antidepressants raise the serotonin level immediately.
- Low levels of neurotransmitter therefore cannot be the simple explanation for depression.
- It may be that the drugs reduce depression by increasing the sensitivity of the receiving neurons, which takes some time to develop and explains how neurotransmitters affect depression.

'One problem is individual differences, drugs affect people in different ways.'

- For example, not every depressed person is helped by taking serotonin-based drugs. This suggests that there are other causes for this disorder besides low serotonin activity.
- If it were, all individuals should improve as a result of the drug.
- This is supported by the finding that some people who have low serotonin levels stay depression free, whereas others do not.

'There is also an issue linking cause and effect.'

- Namely, is it serotonin which causes the symptoms of depression, or could it be that the symptoms of depression cause low levels of serotonin?
- Martin *et al.* (2001) compared the effects of anti-depressant drugs with therapy using brain scanning and found patients showed the *same* changes in levels of serotonin.
- This shows neurotransmitter levels such as serotonin *can* be caused by psychological factors such as mood, rather than just the other way around (i.e. serotonin causing changes in mood).

'Some argue that while serotonin is a factor in depression it does not cause the illness.'

- Delgano *et al.* (1990) suggest it is more likely that serotonin plays a *contributing* role in mood regulation as opposed to a *causal* role in depression.
- They support this by saying it is a mistake to think depression is caused by decreased serotonin just because serotonin-based drugs reduce depression.
- In a way, this is like saying a lack of rash cream (corticosteroids) causes rashes, just because you observe that rash cream (corticosteroids) reduces a rash.

References

Delgano, P. L., Charney, D. S., Price, L. H, Aghajanian, G. K., Landis, H. & Heninger, G. R. (1990). Serotonin function and the mechanism of antidepressant action. Reversal of antidepressant-induced remission by rapid depletion of plasma tryptophan. *Archives of General Psychiatry*, 47, 411–18.

Martin, S. D., Martin, E., Santoch, S. R., Richardson, M. A. & Rovall, R. (2001). Brain blood flow changes in depressed patients treated with interpersonal psychotherapy or venlafaxine hydrochloride. *Archives of General Psychiatry,* 58, 641–8.

V ✓ A ✓ K ✓ ORG HANDOUT 121

TOPIC: Psychological explanations of depression

CONSIDERATION CONTINUUMS

Initially students are asked to identify and outline one psychological explanation of depression in six sentences. This will help them create a revision summary for their chosen theory. To complete this first section students could work in small groups to list as many points relating to one explanation as possible. They could then use this to identify the six points they wish to record on their handout. Students then need to identify research that supports the theory. Again in a group, they discuss the strengths and weaknesses of the supporting evidence. For example, small sample size, issues with internal validity, only applies to mild/moderate depression.

Following this, students represent their opinion of the supporting research by placing an X on the first continuum, which ranges from 'there is strong support for the explanation' to 'there is little support for the explanation'. In the box below, students explain their decision based on their group discussions. The same process is then repeated for the general psychological approach upon which the depression theory is based. Groups could be provided with a range of research from which to develop their opinions. This could be differentiated for each group, challenging more able students with research that has less obvious flaws or a range of findings.

As a plenary, I (RCG) would ask groups to place their X for each continuum projected onto the board and explain the reason for their choices.

TOPIC: Psychological explanations of depression

COBWEB COMMENTARY

This is similar to the Developing Depression Discussions handout (see page 62), students are challenged to identify related statements that can be used to develop a basic point. This activity also aims to highlight the need to develop evaluative comments to meet the requirements of the higher mark bands. As an extension students could create their own questions and ask others to answer them or address them themselves. More able students could try to add their own final box where they consider the value of the research evidence, or identify additional studies from their own research. Less able students could choose one or more cobweb strands and create a mini-version recorded onto a note card that can be learnt for revision.

Reference

Gotlib, H. I. & Hammen, C. L. (1992). *Psychological aspects of depression: Towards a cognitive-interpersonal integration*. Chichester: John Wiley & Sons.

TOPIC: Biological therapies for depression

FORMULATING EVALUATIONS

Having completed the two previous handouts that encourage the development of evaluative comments, students should be prepared for the reduced structure of this task. Each picture relates to an evaluation point that could be made about the use of antidepressants. For example: the first image could represent the placebo effect; the third, publication bias. Students use information from their textbook to explain what the image represents (the point). They then identify research evidence that supports the point made. Following this, students develop the comment by expanding or evaluating; for example, additional support, refuting research, comment on methodology, alternative viewpoints.

Students who may struggle to identify information in the text could be provided with information on separate cards for them to decide where these could be placed on the handout.

HANDOUT 124

TOPIC: Psychological therapies for depression

QUICK QUESTIONS

Students are asked to answer one question from the bottom row (AO1), one from the second row (AO2) and a third from the top row (Synoptic). Along each row questions vary in difficulty, allowing students to choose one they feel suits their ability. For the AO2 question students should be encouraged to include specific research evidence to support their point, and if possible to consider the validity of these studies. Students then form pairs to address the following question: 'Outline and evaluate one psychological therapy used in the treatment of depression' (25 marks). The questions on the handout act as a writing frame that will help students build their response.

As an additional task I (RCG) would ask students to read each other's answers in a later lesson and try to identify the questions used to build the essay.

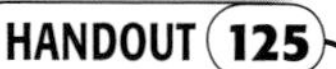

HANDOUT 125

TOPIC: Psychological therapies for depression

SUGGESTING SOLUTIONS

This activity requires students to reflect on the various treatments (biological and psychological) for depression. After reading Greta's case study, students are asked to decide on a suitable therapy and give reasons for their decision. They are further asked to explain which treatment they would not recommend for the client. More able students could go beyond their lesson notes by researching each therapy covered.

The Psychologist magazine (available online) often reports on research into various depression treatments.

Students could undertake their own research using this publication or other textbooks and journals before attempting the handout.

http://www.thepsychologist.org.uk/

V✓ A✓ K✓ HORGS

TOPIC: Classification and diagnosis of phobic disorders

KEY WORD CONNECTIONS

This could be a simple but thoughtful start to the topic and also tick some of the 'literacy across the curriculum boxes'!

In groups (you could use a collaborative learning structure, see page 3), have your students try and define the words **fear, excessive,** and **anxiety.**

Once they have done that, ask them to produce a definition of **phobic disorders**. By considering the other key words first, you will provide them with a good foundation.

TOPIC: Classification and diagnosis of phobic disorders

SCARY ROLLING SHOW

Another great way to start the topic and the lesson is through a 'scary' rolling show.

Rolling shows and how to construct them are described on page 5.

Consider using images of spiders, rats, slugs, insects, snakes, etc., and watch your students squirm as they come into lesson!

It could be a 'nice' way to stimulate discussion about what the students are scared of and their explanations of why they think they are afraid.

V✓ A K✓ OS HANDOUT 126

TOPIC: Classification and diagnosis of phobic disorders

CLINICAL CHARACTERISTICS CROSSWORD

Handout 126 contains a 'Clinical characteristics crossword' with 11 questions to answer.

This might be a good activity to use once you have taught a lesson or two on the topic in order to recap learning or test their understanding.

This is actually quite a challenging activity so you may wish to reserve it for use with your gifted and talented.

The correct answers are displayed below.

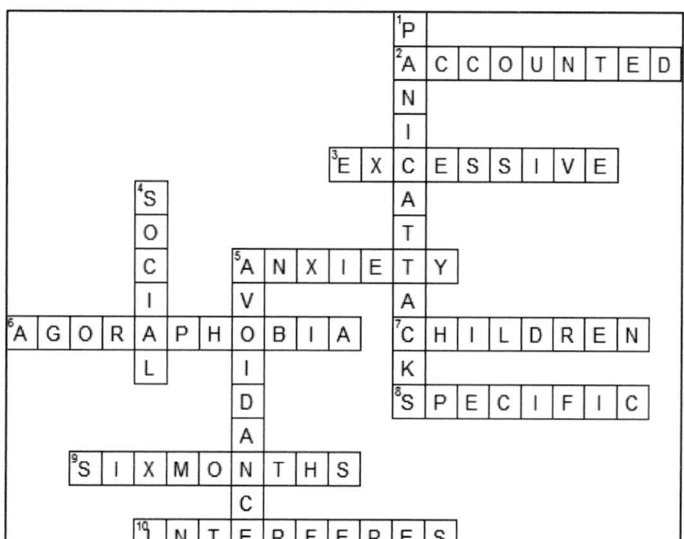

V ✓ A ✓ K ★ HOGS

TOPIC: Biological explanations of phobic disorders

ODD ONE OUT

An 'Odd One Out' activity entails displaying four key words or images and asking the students which one they think is the odd one out, like on the quiz show *Have I Got News for You*.

To introduce the evolutionary explanations of phobic disorders consider displaying three images that relate to 'ancient' fears (such as a snake, spider and heights) and displaying one image that relates to a modern-day fear (such as a car or gun).

Obviously as a teacher you know the 'answer' but actually, this is a particularly good starter activity because it gets students thinking straightaway in the lesson. It is good to encourage the idea that there is no definite answer.

You could also use a collaborative learning structure for this activity (see page 3).

V ✓ A K ✓ ★ OS

TOPIC: Biological explanations of phobic disorders

UNDERSTANDING TWIN STUDIES

The genetic and evolutionary explanations of phobic disorders often rest heavily on the evidence from twin studies.

In the past, I (MWG) have found that many students struggle to understand and interpret the results of twin studies.

Consider using (and possibly adapting) **Handout 65** as a way of introducing the logic of twin studies. The activity was described earlier on page 38.

V ✓ A K ✓ ★ HORS

TOPIC: Biological explanations of phobic disorders

EVOLUTIONARY MONSTERS!

Students will understand the evolutionary explanations in much more depth if they first get to grips with the principles of evolutionary explanations of behaviour.

The **evolutionary monsters** activity is a fantastic way to help students with this (see page 15 for a full description and link to **Handout 21**).

V ✓ A K ✓ ★ HORS HANDOUTS 127-128

TOPIC: Biological explanations of phobic disorders

PREPOTENCY AND PREPAREDNESS

This was once a favourite topic for coursework (when everyone had to do one non-experimental study). It could be used now as a good starter activity or whole lesson investigation into evolutionary explanations of phobic disorders.

Carrying out various psychology studies with your classes is even more important now that 'How Science Works' has taken such a prominent role in the specification and examination papers.

Handout 127 briefly describes the evolutionary explanations of phobic disorders, in particular, the theories of prepotency and preparedness. It also provides a description of a correlational study you could ask students to conduct along with some discussion questions to consider after they have collected and analysed their data.

Handout 128 contains a questionnaire that could be used in order to complete the study.

If you do it as a class activity the data can be analysed as follows:

- For each participant (or for the whole class) calculate the correlation coefficient for fearfulness and harmfulness.
- For each participant (or for the whole class) calculate the correlation coefficient for fearfulness and strangeness.

Calculating a correlation coefficient

You can calculate the correlation coefficient using Excel (for newer versions of Excel the process may be slightly different):

1. Open a new document in Excel (select <File> <New> <Blank workbook>).
2. Enter the two columns of data: fearfulness and harmfulness or fearfulness and strangeness.

3. To calculate correlation coefficient: Place the cursor in an empty box. Select <Insert> <Function>. In top box type 'correl' and press 'go' and then <OK>.
4. Screen now says 'array1' and 'array2'. Click in 'array1' and then move cursor to top of first column of your numbers, click and drag to bottom of column. Do the same for 'array2'.
5. To plot a scattergraph. Place cursor at top of first column and drag to bottom of second column. Select <Insert> <Chart> <XY (Scatter)> and press <next>.

Which coefficient is larger, fearfulness and harmfulness or fearfulness and strangeness? What conclusions can be drawn as a result?

Reference

Bennett-Levy, J. & Marteau, T. (1984). Fear of animals: what is prepared? *British Journal of Psychology,* 75, 35–42.

TOPIC: Psychological explanations of phobic disorders

THINKING COLLABORATIVELY

As a starter to this topic, display this question to your students:

Assuming phobias ARE NOT the result of biology and evolution, why is it that some phobias are very common (e.g. snakes, spiders, heights)?

Use a collaborative learning structure such as **Random numbers** to ensure good differentiation (see page 3).

TOPIC: Psychological explanations of phobic disorders

WHAT DOES THIS EQUATION MEAN?

Another way to get your students working collaboratively is using **Group statements** (see page 3).

Display this equation on the board.

Loud noise (UCS) Fear → (UCR)
Loud noise (UCS) + Rat (NS) Fear → (UCR)
Rat (CS) Fear → (CR)

Ask your students to use their knowledge of classical conditioning from their AS studies to write a statement explaining what this equation means (you may recognise this from the 'Little Albert' study).

TOPIC: Psychological explanations of phobic disorders

BROKEN PIECES

This activity is intended to help students learn the evaluations of the behavioural approach to phobic disorders.

It requires that they work collaboratively and analyse statements in order to complete the activity successfully.

Arrange the students into groups of about four. Cut out the statements on **Handout 129** and share them out equally within the small groups (i.e. each small group has one handout each).

The rules are that students can only read their statements to others in the group, they are not allowed to swap them or show them to anybody else in the group.

Their task is to work out and write down (maybe on an A3 sheet in the middle of their table) three fully elaborated evaluation points.

This will mean that students will need to read out their statements and the group will need to listen carefully in order to try and connect the statements with their own. Not an easy activity!

If they are struggling to do this, perhaps you could give them one completed example.

Answers

Evaluation – recall of traumatic events

- One supporting argument for the conditioning explanation is that people with phobias can often recall a specific incident when their phobia appeared (Sue *et al.*, 1994).
- This supports the explanation because it verifies the suggestion that phobias occur when a person associates a previously neutral stimulus (e.g. dog) with a fear response, i.e. that phobias are learnt as a result of the environment.
- However, not everyone who has a phobia can recall an incident when it occurred. Although, on the other hand, it could be argued that these events did happen but have been forgotten (Ost, 1989).
- Another problem with this evidence is not everyone who has been bitten by a dog develops a phobia of a dog (Di Nardo *et al.*, 1988). The principles of conditioning suggest that they should.

Evaluation – evidence of social learning

- One strength of the behavioural approach is that the role of social learning has been demonstrated experimentally.
- Bandura and Rosenthal (1966) showed that an observer who watched a model apparently experiencing pain every time a buzzer sounded, later demonstrated an emotional reaction to that sound.
- This appears to show that phobias can also be learnt via observation, and that direct experience of a traumatic event is not always necessary for the development of fear associations.
- However, this explanation also struggles to explain some individual differences. For example, why one sibling might fear dogs but another does not, when they had both previously observed their mother being bitten by a dog.

Evaluation – phobias are inherited

- A major claim made against the behavioural explanation is the idea that phobias are *inherited* rather than *learnt.*
- For example, Seligman (1970) suggests that we are biologically prepared from birth to rapidly learn a fear association (phobia). Others suggest we inherit phobias of certain types of objects (*prepotent objects)*.
- Indeed, this would be better able to explain the fact that not all people who experience a traumatic event go on to develop a phobia related to it.
- As such, the argument made against this behavioural explanation is that it is too focussed on the role of nurture and therefore ignores the evidence that nature also has an influence.

References

Bandura, A. & Rosenthal, T. L. (1966). Vicarious classical conditioning as a function of arousal level. *Journal of Personality and Social Psychology*, 3, 54–62.

Di Nardo, P. A., Guzy, L. T. & Bak, R. M. (1988). Anxiety response patterns and etiological factors in dog-fearful and non-fearful subjects. *Behaviour Research and Therapy*, 26(3), 245–51.

Ost, L. G. (1989). Blood phobia: A specific phobia subtype in DSM-IV. Paper requested by the Simple Phobia subcommittee of the DSM-IV Anxiety Disorders Work Group.

Seligman, M. E. P. (1970). On the generality of the laws of learning. *Psychological Review*, 77, 406–18.

Sue, D., Sue, D. & Sue, S. (1994). *Understanding abnormal behaviour (4th edn)* Boston, MA: Houghton Mifflin Co.

TOPIC: Biological therapies for phobic disorders

MODELLING NEURAL NETWORKS

Like many areas of psychology, there really is little point talking to students about the role of neurotransmitters, synapses and neural pathways in phobic disorders unless they have a basic grasp of biological mechanisms in the brain!

This modelling activity is described earlier on page 37.

You could extend this activity by asking your students to model the action of certain drugs.

TOPIC: Biological therapies for phobic disorders

TRIPLETS

The words shown at the start of **Handout 130** all relate to chemotherapy (a biological therapy for phobic disorders).

For each set, students choose three words that link together in some way. The lines to the right of the set give students the opportunity to explain the connection between the words.

Differentiation can take the form of must, could, should: all students must do one set, most could do two sets, some should try to aim for three or more.

For example, benzodiazepines – central nervous system – GABA. Explanation: Benzodiazepines slow down the activity of the central nervous system by enhancing the activity of GABA. This makes the person more relaxed and less anxious.

TOPIC: Psychological therapies for phobic disorders

CHARLIE BROWN STARTERS

Ellis (1957) proposed that the way to deal with irrational thoughts was to identify them using the ABC model.

'A' stands for the activating event – a situation that results in feelings of frustration and anxiety.

Such events lead to irrational beliefs (B) and the beliefs lead to self-defeating consequences (C).

For example:

A: A friend ignores you in the street.
B: He must have decided he doesn't like you; no-one likes you and you are worthless.
C: Avoid social situations in the future.

It is not possible to reprint the cartoons here for copyright reasons but some of the 'Peanuts' cartoon strips starring Charlie Brown are absolutely perfect for finding examples to analyse using the ABC model.

Perhaps try and find some on the Internet and give them to your students to try and analyse.

Reference

Ellis, A. (1957). *How to live with a 'neurotic'.* Hollywood, CA: Wilshire Books.

TOPIC: Psychological therapies for phobic disorders

REBT REVISION CARDS

A particularly successful lesson structure for me (MWG) has been this very simple one:

- Starter.
- Introduce a revision technique to students.
- Students use that revision technique to learn and remember a topic.
- Plenary – test the students at the end of the lesson either with a quiz or exam-style question.

These lessons seem to work particularly well because students are motivated to learn the material you give them (because they know they will be tested!), but also because they get to evaluate different revision techniques.

Handout 131 contains five revision cards relating to the cognitive behavioural therapy REBT (Rational-Emotive Behavioural Therapy). Students can cut these cards out, and write their answers on the back. They should be able to find the information in their textbooks (page 198 in the *A2 Complete Companion*), or alternatively on the Internet.

When they have finished, they test themselves and each other (i.e. by picking a card, answering it, and then checking the answer on the back).

At the end of the lesson, provide some kind of test, quiz, or exam-style question that will assess how well the revision technique worked for each student.

Reference

Ellis, A. (1957). *How to live with a 'neurotic'.* Hollywood, CA: Wilshire Books.

V A✓ K✓ HOG HANDOUT 132

TOPIC: Classification and diagnosis of OCD

WHAT IS OCD?

This handout acts as an introduction to OCD, aiming to help students differentiate between obsessions and compulsions. Students could be numbered and all odd numbers assigned the task of researching obsessions while those with even numbers investigate compulsions. Any information gathered is recorded on the relevant clipboard. I (RCG) find a helpful place to start is with the DSM-IV-TR criteria for obsessions and compulsions (see page 204 of *A2 Complete Companion*).

Even numbered students then find an odd numbered student to form a pair and share the research they have found. Once that is completed students could join another pair or find a new partner to complete the second task. The latter task requires higher order thinking as students try to draw out similarities and differences between obsessions and compulsions.

As a homework activity students could use the completed handout to write a hypothetical case study for an OCD sufferer or, for less able students, identify the obsessions and compulsions described in a case study example.

V✓ A✓ K HOR HANDOUT 133

TOPIC: Biological explanations of OCD

BIOLOGICAL BREAKDOWN

The layout of the handout can be used for any topic: just change the heading or keep it the same if looking at depression or schizophrenia rather than OCD. Students need to identify information relating to biological explanations of OCD (or the mental disorder you have chosen) this could be organised under headings such as: explanations, supporting research, refuting evidence, etc. Once information has been gathered, students decide where to place their knowledge in the various boxes in the handout. For more able students this could take the form of an argument flowing through the boxes. For example, the cause of OCD is explained as.... ➲ this is supported by... ➲ however, this evidence could be criticised because... ➲ yet further support is found from... ➲. Some students may find modelling this format helpful before beginning the task. Students do not need to be limited to writing; they could draw pictures or stick in images they have found. You could offer a prize for the most imaginative breakdown.

As a starter for the following lesson, students could receive another student's breakdown handout and record five points from their peer's work in their own notes, or work in pairs to identify points both breakdowns display and any information their own handout did not show yet their peer's did.

V A✓ K✓ HOG HANDOUT 134

TOPIC: Psychological explanations of OCD

PSYCHOLOGICAL EXPLANATIONS

Each question on the handout relates to one of the levels of thinking in Bloom's Taxonomy (see page 4 *AS Teacher's Companion*). You could challenge students to complete all six questions or state tasks 1 to 3 should be done alone, 4 and 5 in pairs and question 6 as a group of four. Another variation could involve students being assigned questions based on ability (less able attempt questions 1 to 3) then form a pair with another who completed different questions to help each other complete the handout. Alternatively students could have the handout close by as the lesson progresses and note down any answers that arise during the course of the lesson.

Like many of the handouts this activity does not relate solely to OCD, the questions could be applied to many areas in Units 3 and 4.

Reference

Bloom, B. (1956). *Taxonomy of Educational Objectives.* Harlow: Longman.

HANDOUT 135

TOPIC: Biological therapies for OCD

TARGET AND CHALLENGE

This is another activity that can be applied to a wide range of psychological topics. Students are given a piece of text to read in a set period of time, this could be set as a reading homework in preparation for this task. The text could be modified to be appropriate for different abilities. Students should be advised to use this time wisely and not simply read over the text but create mindmaps, lists, tables. After the allotted time students are asked to hide away the text in their folders. Using only their memory, students work alone to record eight points from the text. These points could include a simple sentence relating to a form of treatment; for example, 'drug therapy is the most commonly used treatment for OCD'. Other points may relate to a specific study, such as, 'Soomro *et al.*'s (2008) review of 17 studies found SSRIs were more effective than placebos in reducing OCD symptoms'. The target of five is expected of all students, the challenge of eight aims to push more able students. Students then join in pairs for the next set of target (9-13) and challenge (14-16) points, adding points their partner had that they did not. The final section asks students to return to the text to meet the final target (17-21) and challenge (22-24) points.

Students should be encouraged to check their own work by reading through each point and checking each one is correct and identifying whether any further details could be added. As follow-up, students could highlight which points are AO1 statements (outlining/describing) and which statements could be used to evaluate the explanations.

Reference

Soomro, G. M., Altman, D. G., Rajagopal, S. & Oakley-Browne, M. (2008). Selective serotonin re-uptake inhibitors (SSRIs) versus placebo for obsessive-compulsive disorder (OCD). *Cross-Cultural Research*, 34, 70–87.

HANDOUT 136

TOPIC: Psychological therapies for OCD

SIX HATS ANALYSIS

After students have developed an understanding of one psychological approach to treating OCD, this activity can be used to consider the appropriateness and effectiveness of this therapy. Assign students to a hat. Students sit with students of the same hat and work together to complete their section. The red and the white hat should be accessible to most students, whereas green hat and blue hat require higher order thinking. Once students have finished their section they then form new groups (three students of different hats for two sessions seems to work better than a single session with a group of six) to share their ideas.

Reference

DeBono, E. (1985). *Six Thinking Hats*. Little, Brown and Company.

TOPIC: Explanations of media influences on prosocial behaviour

THE MEDIA AND PROSOCIAL BEHAVIOUR

Handout 137 provides various explanations for prosocial effects of the media and requires students to suggest how these explanations might apply to familiar TV programmes. The explanations are fairly basic, though you may want to work through one example to help students.

This could be a good introduction activity to the topic.

TOPIC: Explanations of media influences on prosocial behaviour

CONTENT ANALYSIS

If you have the time within lessons you could conduct a content analysis of children's TV programmes to investigate the frequency of different prosocial behaviours. Alternatively you could set this as a homework.

The benefits of conducting different types of psychological studies is that students get a more rounded understanding of 'How Science Works', which would prepare them in particular for PSYA4, where they need to have a good knowledge of different types of research methods and techniques.

The key decisions for conducting a content analysis will need to be the sample, i.e. which programmes will be used and why? For example, you could look at 5-minute clips of the five most popular programmes according to viewing ratings.

The next key decision is what behavioural categories you will use to operationalise 'prosocial behaviour'. For example, helping, sympathising, comforting, supporting, admitting fault, etc.

You could even conduct an analysis of the frequency of prosocial behaviours vs. the frequency of antisocial behaviours.

TOPIC: Explanations of media influences on antisocial behaviour

DODGY CONCLUSIONS

Handout 138 describes a fictitious study into the link between exposure to media violence and aggression.

The activity for the students is to identify as many problems with Dr Psychologist's conclusion as they can.

Again, this is an extremely important skill for them to practise as students may be expected to discuss fictitious studies using their knowledge of certain topics. As such, it is really important that they can do this independently.

One of the ways in which they can 'discuss' such studies is to provide some evaluation.

Problems students might identify

- Population validity – the study only uses boys and therefore the results may not generalise to girls. Perhaps boys are more likely to be influenced by aggressive media because it arouses a more instinctive aggressive nature.
- Population validity – the study uses 3–4 years olds. It could be argued that this age group are more impressionable than older age groups because they are still at an early stage of moral development. On the other hand, it might be argued that they are *less* likely to be influenced by the video clips because they do not have the cognitive capacities to generalise from what they see to their own lives.
- Short-term effects – the study tests for the boys' aggression immediately after showing them the video clips. As such, we do not know whether the boys would be affected later on, for example four hours later.
- Ecological validity – the boys only watch the media clips for 10 minutes and are then tested for aggression. In reality, people are worried about prolonged exposure to media violence (i.e. over a long period of time) so it is difficult to generalise from these results.
- Extraneous variables – it could be that the violent media arouses the children, which makes them appear more aggressive, rather than the media directly causing aggression. Equally, the distraction task may arouse the children.
- Operationalisation of aggression – it could be questioned whether pricking a balloon with a pin is really a valid measure of aggression.
- Oversimplified conclusion – it is too much of an over-simplification to suggest that TV should be banned. It makes television the scapegoat for aggressive behaviour and does not consider any other variables that might be involved.

V A✓K HOGS

TOPIC: The effects of video games and computers on young people

COLUMBINE MASSACRE – CAN WE USE THIS AS EVIDENCE?

In 1999 Eric Harris and Dylan Klebold walked into Columbine High School in Colorado where they were students and embarked on a massacre.

They killed 12 of their fellow students, 1 teacher, and injured another 21, before both committing suicide.

It was said that they were both obsessed by the violent video game called 'Doom'. Many hypothesised that their violence was influenced and encouraged by such games and the victims' families even tried to sue the makers of the game.

It is quite understandable that students will make references to such examples when considering the effects of video games on young people. They are also likely to make comments such as: 'I play loads of video games and I don't consider myself to be violent or aggressive'.

However, we should probably be encouraging our students to develop a more scientific stance on this topic, rather than an anecdotal one.

Pose your students the following question:

Why should we never rely on one-off events as evidence for a link between violent video games and real-life violence?

Use a collaborative learning structure such as **Random numbers** or **Group statements** (see page 3) to ensure accountability and differentiation.

V✓A K✓ HORS HANDOUT 139

TOPIC: The effects of video games and computers on young people

ELABORATION LADDERS

This is an idea also described in the *AS Teacher Companion* and is useful for many topics really.

The activity and evaluation technique was born in frustration with rudimentary essay comments such as: 'The ecological validity of the study is low because it is not like real life' Aaaaggghhh!

Of course, our job as teachers is to help students to elaborate their evaluative comments – something they seem to find really hard, but undoubtedly has a significant impact on their grades if they can develop the skill.

Having read the above statement in an Asch essay for the thirtieth time a couple of years ago, I (MWG) decided to try and devise a memorable teaching technique to help students with this skill.

The central idea behind the elaboration ladders (**Handout 139**) is that students start with an introductory evaluation comment at the bottom of the ladder and then gradually elaborate this comment further and further until they reach the smiley face at the top! The box on the right-hand side is designed to prompt students into thinking of ways they could elaborate their evaluations, for example 'Have I got evidence?'.

By going through this process, the hope is that the student is able to discuss their evaluation and its implications in more depth. This visual technique, used in conjunction with the prompts on the right, seems to have been very successful in developing elaboration skills in the students at our school.

Handout 139 is obviously focussed on evaluating research into the effects of video games on young people and some hints are provided for the students to help them along the way.

V A K✓ HORS HANDOUT 140

TOPIC: The effects of video games and computers on young people

EXAM PRACTICE: VIDEO GAMES

I think the most daunting type of exam question in PSYA4 will be of the type included on **Handout 140**.

It describes a fictitious study on the effects of video games and then asks students to discuss this study in relation to their knowledge of media and aggression for 15 marks.

Such a broad and unstructured question is likely to intimidate even the most confident psychology students.

With this in mind, **Handout 140** attempts to help students plan how they can break down their response into smaller and more manageable chunks.

Following completion of their plans, you could then set this as a homework task or timed assessment.

V✓ A✓ K HOS

TOPIC: Persuasion and attitude change

'BECAUSE I'M WORTH IT'

A good way to introduce the persuasion and attitude change topic is to look at some TV adverts and discuss with your students what makes them so effective.

I (MWG) showed my students this Loreal advert with Jennifer Aniston.

http://www.youtube.com/watch?v=YxdL5Wgnsjw

The students came up with some excellent suggestions as to why it might be effective.

For example:

- She is a role model for many women because she is attractive.
- She is well known for her hair, so it is effective because she is endorsing a good shampoo.
- The advert tries to put across the idea that you are buying more than a shampoo – you are buying a relationship!
- The advert suggests that the shampoo will increase your self-esteem 'because I'm worth it'.
- It includes 'scientific' information, which persuades you that the shampoo must work.
- The 'science bit' isn't explained by Jennifer Aniston but by a man who presumably is a more credible source (we also discussed stereotypes of 'scientists' here).
- The advert is very light and white, which is associated with cleanliness.
- The background music has an upbeat tempo, which makes you want to go out and buy it. It also makes you feel 'upbeat' about the shampoo.

...and finally (and this is a direct quote...)

- 'Because she is hot sir.'

V A K✓ HORS HANDOUT 141

TOPIC: Persuasion and attitude change

HOVLAND-YALE (PERSUASION REPORT)

To take the activity previously described a little further, you could turn this into a written exercise with more of an emphasis on theory and evidence. For example, students could produce a report explaining how and why a particular advert is (or isn't) effective according to the theory and/or research.

Handout 141 provides an example of how students might structure this report for the Hovland-Yale model of persuasion.

You could produce an equally useful report structure for the elaboration-likelihood model.

V A K✓ HORS HANDOUT 142

TOPIC: Influence of attitudes on decision making

DOING AO2 – TESTING HYPOTHESES

Throughout A2 Psychology, there should be a consistent emphasis on 'How Science Works'.

In its simplest terms you can explain to your students that science is a process of observing, developing theories and hypotheses, testing those hypotheses and then drawing conclusions.

A good way to put this into context is by evaluating theories based on this process and emphasising the idea that theories can be evaluated by testing hypotheses that are based on the logic of the theory.

As such, **Handout 142** encourages students to consider this process of science with the end result being a nicely structured evaluation of cognitive dissonance or self-perception theory based on evidence.

References

Cooper, J. & Fazio, R. H. (1984). A new look at dissonance theory. *Advances in Experimental Social Psychology,* 17, 229–65.

Festinger, L. & Carlsmith, J. M. (1959). Cognitive consequences of coerced compliance. *Journal of Abnormal and Social Psychology,* 58, 203–10.

Kleinjan, M., Egels, R. C. M. E., Van Leeuwe, J., Brug, J., Van Zundert, R. M. P. & Van den Eijnden, R. J. J. M. (2009). Adolescents' rationalisations to continue smoking: the role of disengagement beliefs and nicotine dependence in smoking cessation. *Addictive Behaviours,* 34(5), 440–5.

V ✓ A K ✓ HORS HANDOUT 143

TOPIC: Influence of attitudes on decision making

LOOKING AT THE BIGGER PICTURE

The activity on **Handout 143** is aimed at helping students with synoptic commentary in this topic.

The information at the top of the sheet details the challenge that dissonance theory presents to the principles of behaviourism. It is an extract from *The A2 Complete Companion*, page 227.

Asking students to read the information is usually not enough, so helping them deconstruct and think about what the extract is saying is more likely to develop understanding and recall.

The activity described on **Handout 143** should therefore help students to make diagrammatic connections within psychology.

Reference

Tavris, C. & Aronson, E. (2007). *Mistakes were made - but not by ME: Self-justification in public and private life.* New York: Harcourt.

V A K ✓ OS HANDOUT 144

TOPIC: Explanations for the effectiveness of television in persuasion

SELF-MONITORING SCALE

Snyder and de Bono (1985) have found that 'hard-sell' and 'soft-sell' advertising approaches have different effects on different types of people.

'Hard sell' refers to when factual information about a product is presented. This links to the idea of a central route to persuasion as in the elaboration-likelihood model.

'Soft sell', on the other hand, is a more subtle and creative technique of persuasion that links in to the idea of the peripheral route.

Snyder and DeBono (1985) found that people who score highly on a test of 'self-monitoring' (i.e. regulating their behaviour so that they will be perceived by others in a favourable manner) had more favourable attitudes to soft-sell advertisements.

Whereas, people low in self-monitoring (i.e. less image conscious) preferred more factual hard-sell approaches.

Handout 144 contains an adapted version of Snyder's (1974) self-monitoring questionnaire to use with your students.

Students have to read the statements and decide whether they are mostly 'True' or 'False' in their case.

A score between 0 and 7 would indicate a low self-monitor.

A score between 9 and 15 would indicate a high self-monitor.

A score of 8 is directly in the middle.

Once the students have completed the questionnaire, read out the question numbers that would indicate a high self-monitor. They give themselves a point for each of these.

Answers that indicate a high self-monitor

1. True
2. False
3. True
4. True
5. True
6. True
7. False
8. True
9. False
10. True
11. True
12. True
13. False
14. True
15. True

References

Synder, M. (1974). Self-monitoring of expressive behaviour. *Journal of Personality and Social Psychology*, 30(4), 526–37.

Synder, M. & DeBono, K. (1985). Appeals to image and claims about quality: understanding the psychology of advertising. *Journal of Personality and Social Psychology*, 49, 586–97.

TOPIC: The attraction of celebrity

CONNECT 4

Handout 145 encourages students to deconstruct the parasocial relationships explanation for the attraction of celebrity into its basic parts, and then to help them link it together. This should help the students to be more analytical in their commentary.

In the grey shaded areas, students should articulate their understanding of the key terms/ideas, i.e. parasocial relationships, celebrity, identification, etc.

In between the grey shaded areas, students should try and explain how the elements of the theory link together.

For example, parasocial relationships are linked to celebrity because we are usually exposed to the celebrities' lives, beliefs and emotions through the media, meaning that the relationship is only one-way, and thus we are likely to form parasocial relationships with them.

TOPIC: The attraction of celebrity

EVOLUTIONARY MONSTERS!

Students will understand the evolutionary explanations for the attraction of celebrity in much more depth if they first get to grips with the principles of evolutionary explanations of behaviour.

If you haven't already done so, consider using the **evolutionary monsters** activity as it is a fantastic way to help students with this (see page 15 for a full description and links to **Handout 21**).

TOPIC: Research into intense fandom

CELEBRITY ATTITUDE SCALE

The major way in which psychologists have measured celebrity worship has been with the 'Celebrity attitude scale'. Most research in this area has used this tool.

The 'Celebrity attitude scale' is a 17-item scale with lower scores indicating more individualist behaviour (e.g. watching or reading about celebrities) and higher score indicating over-identification and obsession with celebrities.

An extended 34-item version of this scale is included on **Handout 146** for you to use and discuss with your students as an introduction to this topic.

It uses a Likert-scale, where strongly agree is equivalent to a score of 5, and strongly disagree equivalent to a score of 1.

Therefore all scores will be between 34 and 170.

TOPIC: Biological models of addiction

UNDERSTANDING TWIN STUDIES

This activity has been described previously and is useful in many topics.

The genetic and evolutionary explanations of addiction often rest heavily on the evidence from twin studies.

In the past, I (MWG) have found that many students struggle to understand and interpret the results of twin studies.

Consider using (and possibly adapting) **Handout 65** as a way of introducing the logic of twin studies. The activity was described earlier on page 38.

TOPIC: Biological models of addition

MODELLING NEURAL NETWORKS

Like many areas of psychology, there really is little point talking to students about the role of neurotransmitters, synapses and neural pathways in addiction unless they have a basic grasp of biological mechanisms in the brain!

Similarly to the previous lesson note, this modelling activity is described earlier on page 37.

You could extend this activity by asking your students to model the action of certain drugs.

TOPIC: Biological models of addiction

PROFILING BIOLOGICAL MODELS OF ADDICTION

Handout 147 encourages students to consider the wider issues in psychology as well as how the biological theories of addiction link to the concepts of 'How Science Works'.

The activity can help students structure their analysis of the theories and provide meaningful and justified commentary to form part of their AO2 marks in an essay.

This activity could be adapted and work with many aspects of psychology, for example profiling studies, approaches, etc.

This handout might also work well in conjunction with **Handout 148** (described on the next lesson notes).

V A K HORS HANDOUT 148

TOPIC: Cognitive models of addiction

PROFILING COGNITIVE MODELS OF ADDICTION

The rationale and basis for this activity is described previously.

Having done the activity twice for different theories it provides a perfect opportunity for students to compare and contrast theories in order to gain valuable AO2 commentary marks.

It might be worth also providing your students with a simple writing frame to give them an idea of how to do this.

For example: *It could be argued that the …. theory of addiction is more determinist because…, whereas the … theory of addiction retains an element of free will because….*

Although we have included this activity under the 'Cognitive models of addiction', it could obviously be used successfully for the learning models also.

In fact, this type of activity could be used in many different areas of psychology.

V A K✓ HOS HANDOUT 149

TOPIC: Cognitive models of addiction

FRUIT MACHINE COGNITIONS

Handout 149 illustrates a man playing on a fruit machine and the kind of thoughts (cognitions) that an addict might have whilst gambling on the machine.

The cognitions included are based on Griffiths' (1994) study of regular and non-regular gamblers and their verbalisations as they played a fruit machine. The study revealed the cognitive bias present in regular gamblers. For example, they believed they were more skilful than they actually were, they tended to personify the machines, and explained away their losses by seeing them as 'near misses' or 'near wins'.

The handout requires students to explain the initiation, maintenance and possible relapse of this man's addiction behaviour.

Students may wish to draw on theories they have covered in class.

This is good practice for the possible application exam questions that could come up in the PSYA4 exam.

Reference

Griffiths, M. (1994). The role of cognitive bias and skill in fruit machine gambling: A personal overview. *British Journal of Psychology*, 85, 351–69.

V✓A K✓ HORS HANDOUT 150

TOPIC: Learning models of addiction

KEY WORD BOXING

This is essentially a variation of the 'Triplets' activity described on page 68.

Students have to place the key words in the appropriate boxes on **Handout 150**. Or rather, write the key words on the appropriate boxes!

Then they must describe how the relevant theories (operant conditioning, classical conditioning and social learning) explain the initiation and maintenance of addiction.

When doing this, they should make sure they use the key words that are in the 'box'.

This encourages students to use key words in their outlining of various theories as well as giving them some guidance and structure to their explanations.

V A K✓ HORS HANDOUT 151

TOPIC: Explanations for specific addictions

DON'T GAMBLE ON THE EXAM!

'Don't gamble on the exam!' – see what we did? This could be a case of making a handout based on a hilarious pun, but actually I (MWG) think that it does have some useful educational purpose.

I think the most daunting type of exam question will be the type of question included on **Handout 151**.

It describes a fictitious man and his addiction to gambling and then asks students to discuss this study in relation to their knowledge of models of addiction, for 15 marks.

Such a broad and unstructured question is likely to intimidate even the most confident psychology students.

With this in mind, **Handout 151** attempts to help students plan how they can break down their response into smaller and more manageable chunks.

Remember to remind your students to make sure that their answers are 'in context' and to keep referring back to Simon's particular case situation.

Following completion of their plans, you could then set this as a homework task or timed assessment.

By practising questions like this, students will be well rehearsed in the skills required to do well and so will not need to guess (or 'gamble') how to do these in the exam!

V ✓ A K ✓ ★ HORS HANDOUT 152

TOPIC: Vulnerability and addiction

DISCUSSING SELF-ESTEEM AND ADDICTION

Handout 152 provides a writing frame with which to discuss the role of self-esteem in addiction.

In order to do this students will need to use evidence, comment on methodological flaws in the research, and include some synoptic material. These are all the elements required in order to succeed in A2 Psychology and PSYA4, so it is well worth getting your students to have a go at this.

They could use their textbooks to help them if you want to make this an independent research activity.

V A K ✓ ★ HORS HANDOUT 153

TOPIC: The role of media in addictive behaviour

THE DANGERS OF ICE CREAM

There is almost certainly a significant statistical relationship between ice cream and the factors mentioned. However, it is important to note that the news report included on **Handout 153** is fictitious and that there are no pressure groups out there campaigning for a ban on ice cream!

The news report and questions included are an excellent way to demonstrate to students the possible dangers associated with misinterpreting correlational studies.

The bottom half of the handout tries to help students link these ideas to some of the methodological flaws in the correlational research in this area of psychology – the role of media in addictive behaviour.

Much of the research is based on correlations, which leads to problems assigning causal relationships.

By considering both sets of questions, hopefully students will gain a much deeper understanding of the issues and of 'How Science Works' (or doesn't as the case may be!).

Suggested answers

***1.** What variables have been measured in this study?*

Ice cream sales, cases of drowning, and use of slot and fruit machines.

***2.** Which variables do you think would have been difficult to measure?*

All variables would have been difficult to measure directly.

***3.** How do you think they were measured?*

Most would need to be measured using some sort of historical records.

***4.** How would you describe the statistical relationship between ice cream and slot machines and fruit machines?*

It is a positive correlation.

***5.** Why would it be a mistake to argue that ice cream causes use of fruit/slot machines or drowning?*

Correlations do not determine cause and effect relationships because they do not have an independent and dependent variable. There could be a third variable that explains the relationship. For example, as the temperature rises, more people buy ice cream and more people visit Blackpool (and so more people are recorded playing the fruit machines as well). As such, it could be argued that the relationship between ice cream and use of fruit machines is a coincidence caused by a hidden variable – temperature.

***6.** Why would it be useful to do an experiment in this area?*

Because an experiment has an independent variable (in this case it could be a group having eaten ice cream, and a group not having eaten ice cream) and a dependent variable (for example, whether or not the participants drown). By manipulating the independent variable we can see whether there is an effect on the dependent variable and therefore determine a cause/effect relationship.

***7.** Why is it difficult to conduct an experiment like this?*

It is difficult to conduct an ethical experiment because the researcher would be putting the participants in a position where they are vulnerable. For example, if we were investigating the cause and effect relationship between drowning, it would be necessary for some of the participants to die during the study!

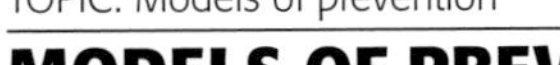

TOPIC: Models of prevention

MODELS OF PREVENTION: TPB

The theory of planned behaviour (TPB) emphasises the belief that behaviour is under the conscious control of the individual.

For example, it would assume that if the individual *intended* to give up smoking, then they would be able to do so.

Ajzen (1989) also stated that the extent to which the individual believes they are able to perform the behaviour in question (perceived behaviour control) acts on the intention to behave in a particular way or directly on the behaviour itself, as well as attitudes about that behaviour and their awareness of social norms surrounding that behaviour.

Handout 154 contains a diagrammatic representation of this model which is taken from page 250 *A2 Complete Companion*.

An activity you could do with your students is to choose one of the specific addictions you have been studying (e.g. gambling, drugs or alcohol) and describe the model in context using the space in the boxes provided.

My (MWG) first reading of the model was that it was quite difficult to understand until I tried to relate it to something specific. I think that the same exercise would help students to understand it too.

As an extension task, students who finish could use the model in order to suggest different ways in which to prevent that addiction from happening in the first place.

These prevention strategies could be in the form of policies or therapies with the individuals themselves.

Reference

Ajzen, I. (1989). Attitude, structure and behavior. In A. R. Pratkanis, S. J. Beckler & A. G. Greenwald (eds) *Attitude, Structure and Function*. Hillsdale, NJ: Lawrence Erlbaum Associates, 241–74.

V A K HOS HANDOUT 155

TOPIC: Types of intervention

EVALUATION AND ELABORATION: INTERVENTIONS

Handout 155 is designed to illustrate to students the level of depth required to achieve top AO2 marks when evaluating biological and psychological interventions for addictions.

Students should start by reading the boxes on the far left-hand side of the page, which outline simple evaluation points. Ask them to highlight (or shade in) each of the boxes in that column with a different colour.

The students should then read the boxes in the next column. Each represents further explanation/elaboration of one of the evaluation points, but they are not in the same order. Students should highlight (or shade in) those boxes with the correct, corresponding colour.

They should repeat this until all boxes in all columns are shaded in. This will require some thought from the students.

Purpose

Explain to students that the more they can elaborate their original evaluation points (e.g. 'It has been said that psychological reinforcement strategies do not address the underlying problems), the more AO2 marks they are likely to get. This is denoted at the top of the handout. The evaluation comments start at 'rudimentary', and then increase in marks the further they are elaborated, through 'basic', 'reasonable' and 'effective'. These are loosely based on the AQA essay mark schemes.

Answers

'There is significant support for CBT as an effective intervention strategy.'

- Ladouceur *et al.* (2001) randomly allocated 66 pathological gamblers either to a cognitive therapy group or to a waiting list control group. Of those who completed the treatment 86% no longer fulfilled the DSM criteria for pathological gambling.
- They also found that after treatment, gamblers had a better perception of control over their problem and increased self-efficacy, showing changes to their thinking.
- As such, this supports the notion of free will, since the gamblers are in control of their own behaviour. If they can change their thought processes, they will be able to change their behaviour.

'It has been argued that psychological reinforcement interventions do not address the underlying problems.'

- Although research has found reinforcement therapies to be effective in reducing addictive behaviour, such interventions do nothing to address the problem that led to the addiction in the first place.
- This means that although a specific addictive behaviour might have been reduced, there is a possibility the person may simply engage in a different addictive behaviour instead.
- A drug addict may, for example, turn to alcohol, but in most cases new addictions tend to be subtle, including compulsive spending or even developing dependent relationships.

'The evidence suggests drug treatments for gamblers can work.'

- Hollander *et al.* (2000) found that gamblers treated with SSRIs to increase serotonin levels showed significant improvements compared to a control group.
- However, the reliability of this evidence might be questioned, since the sample size was very small (n = 10) and the study was short in duration (16 weeks).

- Indeed a larger and longer study (Blanco *et al.*, 2002), involving 32 gamblers over six months failed to demonstrate any superiority for the drug treatment over a placebo.

'One issue with methadone treatments is the problem of substitute addiction.'

- Many drug addicts who are on the methadone programme become as reliant on methadone as they were on heroin.
- Indeed the problem is so great that the unsupervised patients have created a black market, with users sometimes selling their doses for only £2.
- The UK statistics authority showed that methadone was responsible for over 300 deaths in the UK in 2007.

References

Blanco, C., Petkova, E., Ibanez, A. & Saiz-Ruiz, J. (2002). A pilot placebo-controlled study of fluvoxamine for pathological gambling. *Annals of Clinical Psychology*, 14(1), 9–15.

Hollander, E., Buchalter, A. J. & DeCaria, C. M. (2000). Pathological gambling. *The Psychiatric Clinics of North America*, 23(3), 629–42.

Ladouceur, R., Sylvain, C., Boutin, C., Lachance, S., Doucet, C. & Leblond, J. (2001). Cognitive treatment of pathological gambling. *Journal of Nervous and Mental Disorders*, 189, 766–73.

V A✓K✓ OGR HANDOUT 156

TOPIC: Issues of pseudoscience and scientific fraud

CONSTRUCT A CONVERSATION

This handout provides students with material to create their own conversations debating whether paranormal psychology is a pseudoscience. Students could be given all statements or a select few and be encouraged to do their own research to gather further points. The form the conversation takes could be decided by each group of students. Possible formats could be: radio show, news report, chat show, heated discussion in the university staff room. The performances could be filmed and used as a later revision aid.

A development of this activity could see students creating their own evaluation sheet for each conversation. Certain topics or research that needs to be covered are decided on, skills such as clarity of speech, dramatic quality and accuracy of information could all be considered. Each group is given an evaluation sheet to assist planning of the conversation then forms are completed by the audience after each presentation by the audience.

For information on Cyril Burt visit: http://www.indiana.edu/~intell/burtaffair.shtml

For information on Occam's Razor visit: http://www.2think.org/occams_razor.shtml

References

Eysenck, H. & Sargent, C. (1982). *Explaining the Unexplained: Mysteries of the Paranormal.* London: Weidenfeld & Nicolson.

Rhine, J. B. (1929). An investigation into the 'mind-reading horse'. *Journal of Abnormal and Social Psychology*, 23, 449–66.

V✓A✓K OGS HANDOUT 157

TOPIC: Controversies: ESP and psychokinesis

CONSTRUCT A COMMENTARY

Students are charged with the task of using a piece of information to add meaning to each box of the handout. This activity could be attempted alone or each student could be assigned a single box and given a short period of time to complete this one area. Students then move around the room to find others who have completed different boxes. Some sections are more obvious than others, so students could be assigned a section based on ability.

If following this format I (RCG) find students often need to be reminded to teach each other their section not simply allow another to copy their handout. One way to solve this is to split the lesson into 'teaching time', where only the 'teachers' of one section are allowed a handout and learners just listen. Learners then retrieve their handout and record what they can recall, asking the teacher for help if needed. Another section is then addressed with new 'teachers'.

References

Bem, D. J., Palmer, J. & Broughton, R. S. (2001). Updating the Ganzfeld database: a victim of its own success? *Journal of Parapsychology*, 65, 207–18.

Hyman, R. (1985). The Ganzfeld psi experiment: a critical appraisal. *Journal of Parapsychology*, 49(1), 3–50.

Hyman, R. & Honorton, C. (1986). A joint communiqué. *Journal of Parapsychology*, 50, 351–64

Milton, J. & Wiseman, R. (1999). Does psi exist? Lack of replication of anomalous process of information transfer. *Psychological Bulletin*, 125(4), 387–91.

V✓A✓K OTS HANDOUT 158

TOPIC: Cognitive, personality and biological factors

WHAT MAKES A SHEEP A SHEEP?

Each image on the sheet relates to cognitive, personality or biological factors that underlie anomalous experience. Students have to apply their knowledge of these factors to identify what each image represents. Once the images have been colour coded students can explain each image in detail: all students MUST outline two images, most students COULD attempt three images while a few students should aim to describe at least four.

To encourage concise accounts, students could be set a word limit of 100 words per factor.

HANDOUT 159

TOPIC: Functions of paranormal and related beliefs

PEER REVIEWS

In their notes, students answer the following question 'Describe, in about 100 words, the functions of paranormal and related beliefs'. Students then swap their work with another student and complete the forms on the handout. Forms encourage students to read another's work for meaning and help their own revision of the work as they write their own version of the description their peer has given. Handing these forms back to the author will help them identify whether they gave full explanations of the functions or beliefs.

Alternatively, the forms could be adapted to enable less able students to work with more able students to complete the forms together before the original question is attempted. Students then use the handout to answer the exam question for homework. This acts as a writing frame for students who struggle with structuring their written work. The handout can also be modified to allow it to be used with other topics in the specification.

TOPIC: Deception and self-deception, superstition, and coincidence

TEACHING IN TEAMS

Students are assigned to a specific group; this could be based on ability. Each group is assigned one area to focus on: deception, self-deception, superstition or coincidence. It is important that students record information in note form and in their own words, as they will be using this handout to teach others later. Once research time is completed (this will depend on your class needs and SOW timescale) students need to decide on a format to supplement their teaching; for example, a poster, PowerPoint, A5 key point card. Once teaching tools have been created, two activities are possible:

1. Teaching tour – one student from the group remains with the 'teaching tool', i.e. the completed handout. Other students from the group are assigned the role of learners and sent to visit other 'teachers' in the class. Teachers then instruct their visitors on the topic they covered. Learners then travel back to their original group and teach each other, including the 'teacher', what they have learnt. To test understanding, a quiz on all areas is sat individually. The students' scores for each group are added and the average found. The group with the highest average are the winners as they have taught each other well on all topics.
2. Teacher time – groups take the role of teacher and teach the class their topic as a whole. Groups could be encouraged to structure their section into starter, main, plenary, if time permits. To test understanding, a quiz on all areas is sat individually (you could ask students to provide the questions for their section). The students' scores for each topic are collated and a class average is found. The topic with the highest scores indicates the group that delivered the most successful lesson.

I find (RCG) testing the class in either activity enables weaknesses or areas of misunderstanding to be identified and addressed in subsequent lessons.

V✓ A✓ K ORS HANDOUT 161

TOPIC: Psychic healing and psychic mediumship

FORMING A CONSIDERED OPINION

This handout could be used for numerous topics in anomalistic psychology and other areas of the course. For example, the notion of psychic healing could be considered. Completing the handout can act as a basic writing frame for students attempting an essay question. Less able students may benefit from the evidence sections being divided into 'Point – Evidence – Evaluation' (see page 11) to help them make efficient use of research evidence.

The level of help students are given to identify relevant information can be varied based on ability. Less able students can be directed to relevant lesson notes while more able students could be asked to provide their own information from the textbook or Internet research.

V A✓ K OTS HANDOUT 162

TOPIC: Out-of-body and near-death experience

ONE MINUTE WONDER

Students have to talk for one minute on the topic of out-of-body experiences or near-death experiences. Once they have decided on the points they wish to include, a script needs to be written. Pester your science department for a set of stop watches (or allow students to use the stop watch on their mobile phone) so students can time themselves and make any amendments to ensure they hit the 60-second target.

To encourage students to read their speeches to the class, a class competition can be held with a leader board to record who comes closest to the 60-second target. Speeches can be recorded to form a podcast for the topic to be used during revision sessions. This handout can be adapted to allow 60-second speeches to be created for any topic from the specification. To challenge more able students they could be assigned more complex topics or evaluation issues rather than simple 'outline the theory of…'. Speeches should be delivered with the aid of key points or words written on a cue card to encourage retention of information.

V✓A K✓ HORS HANDOUT 163

TOPIC: Science

PLANNING A STUDY

One of the best ways for students to learn 'How Science Works' is for them to plan scientific studies and carry them out.

Handout 163 provides students with a format to plan their experiment and think about how they will analyse their data.

In the PSYA4 exam, students may well be expected to design and describe a detailed study in a prescribed area. This type of handout will also help them to prepare for these types of exam questions.

V✓A✓K HORS HANDOUT 164

TOPIC: Science

STORY TIME

Handout 164 describes a story about a girl and her carrier bag woes!

Students love to be read the stories like primary school children. I (MWG) often turn out the lights and provide illustrations on a PowerPoint for extra effect!

The questions at the bottom of the sheet are designed to encourage students to think about the scientific process, in particular the use of independent and dependent variables in gathering causal conclusions.

(Another excellent custom-written story by Alana Clogan, thank you!)

V✓A K OS HANDOUTS 165-166

TOPIC: Science

HOW SCIENCE WORKS – HARLOW'S MONKEYS

A good way to help students consider the scientific process is to ask them to deconstruct existing studies and how they work.

Handouts 165 and **166** provide students with an opportunity to do this. The first handout describes Harlow's monkey study, which your students may have considered during their AS studies. The second handout is a deconstruction handout for your students to complete.

Reference

Harlow, H. F. (1959). Love in infant monkeys. *Scientific American,* 200(6), 68–74.

V A✓K HOS HANDOUT 167

TOPIC: Validating new knowledge

TRIPLETS

The words shown at the start of the handout all relate to establishing the value of any research. For each set, students choose three words that link together in some way. The long lines to the right of the set give students an opportunity to explain the connection between the words.

I (RCG) remind students there are no right or wrong answers as long as a connection can be made. Differentiation can take the form of must, could, should: all students MUST do two sets, most COULD do three sets, some SHOULD try to aim for four or more.

Triplets could be made into triangle posters and displayed around the classroom: each point of the triangle displays one of the triplet words with the explanation of the link between these words written inside the triangle.

V A K✓ ☆ O S HANDOUT 168

TOPIC: Research methods and concepts

DO YOU KNOW YOUR METHODS?

This is a simple matching exercise for your students to complete.

Probably the easiest way to do this is to cut out the boxes and rearrange them.

Students will be expected to know a variety of different research methods used in psychology as well as their advantages and disadvantages.

This activity could be used as a plenary or revision exercise.

V✓A✓K ☆ O S HANDOUT 169

TOPIC: Issues of reliability, validity and sampling

VALIDITY WORD WALL

Students seem to be able to understand reliability and validity when responding verbally to questions in class but use the terms interchangeably in their written work. This task aims to produce a glossary of the four terms for students to refer to when completing written tasks.

1. Students assign a colour to each of the terms shown in bold at the top of the wall.
2. They then colour code each brick below the terms so that it relates to the correct word displayed at the top of the wall. Each term has four related bricks.
3. Students then use relevant bricks of one colour to write a definition of the related key word.

This task could be differentiated by stating all students MUST produce one definition, most COULD create two definitions, a few SHOULD try to complete all four definitions. The class can feed back their definitions by asking one student to read a definition out while the class listen and check all four bricks were referred to. This could then be done for the remaining three words. Alternatively, working in small groups students could check each other's definitions.

Answers

External validity: includes ecological, population and historical, generalisable, representativeness, can be applied to other situations.
Internal validity: Measures what it intends to measure, can be affected by observer bias, face validity, concurrent validity.
External reliability: consistency over occasions, repeat test at a later date, test-retest method, check by making comparison of findings.
Internal reliability: consistency within itself, inter-interviewer reliability is important, inter-observer reliability should be checked, split-half method.

Starter activity

The following lesson, the word wall can be used for a quick game of taboo. Students have to describe one form of validity or reliability without using that word's four words from the wall.

V A✓K ☆ O HANDOUT 170

TOPIC: Issues of reliability, validity and sampling

SAMPLING TECHNIQUES

This homework activity can be used following the 'selecting participants' lesson. After reading the different situations, students identify the sampling technique used, recording this in the box below each stimulus, then suggest possible strengths and weaknesses of the technique for the specific situation.

This task aims to reinforce the need to refer to context in their responses in exam questions.

V A✓K ★HOS HANDOUT 171

TOPIC: Ethical considerations in psychological research

CONFORMING TO THE CODE

This activity can be used to help refresh students' memory of AS and A2 topics to encourage their use of synopticity and help revise studies that can be used in the PSYA3 and 4 exams. Students need to outline the four ethical principles in the left-hand boxes. This task could be divided amongst the class with a group of students responsible for one principle; students then gather the other three principles from their peers. The second column of boxes is more challenging, as students are asked to identify one research study that illustrates failing to meet the principle. Less able students may benefit from a sheet of research studies from which to select a relevant example. More able students could be challenged to provide their own examples through library research. The final column involves higher order thinking as students are required to think beyond simple reporting of information.

For information on British Psychological Society ethical guidelines visit: http://www.bps.org.uk/document-download-area/document-download$.cfm?file_uuid=E6917759-9799-434A-F313-9C35698E1864&ext=pdf

TOPIC: Inferential analysis, probability and significance

MATCH UP

A simple task that provides students with a glossary of technical terms to help their understanding of subsequent reading, improve essay style or act as a revision tool. Students can colour code or draw lines to match the key words to the definitions or alternatively cut out the information and stick definitions alongside the relevant term.

The information could be used to create a crossword; there are lots of free crossword creators on the Internet.

TOPIC: Inferential tests: Spearman's Rho

CORRELATIONS AND SPEARMAN'S RHO

The PSYA4 exam could ask students to devise a research procedure, for 12 marks. This requires students to develop a hypothesis, operationalise variables and create a workable methodology. The top mark band states decisions must be well reasoned.

When I (MWG) initially starting teaching this aspect of the unit, I began by providing students with a plan for a psychological study and asked students to justify the chosen sample method and aspects of the procedure. You will see that the next few lesson notes provide some ideas for investigations you could carry out.

Handout 173 gives your students some options for carrying out a *correlational investigation* and a form for planning, recording and reporting the results.

V A✓K✓★OS HANDOUT 174

TOPIC: Inferential tests: Chi-squared test

RESEARCHING WARM AND COLD COLOURS

This activity involves carrying out the experiment as a class to give students an understanding of the method they will later be asked to justify. Students are presented with chocolate beans of various colours and, as a class, decide which colours would be seen as warm (for example, red, orange) and which would be cold (blue, green). Some colours may elicit mixed views (lilac), so the majority vote is taken. These colours are then recorded in the warm and cold boxes on the handout. The class could discuss why colours were chosen in this way rather than one person making the decision.

Students then carry out the experiment. Anyone who does not wish to eat a chocolate bean can take the role of researcher. Researchers provide each participant, whose eyes are closed, with one bean that they place on their tongue and let dissolve. The participant then states what colour they think the bean was. Researchers record whether they correctly identified a warm or cold colour. For example, if the bean was red and the participant stated orange this could be identified as a correct identification of a warm colour. Chi-squared is used due to data being categorical and students must only give one response, i.e. they should test only one bean.

	Given warm colour	Given cold colour
Correctly identified colour		
Incorrectly identified colour		

As an extension or homework, students can be asked to design their own research into a related area or an area of their own choosing. The handout can be modified so only the titles of each cell remain to act as a writing frame.

V A✓K✓★OS HANDOUT 175

TOPIC: Inferential tests: Mann-Whitney *U* Test

TESTING THE DIFFERENCE IN COOKIES

In my (MWG) experience, students love to do this investigation because it is messy and they can eat the chocolate chips afterwards!

Handout 175 is fairly self-explanatory in terms of how the investigation works. Students could either bring in their own cookies and work in small groups, or you could conduct this as a whole class experiment.

The students can plan, record and report the findings on the sheet provided.

V A✓K✓★OST HANDOUTS 176-177

TOPIC: Inferential tests: Wilcoxon *T* test

WILCOXON *T* TEST INVESTIGATION

Whether you are teaching Unit 3 before Unit 4 or vice versa, research methods activities can be linked to material from PSYA3. So students are learning information for one exam and preparing themselves for the second. This activity is based upon Garg *et al.* (2007), part of the PSYA4 eating behaviour topic (AQA).

The task asks, 'Could it be that knowledge of nutritional information has an impact on our food choices?' Food packaging now displays the fat, salt and calorie content of a product, often colour-coded red, amber or green. Is this information used by shoppers to inform their diet? Students aim to identify whether a difference exists in how appetising unhealthy foods are found to be when nutritional information is presented compared to when no such information is given. My (RCG) students hypothesised that unhealthy food will receive lower appetising scores when nutritional information is displayed compared to when no such information is provided. They felt knowledge of fat and calories would make the foods less appealing.

The investigation can be conducted on the class, or students can act as the researcher and find their own participants and run the study. Half of the sample complete the rating of chocolate, crisps and pizza shown alone, the other participants rate the same foods but with the nutritional information displayed. The procedure is then repeated with each group experiencing the other condition, so the procedure is counterbalanced. Once all data is collected, students conduct their own statistics test on their data.

As an extension, students could create a discussion for the study, based upon the old AQA coursework. The discussion consists of four sections: explanation of the findings, relating this investigation's findings to previous research in this area, give limitations of the study and suggest how these could be improved, suggest ideas for further research and discuss implications of the investigation's findings.

Reference

Garg, N., Wansink, B. & Inman, J. J. (2007), The influence of incidental effect on consumers' food intake. *Journal of Marketing*, 71(1), 194–206.

TOPIC: Descriptive and inferential statistics

DATA DECISIONS

To continue the theme of this section, **Handout 178** encourages you and your students to carry out some sort of investigation in order to put some of the concepts involved in descriptive statistics in context.

The whole feel of PSYA4 and the research methods section, in particular, is much more applied, so it makes sense to teach these ideas in an applied fashion.

The handout provides areas for students to record data from an experiment that involves two conditions. They then have to calculate mean, mode, median, range and standard deviation and decide which are the best descriptive measures of the data and why.

I did this with my classes with the game penguin swing (search for it on Google) and played girls vs. boys on the digital projector. The game displays the distance you were able to launch a penguin to. Often the scores will be 0, which will be useful when you come to discuss the mode and its effectiveness in describing the data's central tendency.

There is also an extension task for the higher ability students.

TOPIC: Analysis and interpretation of qualitative data

QUALITATIVE CROSSWORD

Students use their textbooks to find the answer to each question and fit them into the grid. To support less able students, groups could be formed and the crossword photocopied onto A3 paper to form a group activity.

Once completed, either individually or in groups, students could colour code each word on the grid to indicate their level of understanding: red = I didn't know the word and needed help; orange = I found this in the text, was a little unsure at first; green = I understood this term quickly, feel confident about this. Crosswords could be taken in to assess class understanding and inform subsequent teaching of this area.

Answers are provided on **Handout 180.**

TOPIC: Psychological research and scientific method

EXAM-STYLE QUESTIONS

Handouts 181-183 are modelled on the exam papers from PSYA4 and could be used as an assessment of student understanding of psychological research and the scientific method at the end of the scheme of work.

Each question displays the mark allocation to help students fully answer each question. On some of the handouts there is more of a breakdown of what assessment objective the question is testing.

Should students struggle with the more extended questions, a writing frame could be provided that contains subheadings to guide students to create a thorough answer: see researching warm and cold colours for a question (g) example (page 88), and planning documents (page 85).

My (RCG) students provided the following suggestions in answer to question (f) on **Handout 183**.

- There seems to be a more balanced outcome in psychology students compared to non-psychology students.
- Non-psychology students were four times more likely to choose more negative words than positive.
- However, in both groups more negative words were chosen.
- Lack of scientific knowledge of non-psychology students may have led to this outcome. The media may have biased views or the name itself 'electro', 'convulsive' both seem dangerous words.
- While psychology students' choices may reflect an understanding of ECT and so have made informed decisions the non-psychology students may not understand the therapy.
- Only 15 people per group (7 + 8 / 3 + 12) so it would not be wise to generalise these findings to the wider population.

Handouts

Introduction to ______ Unit ____ Section ____

KEY WORDS

Term	Definition

SPECIFICATION TOPICS

SKILLS REMINDER

AO1	**Outline of theories, studies explanations, therapy**
AO2	Evidence Appropriateness Justification
AO3	Synopticity: Issues/debates Methodological evaluations

ESSAY AO2/3 REMINDER

P	**Make the point**
E	Give evidence/comment/ example/quote that relates to the point made
E	Expand by explaining HOW the 'E' relates to the point. Comment on the validity of the 'E'. Could there be an alternative view/ explanation? What issues does 'E' raise?

▶ General topics p.1&9

How Science Works – project mark scheme

Abstract - 150 words

To be included: aim, hypothesis, brief comment on sample and method, statistics, conclusion reached.

All points included in a concise, coherent manner.	3 marks
Most points included in a coherent manner.	2 marks
Some points covered or all points covered but muddled, lengthy style.	1 mark
Absent, incorrect or lacks detail to give reasonable summary of the project.	0 marks

Introduction – background research – 1200 words

To be included: three research studies and/or theory directly relating to the project, or well applied to aim if specific area lacks direct study.

Studies and/or theory are well chosen, explained in detail and explicitly related to project's aim.	4–5 marks
Research is relevant to area of study and reasonably explained. Some links made to aim of project.	2–3 marks
At least two research items are mentioned in brief detail. Implied link to aim at times.	1 mark
Research does not relate to project aim and/or lacking in detail. No links made to project aim.	0 marks

Introduction – organisation and explanation – 300 words

To be included: initial introduction statement to general area of study, relevant research - final item is on linking most closely to aim (see mark scheme above), explanation of why specific aim was chosen.

Well-structured introduction, general area of study and explanation of aim shows good understanding.	2 marks
General area and aim reasonably explained but structure may be a little muddled.	1 mark
Explanations lack depth and/or structure lacks logical flow.	0 marks

Hypothesis – 200 words

To be included: fully operationalised experimental/alternative hypothesis, including explanation of the direction, and null hypothesis.

Both hypotheses are fully operationalised and direction explained.	2 marks
Both hypotheses given but not fully operationalised. Attempt made to explain direction.	1 mark
Missing one hypothesis or both lack detail to make them untestable or incorrect.	0 marks

Method – 500 words

To be included: research design (including how groups were formed), IV and DV, sample method, sample size and relevant demographics, materials and apparatus (examples in appendix), method (including ethics).

All areas mentioned in sufficient detail to allow full replication of the project.	4–5 marks
Areas mentioned in some detail to allow replication of project, only minor details missing.	2–3 marks
Replication of project is just possible, though some details are omitted.	1 mark
Replication of procedure is not possible due to absence of key aspects or materials.	0 marks

▶ General topics p.7

How Science Works – project mark scheme

Results – explanation of results – 300 words

To be included: full justification of statistics test chosen, appropriate probability set (P= 0.05), description of data trends and anomalies, test value and critical value recorded, explanation of hypothesis chosen.

Full justification of statistics test, data is well described and correct hypothesis chosen.	2 marks
Partial justification of statistics, description of data is reasonable, correct hypothesis retained.	1 mark
Statistics test not justified or incorrect test used. Incorrect hypothesis selected.	0 marks

Results – presentation of results

To be included: fully labelled graph of data, raw data in appendix, full statistics test calculations in appendix.

Appropriate graph chosen to display data, calculations and raw data clearly presented.	2 marks
Graph may lack suitable title but axes are labelled. Data and calculations could be clearer.	1 mark
No raw data, calculations not shown. Graph missing or unlabelled.	0 marks

Discussion (a) review of findings – 200 words

To be included: statement of hypothesis accepted, test and critical value, probability level set, trends/anomalies.

All information included. Trends and anomalies well explained.	2 marks
Most information included. Attempt to explain trends and/or anomalies.	1 mark
Hypothesis accepted not stated, little attempt made to discuss data.	0 marks

Discussion (b) relating findings to background research – 400 words

To be included: project's data is related to research discussed in the introduction.

Detailed comparison made with attempts to explain reasons for differences in data.	3 marks
Reasonable attempt made to compare and contrast findings to previous research.	2 marks
Implied links to previous research, student tends to simply describe previous work in this area.	1 mark
No attempt made to relate findings to previous research mentioned in introduction.	0 marks

Discussion (c) limitations and modifications – 400 words

To be included: three limitations, each one given appropriate modification.

Three specific limitations with appropriate modifications given for each point.	3 marks
Two limitations relating specifically to method/apparatus used in the project and modifications.	2 marks
One or two general limitations, e.g. small sample size, lacking in population validity.	1 mark
No attempt made to identify limitations of study.	0 marks

Discussion (d) implications and future research – 400 words

To be included: implications of project for wider society and two ideas for future research.

Two research ideas given in good detail and thoughtful discussion of implications of findings.	3 marks
One or more research ideas in reasonable detail with brief comment on implications.	2 marks
Either one research idea in brief detail and/or vague comment on implications.	1 mark
No attempt made to discuss future research and/or no implications discussed.	0 marks

▶ General topics p.7

How Science Works – project mark scheme

References

All research fully referenced in correct format.	2 marks
References in correct format, some omissions, however.	1 mark
No references, or references not in acceptable form.	0 marks

Project style

Formal, scientific style used throughout. Appropriate sections in correct order.	2 marks
Generally scientific reporting style and coherent in nature.	1 mark
Scientific style not used (written in first person/informal), lacks coherent structure.	0 marks

Student input

Student worked alone with little teacher input.	2 marks
Student worked in small group with little teacher input.	1 mark
Significant support and guidance needed from teacher.	0 marks

Design decisions

Full consideration of issues such as counterbalancing and great care of ethical issues.	2 marks
Most decisions suited aim of investigation.	1 mark
Incorrect decisions made that impacted greatly on validity of project.	0 marks

Total mark out of 40 = ____________ Grade awarded ____________ Target grade ____________

Comments

▶ General topics p.7

How Science Works – study deconstruction 1

Study	
Research aim(s)	
Research method Investigation design	
Sample Sampling method	
Independent Variable (operationalised) *...or covariable 1 if correlation*	
Dependent Variable (operationalised) *...or covariable 2 if correlation*	
Hypothesis Null hypothesis	
Statistical test Justification	Study was looking for a difference / relationship Study gathered unrelated / related data Study gathered nominal / ordinal / interval data
Results	

▶ General topics p.8

How Science Works – study deconstruction 2

Conclusions	
Potential ethical issues	1 – 2 –
How they were/could have been dealt with	1 – 2 –
Internal validity	
External validity	

Internal validity - Think about the operationalisation of the IV and DV. Think about extraneous variables, e.g. demand characteristics, social desirability, Hawthorne effect. Think about experimental design and the weaknesses of that design in the context of the study.

External validity - Think about the sample and the sampling method (population validity). Think about the research setting and whether the results could be generalised to different settings (ecological validity).

▶ General topics p.8

FOLDER INDEX

	DATE	TITLE	AIM	☺ 😐 ☹
1				
2				
3				
4				
5				
6				
7				
8				
9				
10				
11				
12				
13				
14				
15				
16				
17				
18				
19				
20				

▶ General topics p.9

FOLDER INDEX

	DATE	TITLE	AIM	☺ 😐 ☹
21				
22				
23				
24				
25				
26				
27				
28				
29				
30				
31				
32				
33				
34				
35				
36				
37				
38				
39				
40				

▶ General topics p.9

Tracking my progress

My Target Grade =

Assignment	What your teacher said you needed to do to improve...	Your mark / out of	Grade	Over / On / Under
1.	• •			
2.	• •			
3.	• •			
4.	• •			
5.	• •			
6.	• •			
7.	• •			

▶ General topics p.9

Tracking my progress

My Target Grade = ______

8.	• •			
9.	• •			
10.	• •			
11.	• •			
12.	• •			
13.	• •			
14.	• •			

▶ General topics p.9

It is absolutely crazy how many students do not read their essays before they hand them in! Use this form to review your work and assess your own areas of strength and weakness. This must be handed in WITH your essay in order for your homework to be accepted.

Indicate in the column on the right whether you (1) strongly agree, (2) agree, or (3) disagree.

Self-evaluation form

In this essay I have...

AO1 - KNOWLEDGE AND UNDERSTANDING

AO1 Marks available in this assignment =

Read and understood the **knowledge** and **instruction** words in the question and what they require you to do (e.g. discuss, outline, evaluate) ☐

Included material that is **relevant** to the question and excluded that which is **irrelevant** (e.g. asks you to outline an explanation or theory.. don't spend all your time describing studies!) ☐

Planned your essay using an essay plan sheet or mind map ☐

Used **key terms** to show your knowledge and understanding ☐

Used those **key terms** accurately and successfully, not just 'dropped' them in ☐

Summarised detail where you do not have enough time to include it all ☐

Paid close attention to **how many AO1 marks are available** and not given too little/ too much detail ☐

AO2/AO3 – EVALUATION, ANALYSIS AND KNOWLEDGE OF HOW SCIENCE WORKS

AO2/AO3 marks available in this assignment =

Paid close attention to **how many AO2 marks are available** and not given too little/ too much evaluation and analysis ☐

Used different **sign posts** to introduce the evaluations (e.g. this is undermined by, this can be challenged by) ☐

Have **fully elaborated** all analysis and evaluation points (e.g. included evidence, examples, supporting statements, counter-arguments, etc.) ☐

Made sure the evaluations are **relevant** to the question (e.g. if the question asks you to evaluate a theory or explanation… make sure your focus is not entirely on evaluating studies) ☐

Stayed very focussed on the essay question/ title ☐

Have included one or two synoptic elements (e.g. link to a psychological issue/debate, link to other area in the specification) ☐

QUALITY OF WRITTEN COMMUNICATION (marked within both sections)

Written **clearly** and **concisely** ☐

Used **paragraphs** for each new point/topic ☐

Linked the paragraphs together seamlessly ☐

▶ General topics p.9

Teacher feedback form

AO1 - Knowledge and Understanding	
8–9 marks	**Awarded**
Knowledge and understanding is accurate and well detailed.	
Good range of appropriately selected material to address the question.	
Organisation and structure of answer is excellent.	
5–7 marks	
Knowledge and understanding is slightly less accurate and detailed (some mistakes).	
Mostly appropriately selected material to address the question (less depth/breadth).	
Organisation and structure of answer is good.	
3–4 marks	
Knowledge and understanding is basic (lack of depth and explanation).	
Some appropriately selected material to answer question (bits missing & irrelevant material).	
Organisation and structure is basic.	
1–2 marks	
Knowledge and understanding is muddled or inaccurate.	
Material selected to answer the question is too brief or irrelevant.	
Lacks organisation and structure.	

AO2/AO3 Analysis, Evaluation & How Science Works	
13–16 marks	**Awarded**
Evaluations are fully discussed and elaborated – showing sound analysis.	
The answer is well focussed on the question and shows clear line of argument.	
Shows substantial evidence of effective IDA – issues, debates and approaches.	
Excellent quality of written communication.	
9–12 marks	
Evaluations are explained and elaborated – showing reasonable analysis.	
The answer is generally focussed on the question and line of argument is evident.	
Shows evidence of reasonable IDA.	
Reasonable quality of written communication.	
5–8 marks	
Evaluations are basic – showing some understanding.	
The answer shows some focus on the question.	
Shows some evidence of basic IDA.	
Quality of written communication lacks clarity and accuracy.	
1–4 marks	
Evaluations are weak – showing little understanding.	
The answer shows little focus on the question.	
Little/no evidence of IDA – or IDA is muddled.	
Poor quality of written communication.	

For teacher comments PTO or see essay. . . . .

Total:	
Grade:	

▶ General topics p.10

Essay targets

Grade	A01	A02/A03
A	Have completed all the targets below with detail, organisation and accuracy. Have demonstrated good understanding (e.g. through examples or explanation).	Evaluations and analyses are discussed and show depth (e.g. use of evidence/counter arguments, etc.). There is a clear line of argument. Clear focus on the question throughout. IDA point(s) is used effectively and the **relevance clearly explained/justified.**
B	Have made very few/no mistakes in the outline of the explanation/research. Have included extra details to show depth of knowledge.	Good organisation and structure. Evaluations and analyses show extra explanation or elaboration, showing sound understanding. Evidence is used to support arguments where appropriate. IDA points are well explained.
C	Have included all the major principles/details. Have included key terms relevant to the explanation/research.	Evaluations and analyses are explained – showing reasonable understanding. Evaluations and analyses are mostly focussed on the essay title. Links to issue or debate are coherent. Evaluation of methodology is reasonable.
D	The outline is beyond brief but missing major elements.	Have shown some understanding of the evaluation points. The emphasis is on *using* material/evidence, rather than *describing* it. Some link to issue or debate. There is some evaluation of methodology.
E	Only included a very brief outline of the explanation/research.	Evaluation points are included. There is some focus on the essay.

If you are scoring low marks it could be because…

- Errors in grammar, spelling and structure.
- No IDA material, or inaccurate.
- Evaluations are inaccurate or not elaborated.
- Material included is irrelevant.
- Arguments make little sense.

▶ General topics p.10

PEE handy statements

P = in support of the theory...

P = However, research evidence is not conclusive...

P = A criticism of this explanation...

P = The explanation may overlook...

P = It could be argued that...

P = Contradictory evidence from...

P = one implication may be...

Evidence
Research study
Concept
Alternative view
Quotation
Issue

E = This evidence adds support as...

E = One methodological problem that may weaken the support provided is...

E = However, the evidence may lack population validity...

E = Although the explanation could offer an insight into the data, findings could also be explained by...

E= The influence of the Biological perspective means that...

E = By only concentrating on nurture this evidence may ignore...

E = The advantages of taking this reductionist approach are...

E = This provides a strong criticism because...

▶ General topics p.11

Filtration

From the text given to you, write down here what you think are the most important studies, arguments, key words, sentences, etc.

Compare with your group/class and decide on the five most important points you wrote above. When you have done this, you could write a brief summary of the text using your choices.

▶ General topics p.13

Treasure or trash?

Read the text and place the most important points in this section – your 'treasure'. You may wish to explain why you are keeping it in another colour.

Place all the bits of the text you are going to lose here - your 'trash'. You may wish to explain why you are rejecting it in another colour, e.g. it is irrelevant to your essay.

▶ General topics p.13

Brief summaries

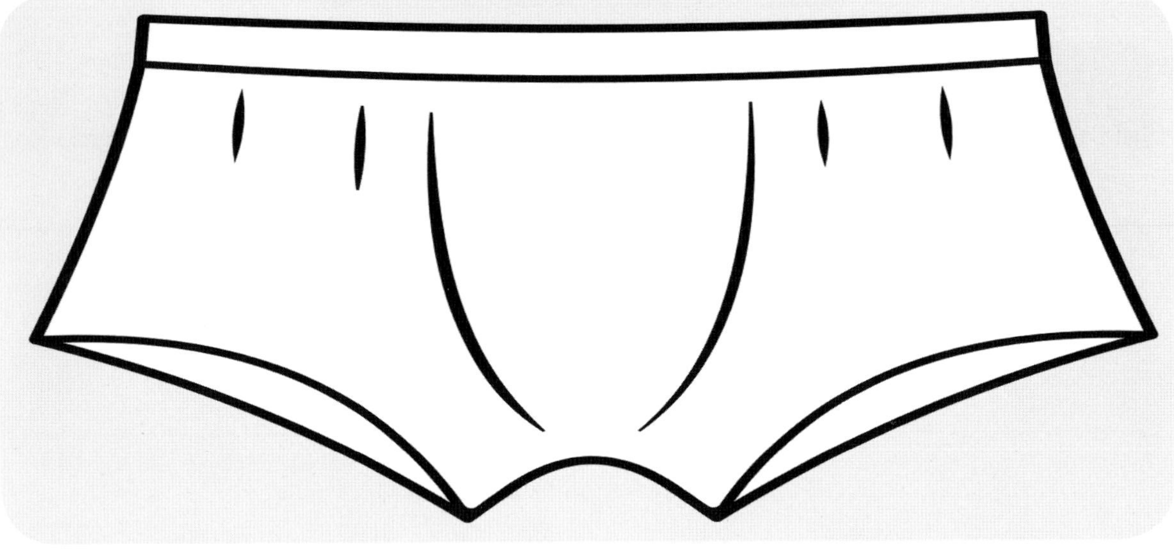

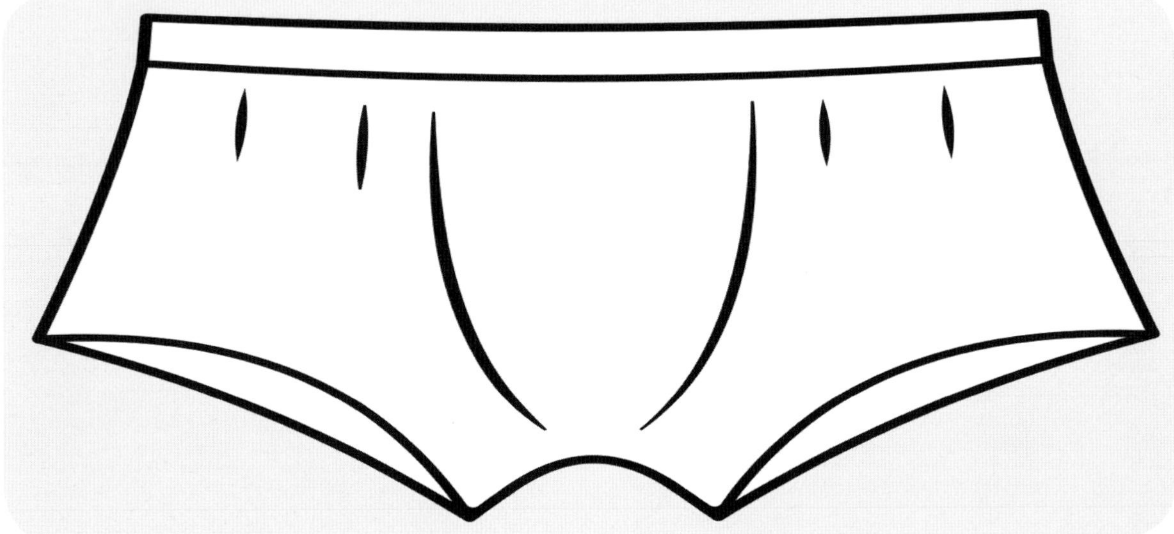

▶ General topics p.13

Extension proforma

READ THE EXTENSION ARTICLE:

1. With highlighters, **select** the most relevant/interesting points in that article (don't fall into the trap of highlighting everything – make considered choices)…

2. **Deconstruct** this article into its three most important points…

- ☐
- ☐
- ☐

3. Can you **assess** and explain the relevance of this article to today's lesson and objectives?

4. Use one of the **higher order thinking** skills in relation to this article and today's lesson objectives *(design, improve, develop, predict, hypothesise, judge the value of, compare/contrast, prove, adapt).*

You must be ready to feedback your considerations to the class without using these notes – be ready to be asked!

▶ General topics p.13

Golden nuggets

There are certain 'all-purpose' criticisms that can be dropped into any essay. These are nifty little gems that will impress the examiner. But you must make an effort to *shape* the criticism to the context through elaboration. And don't look a fool – make sure the criticism does apply. Finally, don't just re-use the same one over and over!

Key idea	Research support	Usage
Demand characteristics. Participants actively try to make sense of what is required of them in an experiment, which means they do not behave as they normally would.	Orne (1962) demonstrated this in an experiment where he asked participants to add up columns of numbers on a sheet of paper and then tear the paper up and repeat this again. If people believed this was part of a psychology experiment, some were willing to continue the task for over six hours! This led Orne to conclude that sometimes people are over-cooperative and behave in quite a different way than they would normally.	Challenges the validity of a study.
Gender bias in experiments Male and female participants are treated differently by the experimenters, which explains why some studies discover gender differences that are not really there.	Rosenthal (1966) found that male researchers were more pleasant, friendly, honest and encouraging with female than with male participants, leading Rosenthal to conclude that, psychologically, participants may simply not be in the same experiment at all.	For studies that show gender differences, challenges validity of the conclusions.
Sample bias (population validity) The findings from psychological research are not only unrepresentative on a global scale, but also within Western culture. College students are not very representative of the general population.	Sears (1986) found that 82% of research studies used undergraduates as the participants in psychology studies and 51% were Psychology students. He pointed out how unrepresentative such research is because of age, intellect and other differences. For example, their self-concept, social and political attitudes are unlikely to be fully formed, they have a stronger need for peer approval, they are selected for compliance to authority, and their social and geographical mobility leads to enhanced instability in peer relationships.	General comment on the relevance of psychological findings for statements about human behaviour. For studies where students used as participants, challenges the validity of the conclusions.
The Hawthorne effect Participants' behaviour is affected by knowledge that they are observed.	Roethlisberger and Dickson (1939) were asked to investigate whether lighting had any effect on production levels at the Hawthorne Western Electric factory. They found that increased lighting led to increased production – but so did decreased lighting. The increased attention acted as a confounding variable.	For studies that show performance has improved – suggests this may be due to the Hawthorne effect rather than any experimental treatment.
Experimenter bias Experimenters unconsciously communicate cues to participants about what they expect to find and this affects participants' behaviour.	Rosenthal and Fode (1963) asked students to train rats to learn their way around a maze. They were told that there were two groups of rats: one group were 'fast learners' having been bred for this characteristic, whilst the other group were 'slow learners'. The supposedly brighter rats actually did better.	Applies to lab experiments, or any situation where a researcher's expectations may be communicated to participants.
Social desirability bias Respondents give answers that show them in a 'good light'.	Crowne and Marlow (1960) developed a scale to assess the 'truthfulness' of a person's answers. This is a way of assessing the validity of the answers given on a questionnaire/interview.	Applies to questionnaires and interviews.
Add some golden nuggets of your own.		

Golden nuggets in use – some examples

One problem in many studies is that male experimenters treat male and female participants differently (Rosenthal, 1966). The consequence is that the conclusion about gender difference may be due to a confounding variable rather than the IV.

This study may lack population validity because the participants were undergraduates. Sears (1986) pointed out that students are not representative for many reasons – they are more intelligent, younger, and their attitudes are not fully formed.

▶ General topics p.14

Useful phrases and connectives

Changing direction
- However …
- Having said that …
- On the other hand ...
- Except …
- … although …

Adding an argument, criticism support or evidence
- In addition …
- Also …
- Moreover …
- Furthermore …

Emphasising
- … above all
- … in particular
- … especially
- … significantly

Illustrating your understanding or argument
- For example …
- Such as …
- For instance …
- In the case of …
- In the context of this study/behaviour …

Using evidence
- Evidence to support/undermine this …
- One research study that supports this theory is…
- One research study that challenges this theory is…
- This hypothesis is supported by…

Comparing
- In the same way …
- Similarly …
- Compared with …
- Likewise …

Contrasting
- Whereas …
- Alternatively …
- … more/less than …
- Instead of …

Drawing conclusions
- This suggests that …
- This supports/undermines the theory that …
- As a result of …
- Therefore …
- Consequently …

Using explanations/theories
- One can explain these findings with…
- These findings imply…
- A different way to explain these findings would be …

Criticising the methodology of a study
- One limitation of this study is …
- One strength of this study is …
- This study lacked ecological validity …
- There may have been demand characteristics …

Applications
- An application of this research is …
- One consequence of this finding is …

Referring to issues, debates and approaches
- This links to the *nature vs. nurture* (or any other) debate in psychology because …
- There is a connection here to another area of psychology …

▶ General topics p.14

Misunderstood monsters

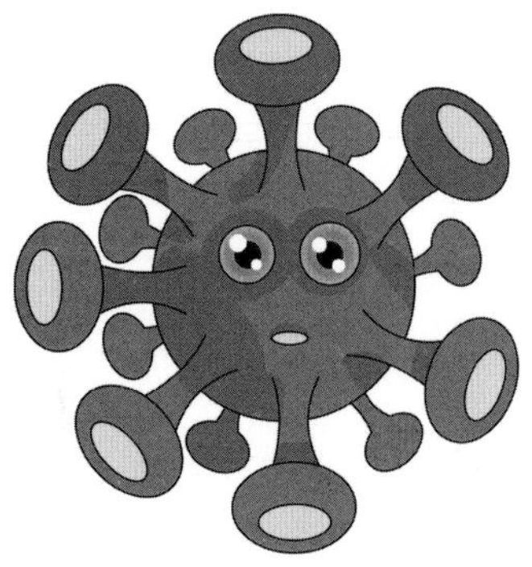

Know your evolutionary principles!

Feel free to be imaginative during this exercise, particularly when thinking about the EEA! Include all the bold words in your explanations.

- Choose one of these monsters.
- Explain how its unique features are **adaptive** to the environment.
- To do this, it will be necessary for you to describe the **environment of evolutionary adaptation (EEA)**.
- Explain the process of how/why their features evolved via **natural selection**.
- Describe their **current environment** (i.e. how the environment has changed).
- Explain how their features are now **maladaptive**.
- Explain the role of **genome lag**.

▶ General topics p.15

Classic AO2 points for evolutionary explanations of human behaviour

Whatever evolutionary theory you are studying, see if you can fit it into the following evaluative frameworks.

You'll probably have to copy them out. With some thought, you should be able to adapt these frameworks to fit any evolutionary theory that you have observed.

It could be argued that <*name whatever theory you are discussing*> theory is speculative, i.e. based on little or no evidence. For example, Hayes has argued that evolutionary psychology has a tendency to ignore 'null' findings (i.e. that facts don't fit the theory being proposed). In this case, this could include <*name anything you can think of that doesn't fit the theory*>. In defence of evolutionary psychology, some psychologists have argued that *all* science does this, not just evolutionary psychology.

Also, it could be argued that, instead of being merely speculative, evolutionary psychology *has* tried to generate testable hypotheses in this area; e.g: <*describe any attempts to generate testable hypotheses in this area*>.

One criticism of the evolutionary approach is that it is determinist because it suggests our genes specify exactly how we will behave. In the case of <*the behaviour you are discussing*>, it is suggested that genes <*briefly outline the role of genes in this behaviour, or why that gene has evolved*>.

This determinist interpretation fails to take into account that genes only predispose us to behave in certain ways, but do not dictate what individuals choose to do. Other factors determine behaviour, such as <*name something in the environment that might contribute to this behaviour occurring*>. This is another example of nature interacting with nurture.

▶ General topics p.15

Know your validity!

Pay close attention to this diagram. Read it through carefully. After a few minutes, see if you can reproduce the diagram from memory.

Once my (MWG) students were able to memorise this diagram, for some reason their evaluation of studies increased threefold!

'The extent to which a research study measures what it is designed to measure.'

INTERNAL VALIDITY	EXTERNAL VALIDITY
What actually happened in the study. Did the IV cause the change in the DV, or was it an extraneous variable?	Can the results and conclusions be generalised outside the study?

NEED TO CONSIDER...

- **Extraneous variables**
- e.g. **Social desirability** (changing behaviour to look good)
- e.g. **Demand characteristics** (changing behaviour because have guessed aim)

NEED TO CONSIDER...

- **Population validity** (can the results be generalised to other populations of people?)
- **Ecological validity** (can the results be generalised beyond to other settings/ situations?)

▶ General topics p.15

Getting to grips with the free will and determinism debate

Working out who says what

Do we really choose our actions? What if you have been hypnotised, or you are a brain in a jar (as in *The Matrix*), or if your biology has been influenced to such a degree by evolution that you only act in accordance with your inherited traits? Is it all just brain-chemistry, governed by physical laws? If you discover, in retrospect, that the actions you thought were free at the time you enacted them were really controlled by your upbringing, your life situation and so on, can you really claim that you chose your actions?

Determinism applies even if there is a 'mind-substance', different from the physical stuff of our brain (and everything else). It seems to imply that there is no freedom for human beings (or for anything else, for that matter). The consequences of determinism seem grave. If no one chooses freely, how can we blame, praise, or punish? How would you look upon another, who acted friendly towards you, if you knew that the person had no choice in the matter? And wouldn't you yourself feel trapped, knowing you could not control your actions (even though you had the *feeling* you could control your actions)?

Some people believe determinism is compatible with free will. Compatibilism says that 'if determinism is true, then we still can have free will'. It does not commit itself to either of these views ('determinism is true', or 'we have free will'), it only states that they are compatible. The view that both statements are true is called *soft determinism*. The incompatibilist view is that both statements cannot be true; hence an incompatibilist would either be a *hard determinist* or a *libertarian*. Hard determinism is the view that determinism is true and that we do not have free will. The libertarian view is that we have free will, and as such, determinism must be false. Libertarians basically think we can tell that we have free will, just by introspecting at the time we make choices. There seems to be a private sphere in our introspection, in which we cannot make mistakes. For example, you cannot be wrong about the fact that you are in pain when you actually are in pain. Who can tell but you? Yet, we might lack the ability to introspect as to the causes of our sensation as they appear in our brains. If you are a smoker, you know that taking a cigarette gives you a kick, a pleasurable feeling, and no one can tell you that you do not. But can you tell that this pleasurable feeling is mediated by dopamine release in the nucleus accumbens? You certainly cannot.

(From http://www.stenmorten.com/English/php/php.htm)

Tasks

1. **OK, you have a lot of difficult philosophical stuff to work out here. Your task is to ensure that you know what all of the big terms mean and start to build it all into some kind of structure. To this end, you need to work on producing a list of the following terms, with a short explanation next to each one:**

   determinism, free will, compatibilism, incompatibilism, hard determinism, soft determinism, libertarianism

2. **Then you have to take each term and plot it on some kind of diagram to show that you understand how they all fit together. There isn't a right answer to this – but you are going to need a clear diagram showing all of the different positions that can be taken with regard to this debate.**

3. **After that, note briefly on your diagram the *consequences* of each position. Whichever position a person takes they can end up reaching conclusions that are difficult or uncomfortable. Briefly indicate next to each position what these are.**

▶ General topics p.16

Ready-made reductionism paragraph

Try the paragraph in the box below in an essay to see if it provides useful AO2 material.

Replace numbers with the following information:

(1) The name of the research (e.g. so and so's theory of such and such).

(2) The behaviour that the research seeks to explain (e.g. bystander behaviour, schizophrenia, moral development, etc.).

(3) The factors that the research concentrates upon (e.g. genes, family life, the role of the media, situational cues, etc.).

(4) The factors that the explanation doesn't concentrate upon.

> It could be argued that (1) is a rather reductionist approach to the study of (2). This means that, in an attempt to isolate and study particular causal factors such as (3) some wider picture may have been lost. It seems likely that (2) is affected by a whole range of factors such as (4), thus it might be useful to develop a more eclectic approach. This criticism may, however, be unjust. All psychological research needs to focus upon particular factors for study and (1) has provided us with a valid insight into the role of (3) in (2).

Try using one or two of the studies below to practise this technique. Then try using it on an A2 topic you are currently covering.

A Peterson and Peterson's research discovered that information in STM was lost after about 18 seconds. However, they had prevented their participants from using verbal rehearsal to keep the information in STM. Information stays in STM for as long as you like if you use rehearsal to keep it there. Of course that would mean that nothing else would be able to be encoded into STM during that time so it isn't a particularly effective technique. This type of rehearsal is also known as maintenance rehearsal because it maintains items in STM.

B Bowlby claimed that the years up until about 2½ were critical in a child's development. This is called a critical period hypothesis. Bowlby claimed that, if a child was denied emotional care during this time, then permanent harm was fairly inevitable.

C As with anorexia, the hypothalamus plays a role in bulimia. Damage to the hypothalamus can result in either overeating or undereating. In animals, damage to the ventromedial hypothalamus (VMH) results in overeating. This happens because the lateral hypothalamus (LH) stimulates eating and the VMH usually stops eating. But if the VMH is damaged then there is no sense of satiety and overeating occurs, and may result in obesity. In an individual who wishes to be thin, overeating is controlled as far as possible but then may result in an excessive binge, which further results in compensation through purging.

D Bickman (1974) tested obedience in a real-life situation, and examined the effects of perceived authority on obedience. Confederates dressed in a sports jacket and tie, a milkman's uniform, or as a guard, and made requests to passers-by; for example, asking them to pick up some litter or to give someone a dime for his parking meter. Participants obeyed most when the confederate was dressed as a guard. This study shows what most of us know – we obey someone who looks like they have authority more than someone who does not.

▶ General topics p.16

Curious Colin's circadian study

Colin is curious: why do most of our bodily functions follow a 24-hour pattern? From visiting the library he understands the circadian rhythm is regulated by an internal body clock (endogenous pacemaker) and that it is readjusted every day according to environmental time cues (exogenous zeitgebers). He wonders what would happen if this internal body clock could run freely without interference from external time cues such as natural light. He is also interested in the effect of altering natural environmental cues.

Colin's friend Nat has agreed to take part in his research. Help Colin's curiosity by devising a study he could conduct into the sleep–wake cycle, either removing all environmental cues or altering a cue to see the impact on the circadian rhythm.

Little literature review – before any research takes place psychologists find out what has already taken place.

Name & date of study	Participants	Procedure	Findings

Confounding variables to consider when designing procedure.

Curious Colin's circadian study
Justify all your decisions!

Participant(s): Colin's friend Nat, a 30-year-old woman, has agreed to help out. Do you think other participants should be included? How many? Should they all be a similar age? Should both genders be included?

Free running or altered cues: Should Colin isolate his participant(s) from all cues? Should he alter one environmental cue, if so how?

Setting: Where should Colin place his participant(s)? Cave? WWII underground bunker? Isolation room in laboratory? Give reasons for your choice.

Validity: What confounding variables does Colin need to be aware of?

Expected findings: Based on the little literature review, what do you expect will happen to the participant(s) bodily rhythm?

▶ Lesson notes p.19

Ultradian update: sleep summary

1. Use your textbook to research the different stages and cycles of sleep.
2. Take 10 minutes to rehearse the information: talk to a friend about what you have learnt or produce a mindmap.
3. Close your textbook and hide your mindmap. Try to complete the summary table below.

Stage	Brain activity (brain wave)	Physical features
1		
2		
3		
4		
REM		

Circle the correct answer.

Each sleep cycle lasts approximately	30 mins in early infancy & 60 mins in adolescence.
	60 mins in early infancy & 90 mins in adolescence.
	90 mins in early infancy & 120 mins in adolescence.
Stages 3 and 4 are also known as	short wave sleep
	spindle wave sleep
	slow wave sleep
The duration of Stages 3 and 4	lessens as the night progresses while REM increases.
	increases as the night progresses while REM decreases.
	remains the same while REM fluctuates.

Reopen your textbook, look back at your mindmap. Check your summary and cycle answers. How well did you do?
Tick the appropriate evaluation on the clipboard.
Set yourself one 'to-do' to help you improve your recall of sleep stages and cycles.

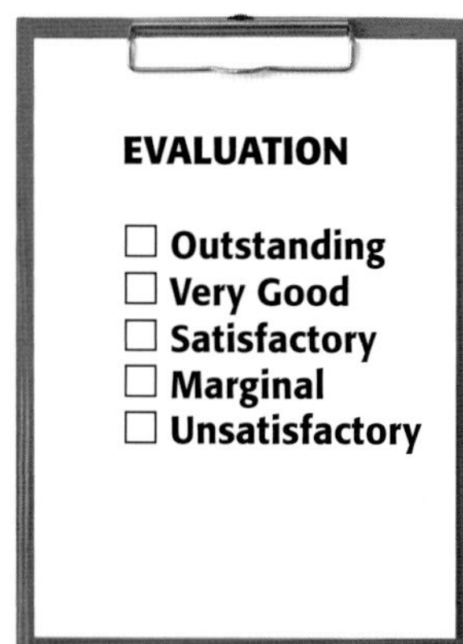

Target:

▶ Lesson notes p.19

Cut and paste – pacemakers and zeitgebers

What do I need to know?

The role of endogenous pacemakers and exogenous zeitgebers

Endo = inside Occurring within the body	Keeps a rhythm	Exo = external Occurring outside the body	German word for time giver

Confidence level: Before

Indicate your feelings towards this topic by circling a smiley.

What aspects do you feel comfortable or confident with?

What are your major worries or concerns about this topic?

Confidence level: After

Indicate your feelings towards this topic by circling a smiley.

Have you addressed areas you were unsure of?

What do you need to do now to cement your understanding and improve later recall of this topic?

- Using the challenge card provided and the images shown below, create a visual representation of the role of the endogenous pacemaker (SCN) and exogenous zeitgebers (light) for the circadian sleep-wake cycle.
- If you need a little extra help, or think you have finished, ask your teacher for the check card.

Pineal gland

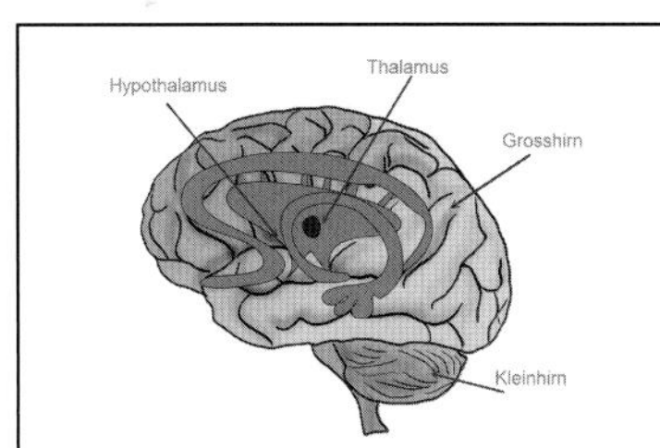

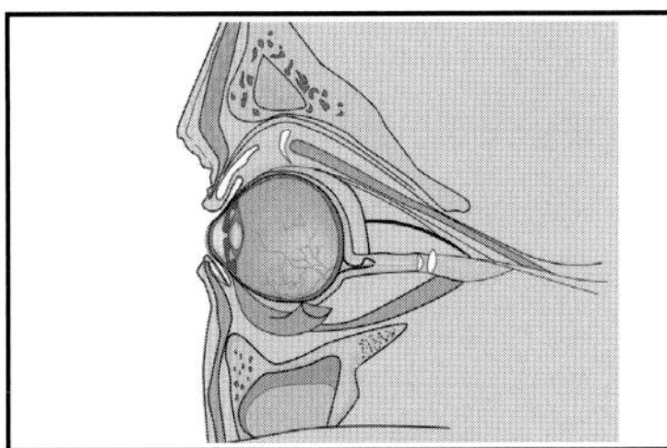

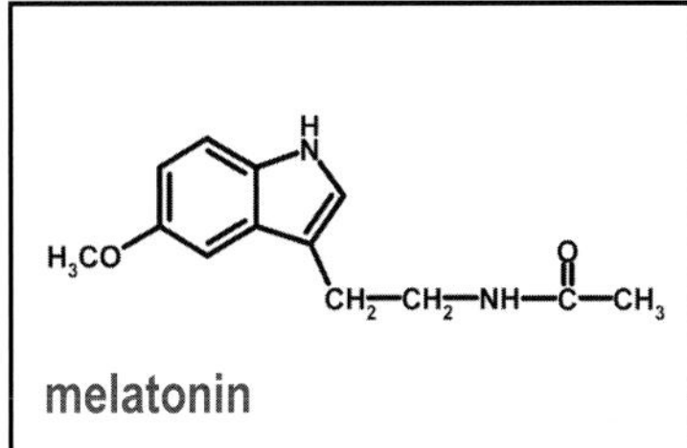

▶ Lesson notes p.19

Challenge and Check cards

Challenge card

In mammals, the main endogenous pacemaker can be found deep in the brain, within the hypothalamus. It is a tiny cluster of nerve cells called the suprachaismatic nucleus (SCN). One SCN sits in the left hemisphere of the brain, the other in the right hemisphere. Both are located just above where the optic nerves from each eye cross over (the optic chiasm). Even with our eyes closed the SCN is able to receive information on light levels from the optic nerve. Special photoreceptors in the eyelids detect light signals and carry them to the SCN. In mammals another pacemaker known as the pineal gland can be found deep in the middle of the brain. This gland is able to receive information about light levels from the SCN as it contains light-sensitive cells. When light is sensed, the production of melatonin in the pineal gland is inhibited. When the level of light falls, the pineal gland is stimulated to produce melatonin. Melatonin is a hormone that induces sleep by inhibiting the brain mechanisms that promote wakefulness.

Check card

When night falls, light lessens. Tiny photoreceptors in the eyes pick up lessening light signals and carry them to the SCN, which lies in the hypothalamus. The main pacemaker in mammals is the SCN, it obtains information on light from the optic nerve. The SCN informs the pineal gland, which produces melatonin (the sleepy hormone). When light is detected, the pineal gland stops melatonin production. Melatonin causes us to become sleepy by inhibiting the brain mechanisms that make us feel awake.

▶ Lesson notes p.19

Cunning commentary

When evaluating the role of endogenous pacemakers it is not enough just to state evidence for their existence, you need to USE the research to address exam questions.
You need to analyse research, consider implications of findings and look at wider psychological issues.

MUST – at least two bold-boxed questions

SHOULD – at least two dash-boxed questions

COULD – at least two star-boxed questions

Conjoined twins share the same blood. As melatonin circulates in the blood, we would expect that conjoined twins would share circadian rhythms, but they do not.
Sackett & Korner (1993)

What might this tell us about the role of melatonin in the sleep-wake cycle?

What methodological issues may arise in carrying out a study into conjoined twins and how might these issues impact validity?

The SCN from mutant hamsters bred to show a circadian rhythm of 20 hours were transplanted into normal hamsters (24 hour rhythm). The normal hamsters subsequently showed the mutant rhythm.
Morgan (1995)

What does this study suggest about the role of the SCN?

Is this study ethically acceptable?
Why or why not?

After 25 days in a cave, Kate Aldcroft's body temperature adopted a 24-hour rhythm, yet her sleep rhythm showed alteration to a 30 hour cycle.
Folkard (1996)

Folkard only studied one participant. Why might this lead us to accept the findings with caution?

What might this imply about the role of SCN in a range of biorhythms?

After destroying the SCN in chipmunks it was found that they were more active at night compared to normal chipmunks.
DeCoursey *et al.* (2000)

How can this study be related to Morgan's work with hamsters?

Is this useful as it was conducted on non-human animals?

▶ Lesson notes p.20

Determining disruption

Lennie is in charge of a busy factory floor. His staff work day and night making large backpacks for travellers. Employees follow a one-week phase advance shift rotation pattern. It has become increasingly obvious that morale on the factory floor is low and the amount of sick days taken is rising. As a caring foreman, Lennie has decided to conduct a survey into the effects of shift work.

What consequences of shift work should Lennie include in his questionnaire?

What questions should he ask to assess the extent of these consequences on his staff?

Which consequences do you feel deserve greater investigation (more questions)?

Practical Points

What type of questions should be asked; open or closed, mixture of the two types?

Do you need introduction questions such as age, gender, length of employment?

How many questions are needed and how will they be ordered?

Wording worries

Will respondents be able to understand psychological terms? Can they be reworded?

Is each question clear and does not lead respondents to a certain answer?

Are there enough options in closed questions and space to write for open ones?

Conduct a pilot of the questionnaire with other students.
Once you have produced your questionnaire you need to justify Lennie using it to research the consequences of shift work. Questionnaires are well known for having a low response rate, so you need to really encourage Lennie's staff to complete the questionnaire.
Write a 200-word speech to be delivered to the employees to encourage them to complete the questionnaire.

▶ Lesson notes p.20

Guess who?

Life stages:
Infancy,
Childhood,
Adolescence,
Adulthood,
Old age

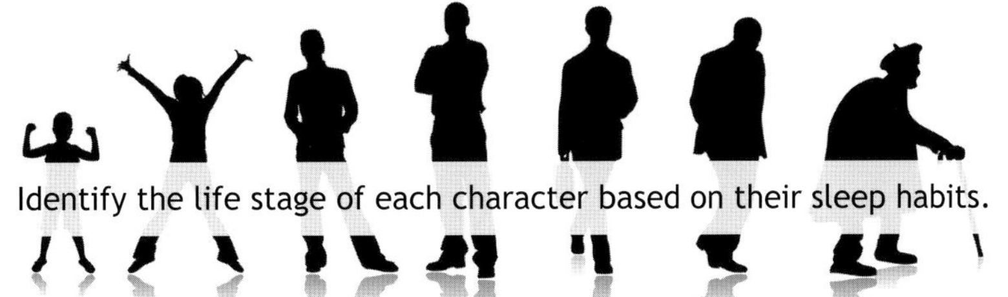

Identify the life stage of each character based on their sleep habits.

Highlight the point in the passage at which you correctly identified the character's age.

I spent a little longer in bed in my previous life stage. Nowadays, two hours a night are devoted to REM, while the remaining six are made up of the other sleep stages. It is rare to find a sleep walker my age or someone who suffers from night terrors; however, people my age can experience insomnia.

Approximately 30% of my total sleep time is spent in REM. I sleep for 12 hours each day, meaning nearly 4 hours of my sleep is REM. Other people my age may experience a form of parasomnia, for example sleep walking.

I have active and quiet sleep, which is a bit like REM and SWS. Early in my life stage about half of all my sleep was active. As I aged, this lessened and I spent more time in deep sleep. Previously I spent about 20 minutes in light sleep before entering deeper stages. Although I get a lot of sleep, around 16 hours, I tend to wake up every hour as my sleep cycle is shorter than people older than me.

I enjoy a nice nap in the daytime. This is probably due to the fact I wake up a lot during the night. I find it hard to go to sleep and cannot seem to sleep through the night. I tend to wake up earlier than other people, too. 20% of my sleep is REM. My SWS accounts for 5% of my total sleep time. As time goes by I've noticed I become sleepier earlier in the evening; sometimes I doze off in front of TV!

I prefer staying up late then lying in, in the morning. I hate the sound of the alarm in the morning; it really is an effort to get out of bed. I'm sure I used to need less sleep but recently I've only felt refreshed if I've had around 10 hours of sleep each night.

Now complete the following statements:

The main difference between an infant's and a 70 year old's sleep is...
Children are similar to adults in that...
As we age the amount of REM experienced...
Older adults may feel more tired than younger people because...
Write two more statements of your own.

▶ Lesson notes p.20

Brain box

Use information from your textbook (pages 12–13 *A2 Complete Companion*) to fill each box with information.
The boxes stack together to produce part of an answer to the following exam question:
'Outline and evaluate restoration theory as an explanation of the function of sleep' (25 marks).
Try to think of other statements that could be built upon in the same way to produce a complete essay.

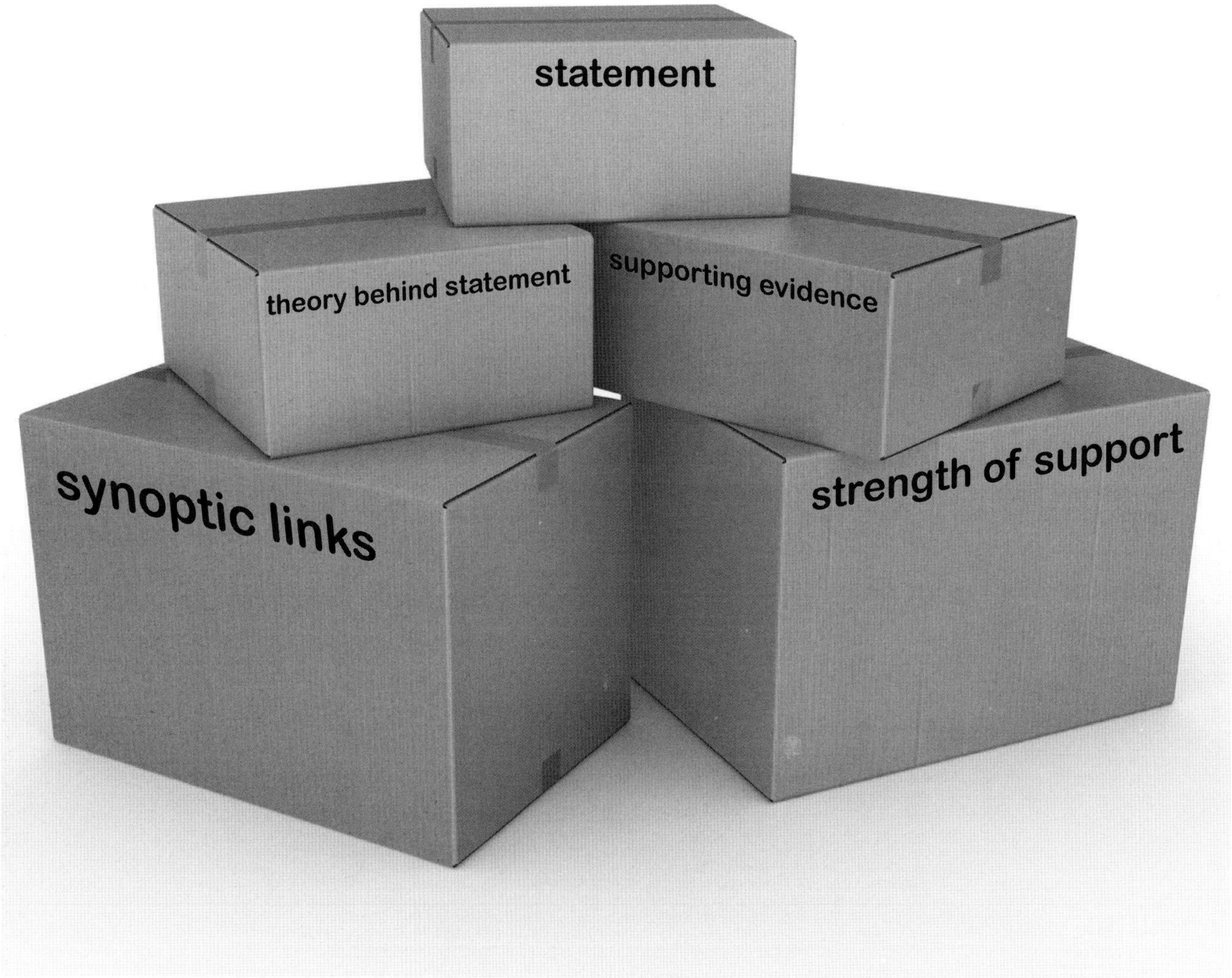

statement

theory behind statement

supporting evidence

synoptic links

strength of support

▶ Lesson notes p.21

Sleepy species

Using Evolutionary explanations (pages 14–15 in *A2 Complete Companion*) explain factors contributing to the total sleep time of the following species.

Sleep times taken from www.bu.edu/phylogeny/

Lion: 13.5 hours

Mouse: 14.5 hours

Cow: 3.9 hours

Brown bat: 19.9 hours

Support for Evolutionary explanations	Contradictory research	Problems with adopting the Evolutionary approach

▶ Lesson notes p.21

Investigating insomnia

After reading the case studies shown below, use your textbook (pages 16–17 in *A2 Complete Companion*) to produce a set of case notes on one or both of the patients.

Deshi occasionally has terrible trouble sleeping. At such times he feels tired but cannot seem to fall asleep. His work as an accident and emergency nurse means he often works night shifts. The changing shift patterns make it difficult to develop a bedtime routine. Deshi enjoys his work but finds the hospital a stressful, high-pressured environment. As a result he often snacks on chocolate and coffee when on a break. He admits he knows this isn't a healthy diet but likes these comfort foods and believes the sugar and caffeine give him the energy needed to cope with a busy shift. Friday night at A&E is especially stressful, Deshi is irritated by those needing treatment for drunken injuries but professionalism means he must keep his frustrations hidden.

What type of insomnia does the patient suffer from; transient, intermittent or chronic?

What kind of insomnia is being displayed; initial, middle or terminal insomnia?

Are they suffering from secondary or primary insomnia?

What seems to be the cause of their insomnia?

Do they display any risk factors associated with insomnia?

Mags is a teacher in her mid 50s. She visited her GP as she has been having trouble sleeping for the last month. She reports she finds herself waking up every few hours through the night. Her GP does not consider her to be depressed but does feel she may have some negative sleeping habits. She tends to stay up late, as she expects she will not be able to sleep through the night so cannot see the point of trying. In the past Mags has been known to grind her teeth when asleep and as a child was a regular sleep walker. Sleep problems have always seemed to be an issue for her. She tries hard to live a healthy lifestyle by avoiding alcohol but cannot resist a 'nice cup of tea' at night to calm her after a busy day at work.

What treatment would you advise for each patient?

What changes could be made to their sleep environment?

What lifestyle changes could they make?

What psychological techniques could be used?

▶ Lesson notes p.21

Rating the reasons

Once you have stated an explanation for the cause of narcolepsy you need to be able to consider the usefulness of that suggestion. One way to do this is to identify supporting research. However, while research may seem to add weight to an explanation, can we confidently accept the research findings?

Research issues to consider…

Was the sample size suitable?
Can we apply animal research to humans?
Could the measurement tool be improved?
Is the study taking a reductionist approach?
Has a nature or nurture stance been adopted?
Does the study provide full support for the explanation?

Narcolepsy is a result of a malfunctioning of the system that regulates REM sleep, e.g. experiencing REM during onset of sleep.

Supporting studies

Reasons for rating

Narcolepsy is linked to a mutation of the immune system: increased frequency of one type of HLA (human leukocyte antigen).

Supporting studies

Reasons for rating

Narcolepsy is linked to the neurotransmitter hypocretin. Hypocretins have an important role in maintaining wakefulness.

Supporting studies

Reasons for rating

▶ Lesson notes p.21

Top-down tag lines

A tag line is a simple sentence or slogan that summarises an event or story. You often see them accompanying film trailers, for example, Shrek (2001) 'The Greatest fairy tale never told'. For each word shown, create a tag line relating to Gregory's top-down theory of perception. The first one has been done for you.

CONSTRUCTION	PERCEPTION CREATED FROM COMBINING DIRECT OBSERVATION WITH STORED KNOWLEDGE.
DIRECT	
INDIRECT	
HYPOTHESES	
INTERACTION	
EXPECTATIONS	
TOP-DOWN	

Now use your tag lines to produce a 300-word description of Gregory's top-down theory of perception.

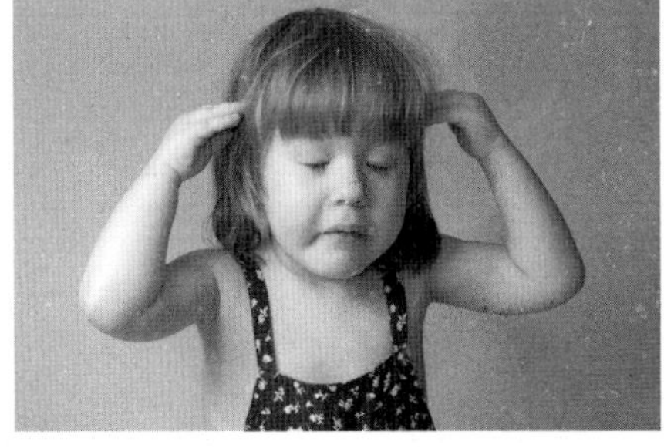

Remember:
The top-down explanation suggests our mind generates expectations about what we are looking at and these explanations help us make sense of what we see.

▶ Lesson notes p.22

Gibson's bottom-up theory of perception suggests that we receive all the information we need from our senses to perceive the environment we are in. We do not need additional information stored from previous experiences (as top-down theory suggests). The changing patterns of light surrounding us are sufficient.

Gibson's theory contains a lot of key vocabulary terms that you should include when describing his ideas.
Match each key word to one of the definitions given below.

Key word	Definition
optic array	As you move towards an object its texture appears coarser, when far away from the object its texture seems finer. You use changes in texture density to judge the distance of objects from you.
optic flow	Each object offers a potential for action. For example, seat-shaped objects afford sitting, objects with handles afford grasping.
texture gradient	Moving towards a point in your environment makes objects directly in front of this point appear still. However, objects to the side of this point seem to move towards you.
invariants	An example of an invariant. The ratio of an object above and below the line of the horizon is a constant for objects of the same size.
horizon-ratio	The changing pattern of light that surrounds you. A bundle of light rays that moves towards you from each point of the illuminated world.
resonance	A vital aspect of your behaviour in order for you to collect perceptual information from your environment.
affordance	The term used by Gibson to summarise how we make sense of the broadcast information once we have picked it up (perceived it).
movement	While some aspects of your environment change as you move around them, others do not. For example, an object's texture will always appear coarser the closer you are to it. This rule is consistent.

▶ Lesson notes p.22

What can newborn babies actually see? What perceptual ability is a child born with (nature) and how much is a result of environmental experience (nurture)?

Before reading research in your textbook (pages 28–29 in *A2 Complete Companion*) indicate your opinion by placing a cross on the continuum below.

Nature ←→ Nurture

Infants are born with perfect perception. They can see objects, understand depth and recognise faces.

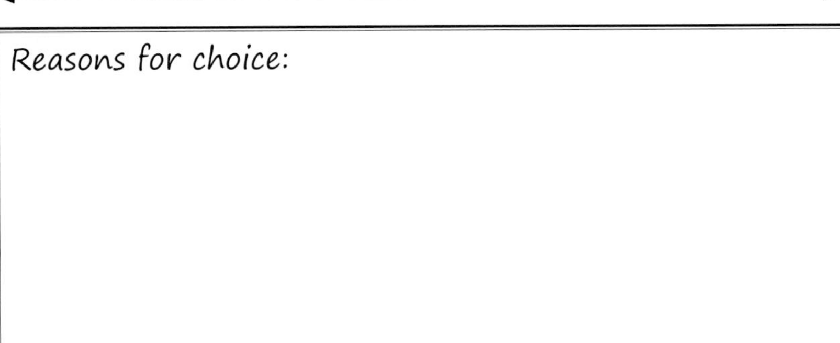

Infants are born with hardly any perceptual ability. They cannot really see objects, understand depth or recognise faces.

After reading the research on infant perception in your textbook outline at least two studies into infant perception. Use a maximum of 100 words per study. You may wish to create a balanced record by including one study that suggests infants are born with sophisticated perceptual ability (nature) and another that suggests some abilities develop as the infant interacts with their environment (nurture).

Remember to include:

- The area of infant perception being researched (for example, depth perception, shape constancy).
- Age of the infant (if known).
- Method used (for example, habituation method, covering one eye).
- Behaviour shown by infants.
- Conclusions drawn as a result of the behaviour seen.

Extension: For each study give one difficulty of using infants in perception research and one criticism relating directly to the method used or conclusions drawn.

Now you have considered research into this area record your informed opinion on the continuum and give a detailed explanation of the stance you have taken.

Nature ←→ Nurture

Reasons for choice:

▶ Lesson notes p.22

Cross-cultural critique

Turnbull 1963

Concluded that because vision is limited in the Congo's Ituri forest BamMbuti pygmies have no great need to make automatic allowances for distance when making judgements on the size of an object. Buffalo in the distance were referred to as insects.

Circle the area researched:
Depth perception
Shape consistency
Size consistency

Hudson 1960

Found nearly all European children nearing the end of primary school could use cues such as occlusion, linear size and object perspective to judge where a spear was pointing. Some Bantu children, however, were unable to use these cues to understand the image.

Circle the area researched:
Depth perception
Shape consistency
Size consistency

Allport & Pettigrew 1957

Argued experience of rectangular windows helped Zulus from urban areas experience the trapezoid window illusion. Zulus in rural areas, where rectangular windows were less common, were less likely to experience the illusion.

Circle the area researched:
Depth perception
Shape consistency
Size consistency

Segall et al. 1963

On showing Zulus the Müller-Lyer illusion the researchers found they were less likely to experience the illusion. This was explained to be as a result of their experience of rooms. The Zulus in this sample lived mostly in circular huts so had little experience of square rooms.

Circle the area researched:
Depth perception
Shape consistency
Size consistency

What do these studies tell us about the nature vs. nurture debate? Are perceptual abilities largely innate or do different environmental experiences impact on perceptual abilities? Record your comments in the box below.

Problems with conducting cross-cultural studies: (Make one comment on each point)

Language and interpretation problems:

Imposed etic:

Natural experiment/anecdotal data:

▶ Lesson notes p.23

Sorting statements

Cut out each statement and sort them into two groups: statements supporting nature's influence on the development of perceptual ability and statements supporting nurture's influence on the development of perceptual ability.

Sensory stimulation alone is not sufficient for perception or perceptual development.

Studies have shown infants to have highly developed perceptual abilities.

We use cognitive schemas (built from experiences) to enrich the sensory data around us.

Cross-cultural studies suggest culture has an impact on abilities such as depth perception and the likelihood of experiencing optical illusions like the Müller-Lyer and trapezoid window illusions.

There seems to be a critical period for squint surgery, if delayed till after the age of four, permanent damage can be seen in the bioculary driven cells of the visual cortex (Banks *et al.*, 1975).

Perception is an innate process.

Slater *et al.* (1990) observed newborns gazed longer at a cube they were unfamiliar with, suggesting they recognised it as a new object.

Top-down theories like Gregory's argue environmental experience is vital in perceptual development.

Gibson's bottom-up theory proposes nothing more is needed than sensory data.

Hubel and Wiesel (1970) used microelectrodes to study different areas of a cat's visual cortex. Simple, complex and hyper complex cells were found, which suggests a biological basis for pattern recognition.

Blakemore and Cooper (1970) found kittens raised in a world restricted to vertical stripes tripped over ropes stretched in front of them. In contrast kittens from horizontally restricted environments were virtually blind to vertical lines once released into real world at five months.

Before two months of age infants shown one playing card placed in front of another view the scene as one object. Only after two months do they begin to perceive it as two separate objects.

Now use the statements to produce your own outline of each position in 150 words.

▶ Lesson notes p.23

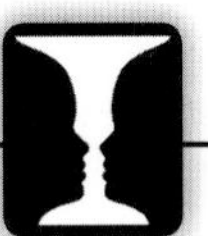

Researching face recognition 1

Follow the instructions to gather data into face recognition abilities in A-level students.

Group 1.

1. Approach a student, preferably not studying Psychology, in a quiet area of your building. Read them the standardised instructions.
2. If they agree to take part, show them the five faces labelled 'Set 1' and allow them to view these images and read the information below each face for 1 minute. Ensure timing is exact by using a stop watch.
3. Remove 'Set 1' and ask the participant to describe their last lesson. This is a distraction task to prevent rehearsal of the faces they have just seen. Use the sheet entitled 'distraction task' to ensure standardisation across each participant.
4. Provide the participant with the form entitled 'Recall sheet' and allow 1 minute for the participant to write the name of each face they have previously seen. Be sure to record that the participant was assigned to Group 1.

Group 2.

1. Approach a student, preferably not studying Psychology, in a quiet area of your building. Read them the standardised instructions.
2. If they agree to take part, show them the five faces labelled 'Set 2' and allow them to view these images and read the name below each face for 1 minute. Ensure timing is exact by using a stop watch.
3. Remove 'Set 2' and ask the participant to describe their last lesson. This is a distraction task to prevent rehearsal of the faces they have just seen. Use the sheet entitled 'distraction task' to ensure standardisation across each participant.
4. Provide the participant with the form entitled 'Recall sheet' and allow 1 minute for the participant to write the name of each face they have previously seen. Be sure to record that the participant was assigned to Group 2.

Decisions to be made:

a) How many participants will be included in each group?
b) Will you have an equal mix of genders within each group? Will you only study one gender?

Questions to answer and tasks to undertake:

a) What experimental design was used?
b) Give one strength and one weakness of using this experimental design to study this area of perception.
c) How could you overcome the weaknesses of this design?
d) Could an alternative research experimental design be used? If so, which one and what are the advantages of using this design?
e) Count the amount of faces each participant correctly named and display the data in a suitable graph. Each participant should receive a score out of 10 (one mark for first name, one for surname).
f) Calculate the mean recall of names for each group.
g) Suggest a suitable statistics test to analyse the data you have gathered.
h) Explain your findings in relation to Bruce and Young's (1986) theory. Try to use FRU, PIN and NRU in your response.
i) Suggest one way the method could be improved, other than changing the research design.

▶ Lesson notes p.24

Researching face recognition 2

Standardised instructions

Thank you for agreeing to take part in this study into perception. You will be shown a set of five faces and given one minute to view these images. After this time the sheet will be removed and you will be asked a series of questions. You will then be given a short memory test. Your results will be kept confidential as your name will not be recorded. You are free to leave the study at any time and can withdraw any data you provide at any point. Do you have any questions? Are you still happy to take part?

Set 1

Julie Marshall
52 years old
Sales rep
Married last year
Friendly

Rav Singh
36 years old
Bank manager
Plays guitar
Ambitious

Paul Davis
40 years old
Self-employed
Vegetarian
Worrier

Tabatha Jones
27 years old
Children's author
Speaks 3 languages
Humorous

Leslie Patrick
61 years old
Runs own spa
Owns a horse
Perfectionist

Set 2

Julie Marshall

Rav Singh

Paul Davis

Tabatha Jones

Leslie Patrick

Distraction task: Ask participants to give verbal responses, you do not need to record this data.

1. Which A-level subject was your last lesson?
2. What topic were you studying?
3. How many male students were in the class?
4. What did you enjoy about the lesson?
5. Describe the appearance of one person you sat next to in the classroom.
6. Explain one activity you undertook in the lesson.
7. Give two key terms from the lesson.

Recall sheet: Group ___________

Please write the name of each person shown (first and last name).
Leave blank any name you cannot recall.

▶ Lesson notes p.24

Agnosia analysis

Explain the difference between apperceptive and associative agnosia.

Complete the sentence:
Sufferers of prosopagnosia cannot:

Two interesting facts about agnosia are:
1.

2.

Advantages of the case study method in this particular study.
Use these points to help you:

Longitudinal, allows patterns of development to be seen over time.

Provides a wealth of data, both qualitative and quantitative.

Disadvantages of the case study method in this particular study.
Use these points to help you:

Usually only one person so generalisation is not possible.

Evidence from studies is often contradictory.

Agnosia case file

Patient name:

Researcher name:

Type of agnosia:

Description of difficulties:

Perceptual ability displayed:

Ethical issues in case studies:

▶ Lesson notes p.24

Statement sorting

1 Research suggests that a process of 'attitude alignment' often occurs with partners modifying their attitudes so they become congruent. One or both partners may do this.

2 We also like people who are associated with pleasant events through classical conditioning.

3 Mutual attraction occurs when each partner meets the other person's needs.

4 People first sort potential partners for *dissimilarity* – avoiding people too different from them.

5 According to the principles of operant conditioning, we are likely to repeat any behaviour that leads to a desirable outcome and avoid behaviours that lead to an undesirable outcome.

6 Research has shown people are generally more attracted to people who share comparable or complementary personality traits.

7 The theory suggests that we enter into relationships because the presence of some individuals is associated with direct reinforcement (positive feelings).

8 If we meet someone when we are feeling happy (positive mood), we are much more likely to like them.

9 We are motivated to seek rewarding stimuli and avoid punishing stimuli.

10 A previously neutral stimulus (stranger who we had no feelings about) becomes valued because they are associated with the pleasant event.

11 Things we find rewarding tend to reflect our unmet needs (e.g. need for company, financial security, etc.).

12 There are two distinct stages in the formation of relationships.

13 This model emphasises the importance of attitudes and personality.

14 Then from those remaining they are most likely to choose someone who is similar to them.

15 Rewarding stimuli produce positive feelings in us (i.e. they make us happy), and punishing stimuli produce negative feelings (i.e. they make us unhappy).

▶ Lesson notes p.25

More to it than Cupid...!

Read the case studies of relationships below and explain the formation of those relationships using one of the theories: Reward/Need Satisfaction Theory (Byrne and Clore, 1970), or Similarity (Byrne, Clore and Smeaton, 1986).

You may wish to incorporate some of the key words provided into your explanation.

Sarah and Asif formed a relationship after meeting each other at work. They were instantly attracted to one another. Sarah was very career minded and was earning a lot of money. However, as a result of letting her work take over, she became quite lonely. Asif, on the other hand, lacked direction in his career and as a result was earning little money and so still living with his parents, who annoyed him.

Key words: Rewarding stimuli, unmet needs, mutual attraction, operant conditioning, reinforcement.

Michael and Alana met at University. They both really enjoyed going to the Student's Union event 'Boogie Nights' and often saw and talked to each other at this event. Eventually they began to form a relationship.

Key words: Classical conditioning, association, pleasant event, neutral stimulus, positive value.

Amie always had a large group of friends and was able to get on with a diverse range of people. However, a few of the boys in her social group were too loud and talkative for her liking. One of those boys, Josh, did share her belief in left-wing politics. Amie and Josh formed a romantic relationship. At first, Josh disagreed with her view on abortion, but changed his mind a few months into the relationship.

Key words: Two stages, dissimilarity, similarity, personality and attitudes, attitude alignment.

Choose a celebrity couple or a couple from a soap who are just starting a relationship.

Explain the formation of that relationship using the theory you think accounts for it best.

▶ Lesson notes p.25

Maintenance strategies questionnaire

Part 1: Data collection
Assure all participants of their anonymity.

Question 1 – Maintenance strategies

We are trying to determine what partners do when they are trying to maintain their relationship in a healthy state.

What do you do now, or have you done in the past, when you are trying to keep your relationship from going downhill? Ask participants to list a maximum of 10 maintenance strategies that they might use.

Question 2 – Repair strategies

We are trying to determine what partners do when they are trying to repair their relationship. This usually happens when one or both partners think that their relationship is not as good as it used to be, that their relationship has gone downhill, and he and/or she wants to restore the relationship to its previous healthy state.

What do you do, or have you done in the past, when you are trying to bring your relationship back to what it was? Ask participants to list a maximum of 10 repair strategies that they might use.

Part 2: Analysing data
For each strategy listed by your participants, decide which category it belongs to and put a tick in that box. Some boxes are likely to have more than one tick.

Categories for analysis	Maintenance	Repair
1. Change external environment		
2. Increase communication with partner (e.g. talk, have symbolic contact, share feelings)		
3. Meta communication (talk about the problem)		
4. Avoid talking about problem, hoping it will pass		
5. Antisocial behaviour (coercive attempts to change partner, e.g. insolence, sullenness, hyper-critical behaviour, refusal to compromise, acting cold, breaking contact)		
6. Prosocial behaviour (friendliness and refraining from criticism when partner is being difficult, being warm, talking about future plans such as engagement, marriage, children, buying a house)		
7. Ritualistic behaviour (celebrating anniversaries, birthdays, giving gifts)		
8. Trying new things		
9. Spending more time together		
10. Spending more time in independent activities		
11. Seeking outside assistance (friends, relationship guidance)		
12. Other		

Part 3: What can you conclude from your study?

▶ Lesson notes p.26

Ethics in breakdown of relationships research

Please examine the research outlines below and then complete the task at the bottom of the page.

A major reason why relationships break down is that one or both partners have an extra-marital affair. Boekhout *et al.* (1999) showed how such affairs might be a direct reaction to the perceived lack of skills and/or stimulation in the current relationship. They asked undergraduates to rate various sexual and emotional reasons for men and women to be unfaithful in a committed relationship. Participants judged that sexual reasons for infidelity (e.g. sexual excitement, boredom) would be more likely to be used by men, whereas emotional reasons for infidelity (e.g. lack of attention, lack of commitment) would be more likely to be used by women.

The importance of social skills deficits in relationship breakdown has been demonstrated in studies that have attempted to *enhance* relationship skills in distressed couples. The Couples Enhancement Training (CCET) programme aims to sensitise couples to issues of respect within their relationship and improve communication and problem-solving skills. Cina *et al.* (2003) compared 50 couples (average length of relationship 12 years) who received CCET training with a control group who did not. Results showed that the CCET group reported much higher marital quality after training.

Tashiro and Frazier (2003) surveyed undergraduates who had recently broken up with a romantic partner. They typically reported that they had not only experienced emotional distress, but also personal growth. These students reported that breaking up with their partner had given them new insights into themselves and a clearer idea about future partners.

Carrying out research into the breakdown of relationships raises particular ethical issues. For example, a woman in an abusive relationship may fear recrimination from her abuser should he discover her participation in the research – as such her privacy and confidentiality should be safeguarded.

Ultimately, the researcher faces a choice of pursuing valuable information or terminating their involvement with a participant to prevent further harm.

Tasks

- *Produce five ethical guidelines for psychologists who wish to undertake the type of research outlined above. You could research the BPS ethical guidelines to help you, but your guidelines must be written specifically with breakdown in relationships research in mind. Each guideline must:*
  - *include advice about situations that are likely to arise*
  - *suggest methods to deal with the situation in order to avoid harm.*
- *Imagine you are a psychologist who receives these new guidelines. Write a letter of complaint that argues that these new guidelines may lower the validity of your research into this area.*

▶ Lesson notes p.27

Report: Relationship breakdown

REPORT

Think of an example of a relationship breakdown that interests you. This could be from something in the news, from a soap, or one of your favourite films.

Using your psychology textbook to help you, write a report on the factors and process of that relationship breakdown.

Your report must include the following:

- Factors that lead to the breakdown (e.g. lack of skills, stimulation, maintenance difficulties).
- Include examples to illustrate your points above (e.g. quotations from interviews, film dialogue, etc.).
- Psychological evidence that this can lead to relationship breakdown (use studies from a textbook).
- A drawn diagram illustrating the model of the breakdown using Rollie and Duck's (2006) model (see right). Make it specific to your case study.
- Potential intervention techniques that could be (or should have been) used and their rationale.

BREAKDOWN
Dissatisfaction with relationship
Threshold: I can't stand this any more

INTRAPSYCHIC PROCESSES
Social withdrawal; 'rumination' resentment
Brooding on partner's 'faults' and relational 'costs'
Re-evaluation of alternatives to relationship
Threshold: I'd be justified in withdrawing

DYADIC PROCESSES
Uncertainty, anxiety, hostility, complaints
Discussion of discontents
Talk about 'our relationship'; equity, roles
Reassessment of goals, possibilities, commitments
Threshold: I mean it

SOCIAL PROCESSES
Going public; support-seeking from third parties
Denigration of partner, alliance building
Social commitment, outside forces create cohesion
Threshold: It's now inevitable

GRAVE-DRESSING PROCESSES
Tidying up memories; making relational histories
Stories prepared for different audiences
Saving face
Threshold: Time to get a new life

RESURRECTION PROCESSES
Recreating sense of own social value
Defining what to get out of future relationships
Preparation for a different sort of relational future
Reframing of past relational life:
What I learned and how things will be different

A summary of Rollie and Duck's model of relationship breakdown.

▶ Lesson notes p.27

Personal ads: Female seeks male

HAPPY go lucky lady, down to earth, 5'4" with medium build, blue eyes & brown hair, loves music & countryside. WLTM honest male for companionship.

HONEST female, 62, WLTM honest & trustworthy male of similar age for friendship.

INTELLIGENT slim blonde, 27 5'9" with GSOH. Seeks tall & honest male of similar age for fun & romance.

YOUNG-AT-HEART fun, outgoing & very caring female seeks similar male, ages 42 to 54, to enjoy quality time with, maybe leading to more.

FUN-LOVING easy-going 23 yr old female, GSOH, separated with a young child WLTM fun, friendly easy-going male for friendship, possibly more.

DIVORCED female, 53, 5'3", likes music & walks. Looking for honest male, taller than her, looks unimportant, for trusting relationship.

ATTRACTIVE BRUNETTE, late 30s, WLTM a dish 35–45, to enjoy the arts, good conversation & even a dance.

WARM ATTRACTIVE FIT F v. young 39, intelligent, sensitive & interesting, into yoga, salsa & interesting conversation seeks sorted, intelligent, caring bloke 36–43, to enjoy life with.

SOCIABLE F, 40 5'11", slim, brown hair, blue eyes, grounded, happy, enjoys cinema, walking, socialising, looking for special M to share these things with.

ATTRACTIVE PROFESSIONAL F, mid 40s, blonde hair, brown eyes seeks attractive M, 40–55, interested in travel, hill-walking, good wine & conversation for friendship, maybe more.

SLIM ATTRACTIVE ASIAN F, grad, early 30s, GSOH, seeks handsome, intelligent Pakistani/Muslim M, 30–40 for friendship.

NO DUMB BLONDE. Sexy, slim, sparky attractive F, 41, into the arts, café culture, adventure seeks playmate/soulmate. Race not an issue.

ATTRACTIVE INTELLIGENT CREATIVE 29, E. Asian background, passionate about arts and travel, would like to meet M with similar interests and GSOH.

GIRL, 39 seeks someone refreshing who is not materialistic or narcissistic and is not interested in the price of tomatoes.

SEXY young 40 yr old brunette, 5'4", GSOH, easygoing, likes holidays, would like to meet tallish gent with GSOH, 33–40, for friendship & possibly more.

HONEST girl, 5'4", likes gardening, outdoors, has dog, would like to meet honest, down-to-earth male for good times & friendship.

LIVING DOLL very attractive, professional lady, slim, 42, long dark hair, seeks tall, handsome bachelor boy/soulmate.

SHY 32 year old female, 5'4" blonde hair and blue/green eyes, likes cinema, music and meals out.

BUBBLY 5'4" blonde likes socialising, cinema and WLTM male who likes the same, to share good times.

EASY GOING F, 53, 5'3" blue eyes, young outlook on life, many interests including gardening, reading, music, animals. WLTM genuine M for friendship, possibly relationship.

GENUINELY GORGEOUS, 30S, confident, petite, stylish, career-oriented F, usual interests, arts and travel etc. seeks stylish, handsome, successful M, 35–50, who loves the pleasures of life, for long-term relationship.

CAREFREE TALL BRUNETTE 26, into music, bars, keeping fit. WLTM superhero, 27–35, to sweep me off my feet.

INTELLIGENT, PASSIONATE F WLTM M 30–45 for passionate and hopefully long-term relationship.

SLIM RELAXED, OUT-GOING male, 28, 5'10" with blond hair and blue eyes, into clubbing. Seeks female to have fun with.

61 YEARS YOUNG, fairly fit 5'4" with medium build, still working full time, loves walking, outdoors, outgoing person with GSOH, not shy but sometimes reserved. WLTM soul-mate to share all of life's ups and downs.

STUNNING BLACK F, 5'9", slim build WLTM ambitious, physically fit, handsome, solvent white M.

BLUE eyes 5'6" blonde hair, likes nights in and out, driving, reading, music & crosswords, WLTM caring, understanding male for fun and possible relationship.

LIFE-LOVING attractive female, 22, medium build, shoulder length blonde hair, enjoys watching sports, golf & dancing, seeks male to enjoy these things and more.

V. BEAUTIFUL sweet, 26, seeks sweet affluent M to adore and be adored by and settle down. Aged 25–50.

THOUGHTFUL F, 49, fabulous, friendly, funny but flawed like everyone else, would like to meet Mr. Right, but not always Mr. Right!!

FUN ATTRACTIVE slim black F, 35, seeks tall, attractive, professional M, 35–44 for friendship and relationship.

BEAUTIFUL F, 30, SLIM Mediterranean-looking enjoys arts, music, travel seeks intelligent, articulate, kind, attractive M, 32–43 for friendship and possible relationship.

BLONDE green-eyed, slim 50 yr old female, GSOH, would like to meet honest, kind male 45–55 for nights out, fun, friendship & possible romance.

PLEASURE SEEKER, 44, blonde, tall, gorgeous and smart, seeks playmate for larks and mischief-making.

GENUINE F, late 40s, likes walking, dancing, cooking, cinema, music. Would like to meet male for friendship, possible relationship.

SOCIABLE F, 28, outgoing, honest, attractive, petite, graduate, enjoys walks, camping, music, nights in/out, seeks fun M, 27–37, GSOH, romantic, genuine for friendship and romance.

FUNKY F, 34 dark hair, green eyes, loves football, dancing, art, seeks similar M 30–40.

SPARKLY ITALIAN BRUNETTE seeks well-educated companion, 35–45, with passion for classical music.

HONEST CARING young-atheart female, 58, enjoys countryside, occasional nights out and animals, would like to meet honest & caring gentleman for friendship & possible relationship.

PROFESSIONAL F, 29, slim, attractive, passionate about the arts and travel, would like to meet M with similar interests.

BIG SMILE AND BARN, F, slim, blue eyes, 50ish, likes plants, words, theatre, walks, travel and seeks intelligent, lively M for balance.

PETITE UNNATURAL BLONDE F, 28, would like to meet dark, handsome M who loves computer games & Star Wars.

SEXY CURVY F seeks M for the usual.

HE WHO DARES WINS this stylish, spirited, intelligent, personable, fit, funny 52 year with whom to laugh at life.

STRONG & SOULFUL 46, beautiful bookworm, into words & music, seeks passionate, grounded, creative mate to share gigs, theatre, humour, stillness & spaces in between.

ALMOST V. HAPPY F, 54, 5'7", attractive & elegant, likes music, singing, books and art, seeks M 50s with warmth and wit.

STUDENT, DARK BROWN HAIR, 30, loves the arts, dancing, laughing and life. Seeks M lover/friend to grow old with.

F 42, as sexy as mango, as comfy as a sofa, as deep as shagpile! Come soar with the swifts oh wise, witty, kind M.

UNUSUAL SORTED SKITTISH SLIM, 5'7" F likes to think she's useful & youthful seeks M in white coat to whisk her off her feet.

FRUIT BAT, versatile, attractive, caring, voluptuous, arcane, F, 31, enjoys gardening, music, art, beachcombing, seeks kind, interesting, like-minded soulmate.

POLITE ATTRACTIVE SLIM PROFESSIONAL F who has lost her way, seeks guiding light, preferably attractive M, 40–60 who is over 5'7" and London based.

▶ Lesson notes p.28

Personal ads: Male seeks female

PART TIME POET, 30, seeks fell-wandering muse to share peaks, valleys, melodies, bass lines, the best of rhymes and puns.

HAPPY OUTGOING male, 52, 5'9", bright blue eyes and cheeky smile, loves nature, music and drama. Seeks female to share life's pleasures.

HONEST AND RELIABLE male, 31, good-looking, very sincere and kind, seeking lady of a similar age for full time relationship.

FIT YOUNG 37 year old single parent with GSOH, up for anything, seeks a female of similar nature, looks not important, for relationship.

RELAXED, OCCASIONALLY WITTY M, 31, seeks intelligent, slim F for drinks and unwise plans.

GENUINE ATTRACTIVE GUY, 41, seeks 30s/40s F into books, films, blues, writing, good conversation, wine, laughter and passion.

BOOGIE NIGHTS, lazy afternoons. Gorgeous M, creative, sexy, confident though occasionally shy WLTM stunning, cheeky, Asian-Mediterranean F, 24–32, for allsorts.

M, 44 SLIM, 5'11", enjoys arts, keeping fit, cinema, music seeks engaging openminded, energetic, fun-loving F for mischievous endeavours.

BUSINESSMAN 45, 5'6", well built, enjoys nights in/out, C&W, music, going to the gym, swimming, WLTM lady 45–55 to share interests.

QUEST FOR CURVES, M, 33, tall, slim artist with specs appeal seeks curvy F for films and fun.

YOUNG 50 year old male, 5'6", black hair, blue eyes, easy-going, smart, varied interests. WLTM similar non-smoker F, attractive, to share happy times.

BELLEVILLE RENDEZ-VOUS, intelligent, creative M, 29, into mountains, Italy and adventure WLTM 21st century F with added sparkle, smart, sensitive and vibrant to share thoughts/dreams with.

GOOD NATURED MALE, 58, 6', well built, brown hair & eyes, caring, honest, easygoing. WLTM slim lady 48–60 to enjoy the outdoors, animals and more.

CUDDLY AFFECTIONATE and loving, arts professional, 50, likes travel, arts, folk, rock, cinema, seeks similar F, no kids, any age, for love/marriage.

WARM TENDER 38 year old M with caring personality, nonsmoker, interested in sports and loves cosy nights in. WLTM similar lady for possible romance.

GOOD-LOOKING M, 25, short dark hair, brown eyes, enjoys going to pubs and clubs, cinema, seeking someone similar to share interests.

TIGER, fit lean male, likes pounding about outdoors, or staying in. WLTM female 26–34, to hold my paw.

MANAGING DIRECTOR, 38, 5'11" attractive, athletic, sincere, and stylish seeks beautiful, classy and sincere F, 20–40, for serious relationship.

KIND-HEARTED ROMANTIC, funny M, young 43, into Green issues and Glastonbury, seeks F to share coffee and carrot cake.

SHARP, GOOD-LOOKER, 38, with wit and vitality, seeks slim, sensual, passionate F, 25–36, with emotional depth, sexy mind and zest for life.

COMPANION AND LOVER with spark wanted to share Brief Encounter in warm climate. I'm 55, good-looking and a bit worn around the edges from love and life.

ROMANTIC professional man, 49, GSOH, loves countryside, travel and good times, looking for lady for friendship, possible romance.

LOVES LABOURS FOUND. Hopelessly romantic dreamer, attractive (apparently), 30s, 6'2" seeks passionate, adventurous, visionary F, 25–35, to embark on that wonderful adventure called life.

WARM AND WITTY, intelligent M, 37, non-smoker, seeks slim F, 20s/30s, must be physically fit, enjoy the outdoors, food and drink, socialising and music, for friendship and romance.

FARMER 5'7", late 40s, blue eyes, keen on music, country walks, days out. Seeks female with similar interests.

BLUES AT TEN. Slim, good-looking blues musician seeks slim, curvy, cute kitten who knows how to dress to please.

HIDEOUS AND STINKY penniless dwarf seeks rich blind F, preferably with no sense of smell.

MOVING ON, sociable M, employed in arts, seeks slim, sociable F, mid-late 30s with zest for life.

SPIRITUAL CREATIVE SOUL, 35, very attractive, welleducated, sensual, loving, passionate, ready to meet slim, attractive F 25–40.

ATTRACTIVE GRADUATE, 40, no ties, 6ft+, enjoys cinema, sport, travel, walking, theatre, looking for F with similar interests. Take a chance, give me a call.

DARK-HAIRED male, 6'2", GSOH, clean shaven, WLTM F for friendship possible relationship.

HOT male, 35, loves nights in and out, not so keen on clubbing, loves romance and would love to give a woman what she wants.

QUITE TANNED 29 year old, separated, like sports, going out, clubbing, etc.

CHEERFUL male 5'9", dark hair, likes pubs, walks, football. WLTM female for friendship possible relationship.

SEEKING INDEPENDENT F. Tall, slim, dependable, happy, cultured M, 60+ seeks independent, sexy F for happy relationship, fun, laughter mutual support, love, sensuality, without ties.

ATHLETIC 29 YEAR OLD, well over 6', does a variety of sports, likes eating out with friends, playing sport, cinema, also likes staying in.

WARM INTELLIGENT left-wing male, young 50s, fit, GSOH, loves travel, jazz, fine wine, good food, walks, seeks slim, attractive, left/lib F for romance and travel.

LOST LAD, 39, seeks guardian angel. Must have GSOH and enjoy life.

ATTRACTIVE AND PROFESSIONAL, good looking, tall, slim, 47, enjoys salsa, film, travel, countryside, seaside seeks F, nationality not an issue, for relationship.

NAUGHTY BUT GOOD MAN, 37, attractive, athletic, cultured, mischievious, spontaneous, very affectionate, seeks petite, sexy woman.

BADLY DRAWN BOY, 34, seeks work of art, 26–36, loves sport, travel, film, walks and maybe you.

OLDER WOMAN WANTED. Attractive 26, slim, graduate, professional seeks attractive, petite, older F, 35+ for fun times.

SOMETIMES GOODLOOKING, often intelligent, always humourous, tall, 45, described as thwarted romantic, enjoys, cinema, music, travel, especially Italy.

ATTRACTIVE GENUINE M, kind-hearted 50, romantic, witty, still young, likes travel and music, seeks attractive and affectionate partner.

FUN LOVING M, 5'10, Dutch/half English with Irish accent into numerology, psychology, Buddhism, outdoor activities, seeking F, 30–45, for once-upon-a-time relationship.

PROFESSIONAL MALE non-smoker, reasonable sense of humour, into films, walks along the coast, WLTM F, 35–45, for friendship and possible relationship.

CREATIVE AND PROFESSIONAL attractive male seeks interesting female, 35–45, to enjoy arts and pleasures, interests and diversions, romance and more.

TALL DARK ATTRACTIVE M, passionate about music and film, seeks reasonably attractive F with passion for outdoors for long term relationship.

FUNNY THOUGHTFUL FRIVOLOUS M, 38, 5'11", medium/large build, brown hair, blue eyes, into music, football, reading, films WLTM liberal-minded F, 34–41, GSOH for long-term relationship.

SENSUAL AND PASSIONATE but shy teacher, 47, seeks soulmate, any age, anywhere, likes travel, cinema, theatre, books, etc. for long term relationship.

▶ Lesson notes p.28

Scoring the ads

There are a number of hypotheses that can be tested:

Wealth/status

- Females will ask for financial resources and economic security more than males.
- Males will offer financial resources more than females.

Physical attractiveness

- Males will ask for traits indicating physical attractiveness more than females.
- Females will offer traits indicating physical attractiveness more than males.

Age

- Females will ask for males who are older than they are (females will prefer to mate with older males).
- Males will ask for females who are younger than they are (males will prefer to mate with younger females).

Family commitment

- Females will ask for family commitment more than males.
- Males will offer family commitment more than females.

For each ad you should record some or all of the following variables:

1. Advertiser's sex
2. Advertiser's age
3. Does advertiser have children? (Assume 'no' if no mention of children is made)
4. Number of relevant terms relating to physical attractiveness offered
5. Number of relevant terms relating to family commitment offered
6. Number of relevant terms relating to wealth/status offered
7. Lower age in the range requested for prospective mate
8. Upper age in the range requested for prospective mate
9. Sex of person sought
10. Number of relevant terms relating to family commitment asked for
11. Number of relevant terms relating to physical attractiveness asked for
12. Number of relevant terms relating to wealth/status asked for

Scoring guide (adapted from Waynforth and Dunbar, 1995)

A Relevant terms for physical attractiveness

Any terms that indicate that the advertiser claims to be good-looking or seeks a good-looking partner

- For both sexes: athletic, beautiful, cute, dazzling, exotic, fit, hot, good-looking, good looks, gorgeous, healthy, medium-build, nice body, nice-looking, sexy, stunning, trim, well-built, well-proportioned, young-looking
- For males: handsome, hunk, masculine, muscular, rugged, tall
- For females: buxom, curvy, feminine, full-figured, petite, pretty, shapely, slender, slim, slim-build
- Also: terms not included here but that are clearly advertisements of physical attractiveness (real example: 40-year-old woman with 'the legs of a 20 year old')

B Relevant terms for wealth and status

Any terms indicating home-ownership, professional status, a specific job, being well-off, a business owner or college-educated as well as any terms indicating above-average lifestyle

- For both sexes: accomplished, affluent, business owner, career, college graduate, comfortable, educated, employed, enjoys good/better things in life, established, financially independent, financially secure, good income, good job, good provider, hard-working, industrious, means, own house, professional (or 'P', see below), prosperous, rich, secure, solvent, successful, sugar daddy, wealthy, well-established, well-to-do
- Also count 'P' as 'Professional' (e.g., as in SWPF 'Single white professional female')

C Relevant terms for family commitment

Any terms indicating a willingness to participate in family affairs

- For both sexes: caring, dependable, family-minded, family-oriented, family time, generous, giving, good cook/housekeeper, kind, likes/wants children, likes to cook, responsible, spending time with family, giving

Use your discretion for terms that are not described here, but do not count descriptive terms that you cannot categorise. For example, preferences for hair or eye colour may vary in ways that are not predictable under our hypothesis, so should not be counted under terms for 'physical attractiveness' (even if they coincide with your own preference!)

▶ Lesson notes p.28

What do mums and dads do? Parental Investment

Let's take a fairly traditional or stereotypical view of the family for this exercise. This might not be what your family is like, but let's stick to something where Dad goes to work and Mum makes the tea, etc.

Evolutionary psychology argues that there's an imbalance or asymmetry between what Mum and Dad put into or 'invest' in their kids. Before we try and explain why this is, we need to look at what sort of imbalance there is between the relative contributions of the two.

See if you can fill in your ideas in the following table.

	DAD'S CONTRIBUTION	MUM'S CONTRIBUTION
Hours of sleep lost in first three years of child's life		
Money contributed to upkeep of child in first three years of life		
Amount of bodily material contributed to conception, to 'making a baby'		
Bodily resources devoted to foetus during pregnancy		
Bodily resources devoted to child during breastfeeding		
Risks taken during childbirth		
Time devoted to childcare during first year of life		

Just out of interest, let's also have a quick look at the following difference, as it might be of interest later on.

	MUM	DAD
How many children *could* each have in a lifetime ?		

▶ Lesson notes p.29

Trivers' predictions

Psychology tries to conduct itself scientifically. This means that its theories of human behaviour must be tested.

In order to do this, hypotheses (predictions) are generated based on those theories and then experiments, observations, interviews, etc., are used to test those predictions.

If the theory is right, those predictions come true! Trivers' (1974) evolutionary theory of parent-offspring conflict makes a series of predictions (see below).

(FYI – that is NOT Trivers on the left!)

Parents and children will be in conflict about the time at which the child should be weaned. Parents want sooner, child later.

Parents will encourage children to value their siblings more than children are naturally inclined to value them.

Parents will tend to punish conflict between siblings and reward co-operation.

Tasks

- Choose one of Trivers' predictions and start an evaluation paragraph by finishing this sentence:

  'One prediction made by the theory is that…'

- Following this sentence, explain why the theory would make this prediction. Use your textbook to help you:

  'This is because…'

- Find a study from your textbook that supports or undermines the prediction made by the theory:

  'This prediction is supported/undermined by…'

- Extension: Make an evaluation of the research method used and comment on how it affects the evaluation, e.g. correlations do not show cause/effect relationships.

▶ Lesson notes p.29

What's going on . . .?

Imagine that a researcher conducts a longitudinal attachment study on 30 infants starting at 12 months of age. Initially, they use the Strange Situation observation technique to classify whether those infants have secure or insecure attachments with their parents/guardians.

They then test the same individuals' romantic adult attachment at 20 years of age using structured interviews.

At both stages the researcher converted the attachment behaviours indicated into an attachment score, with a high score indicating more secure attachment behaviours shown.

The researcher correlated infant attachment scores with their adult attachment scores in order to discover whether there had been **attachment stability** – i.e. whether the attachment styles had remained the same over the course of their life.

Correlation coefficient was calculated at +.52. The scattergraph below shows the results.

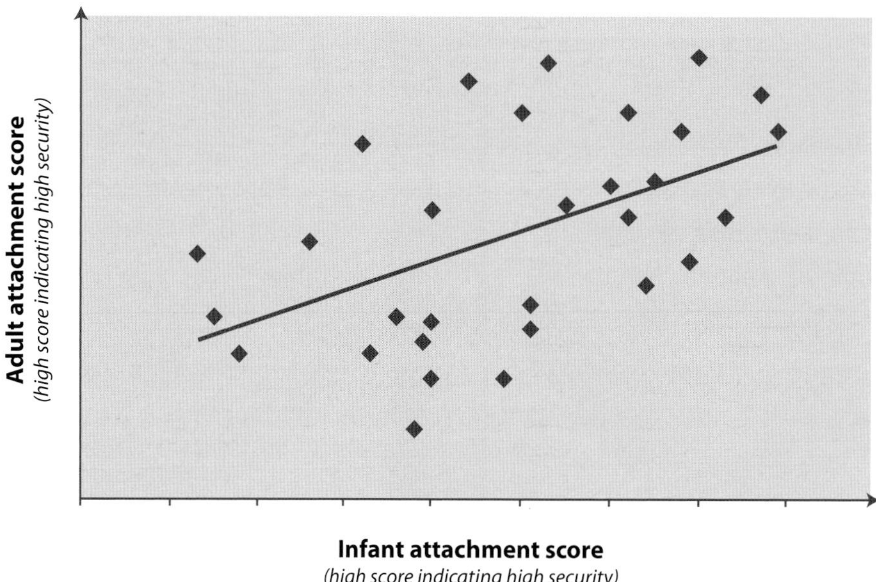

Tasks

- Cast your mind back to AS level and brainstorm what you can remember about the terms **secure attachment, insecure attachment,** and **internal working model** (Bowlby).
- Describe the findings of the correlation study described and illustrated above.
- What would you conclude about the influence of childhood experiences on adult relationships from this study?
- What potential limitations are there to this study, for instance the methodology used?

▶ Lesson notes p.30

LOVE Quiz!

A short version of the love quiz

Question 1: Which of the following best describes your parents' relationship with each other?

(a) My parents have a caring relationship and are affectionate with each other.
(b) My parents appear to have a good enough relationship with each other but are not especially affectionate.
(c) My parents have a reasonable relationship and are sometimes affectionate towards each other.

Question 2: Which of the following best describes your relationship with your mother?

(a) My mother treats me with respect and is accepting and not demanding. She is confident about herself.
(b) My mother is humourous, likable and respected by others. She treats me with respect.
(c) My mother treats me with respect but is sometimes cold and rejecting.

Question 3: Which of the following best describes your relationship with your father?

(a) My father is sometimes affectionate but can be unfair.
(b) My father is caring, affectionate and humourous.
(c) My father is reasonably caring.

Question 4: Select the statement that best describes your experiences of intimacy.

(a) I find that others are reluctant to get as close as I would like.
(b) I find it relatively easy to get close to others and am comfortable depending on them and having them depend on me.
(c) I am somewhat uncomfortable being close to others; I find it difficult to trust them completely, difficult to allow myself to depend on them.

Question 5: Select the statement that best describes your experiences of intimacy.

(a) I don't often worry about being abandoned or about someone getting too close to me.
(b) I often worry that my partner doesn't really love me or won't want to stay with me.
(c) I am nervous when anyone gets too close, and often romantic partners want me to be more intimate than I feel comfortable being.

Question 6: Select the statement that best describes your experiences of intimacy.

(a) I enjoy relationships but am generally quite self-sufficient.
(b) I have been lucky in love and most of my relationships are rewarding. I still like the people I was involved with.
(c) At times I wish I could just melt into someone so we could get beyond our separateness.

Question 7: Select the statement that best describes your attitudes towards love.

(a) The kind of head-over-heels love that is depicted in novels and in the movies does not exist in real life.
(b) It is easy to fall in love and I frequently find myself beginning to fall in love, though I am not sure that it really is love.
(c) Love is a positive and real experience.

Question 8: Select the statement that best describes your attitudes towards love.

(a) It is rare to find a person one can really fall in love with.
(b) In some relationships romantic love never fades.
(c) Most of us could love many people equally well, there is no 'one true love'.

Question 9: Select the statement that best describes your attitudes towards love.

(a) I think that romantic feelings do wax and wane.
(b) Romantic feelings wax and wane but at times they reach the intensity experienced at the start of a relationship.
(c) Intense romantic love is common at the start of a relationship but rarely lasts.

▶ Lesson notes p.31

Spot the cultural difference!

Use your textbook to draw/illustrate **two** differences in relationships between individualist and collectivist cultures (e.g. use stickmen/speech bubbles, etc.).

Then provide an explanation of this difference and find/describe the psychological evidence from your textbook below.

Individualist	**Collectivist**

Explanation:

Evidence:

Individualist	**Collectivist**

Explanation:

Evidence:

▶ Lesson notes p.33

SOCIAL LEARNING THEORY BINGO

Specifics of aggressive behaviour	Direct reinforcement	Bobo doll
Bandura *et al.* (1961): Independent variable	Demand characteristics	Bandura and Walters (1963): Independent variable
Bandura *et al.* (1961)	Phillips (1983)	Context-dependent learning

Specifics of aggressive behaviour	Mental representation	Imitation of behaviour
Bandura *et al.* (1961): Independent variable	Demand characteristics	Ecological validity
Bandura and Walters (1963): Dependent variable	Bandura and Walters (1963)	Nurture

Specifics of aggressive behaviour	Vicarious reinforcement	Direct reinforcement
Imitation of behaviour	Bandura *et al.* (1961): Dependent variable	Demand characteristics
Bandura and Walters (1963): Independent variable	Bandura and Walters (1963): Dependent variable	Bandura and Walters (1963)

▶ Lesson notes p.34

SOCIAL LEARNING THEORY BINGO

Vicarious reinforcement	Mental representation	Direct reinforcement
Imitation of behaviour	Bobo doll	Bandura *et al.* (1961): Dependent variable
Ecological validity	Bandura and Walters (1963): Dependent variable	Bandura and Walters (1963)

Mental representation	Imitation of behaviour	Bobo doll
Bandura *et al.* (1961): Independent variable	Bandura *et al.* (1961): Dependent variable	Ecological validity
Bandura and Walters (1963): Dependent variable	Bandura and Walters (1963)	Nurture

Specifics of aggressive behaviour	Self-efficacy	Imitation of behaviour
Bobo doll	Ecological validity	Bandura and Walters (1963): Independent variable
Bandura *et al.* (1961)	Nurture	Bandura *et al.* (1961): Dependent variable

▶ Lesson notes p.34

Links – Turning study evaluation into theory evaluation

- In order to gain AO2/AO3 marks in PSYA3 and PSYA4, you need to use research studies in your evaluations and, further, to evaluate these studies. But most importantly such **evaluations of the studies must link to the theory**. **You must** show that you can **evaluate the methodology of studies** and explain the **impact that has on our acceptance of a theory.**
- Very often, the essays will ask you to discuss **theories** but NOT **studies**. This means that in order to gain the AO2/AO3 marks you have to evaluate the studies you have used to evaluate the theories! For example, evaluate Bandura's Bobo doll study, which you have used to support Social learning theory.
- What the hell does that mean?! This means that you need to **link** (hence the graphic below!) your evaluation of a study, back to the evaluation of the theory in order to make it relevant to the essay – and get the marks!

➡ Use the framework below to help you make these links!

1. Introduce your evaluation of the study methodology.	2. Explain and elaborate on this evaluation point.	3. Explain how it affects the reliability/validity of the evidence.	4. Explain the impact this has on our acceptance of a theory.
e.g,. One problem with Bandura's study is ecological validity…	*…This is because the children only hit an inflatable doll, rather than a real person who might hit back.*	*…This means the results may not generalise to other settings where children may be given the opportunity to engage in aggressive acts against humans.*	*…As such, we cannot be sure from this study that social learning theory and vicarious reinforcement can explain the performance of aggressive acts against other humans.*

▶ Lesson notes p.35

Situational factors in aggression

A.

B.

C.

D.

E.

F.

▶ Lesson notes p.35

Getting shirty!

THE DAILY NEWS

MINISTER PROPOSES BAN ON FOOTBALL SHIRTS!

The government Minister for Sport, Alana Clogan, today announced plans to ban football supporters from wearing their team's shirts within 24 hours of a game being played.

The move comes after a string of violent incidents involving sets of fans before and after games. Clogan said, 'Having listened to social psychological theories of aggression, it seems clear that the wearing of team colours contributes to the likelihood of hooliganism occurring through a process of deindividuation. By removing the wearing of team colours and shirts, we feel confident that aggression and violence will be reduced at football games.'

Get off the fence!

Imagine you are a social psychologist who has heard about Alana Clogan's plans to ban the wearing of football shirts and colours. You must take a **strong view** on this issue and write a letter to the Minister outlining an argument **against** the proposals.

Your letter must:

- Focus on **psychological arguments and evidence.**
- Include at least **one study** which supports your view that the proposals are flawed.
- Explain how that study relates to this issue.
- Include at least **one study** that DOES support the proposal, but then discredit that evidence (e.g. the methodology used).
- Outline alternative factors/explanations/variables that account for football hooliganism, supported with evidence.
- Suggest your own proposals, based on the psychological evidence.
- Include a brief conclusion at the end which summarises your main arguments.

▶ Lesson notes p.36

Why? Why? Why?

- **Institutional or group level aggression** may occur *within groups* or institutions such as the armed forces or prisons.
- It may also occur *between groups* in cases such as genocide (e.g. the murder of six million Jews by Nazis during World War II).

Write down a brief description of institutional aggression that you have looked at:

Brainstorm reasons **why** you think this happened/happens. Start with a very simple reason **why** at the top, then explore that reason in more depth, keep asking yourself why, why, why?! Try to bring in elements of psychology if you can. You may well need a large piece of paper to do this, A3 for example.

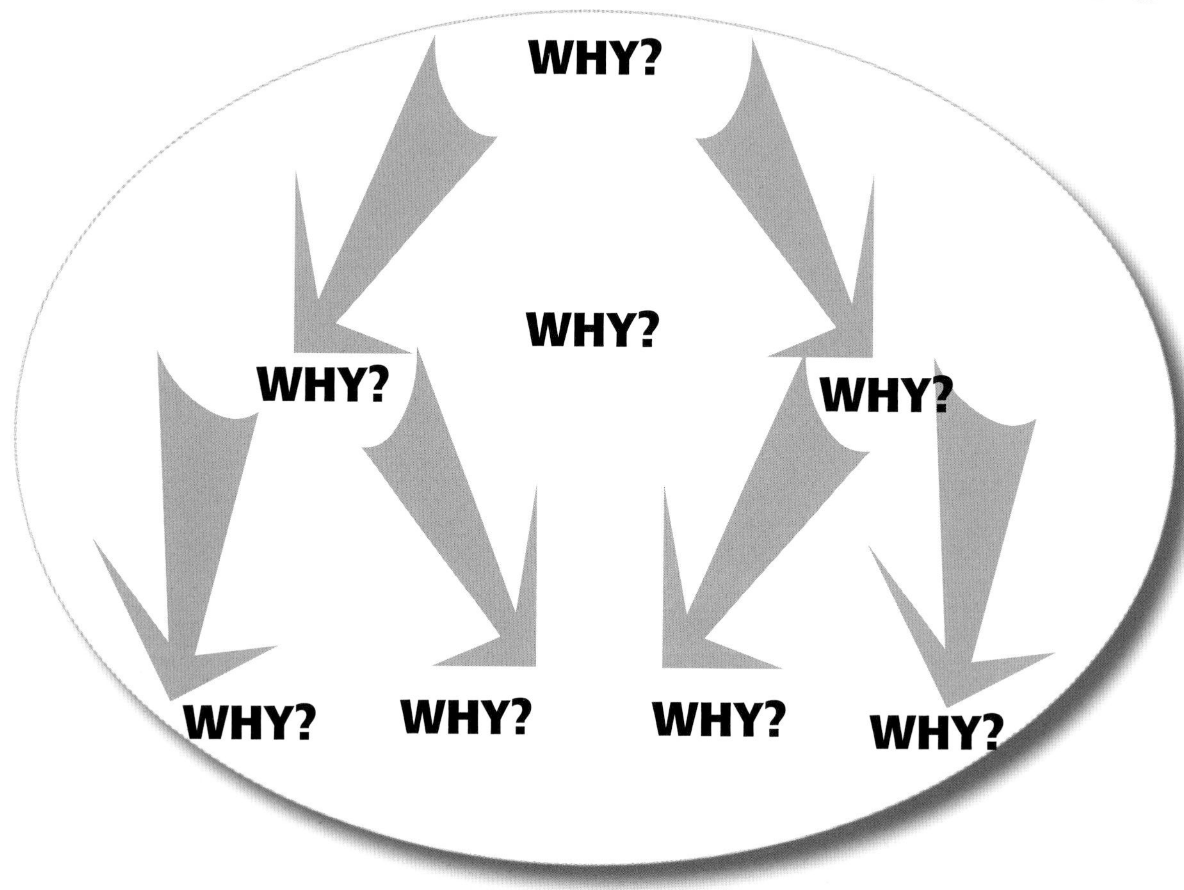

▶ Lesson notes p.37

'Brief' summaries

Making notes on **neural and hormonal mechanisms in aggression** in these 'briefs' will force you to summarise the information. Use your textbook (e.g. page 66 of *A2 Complete Companion*) or the Internet to help you. Try and include the key words written beneath the 'briefs' in your summaries.

The role of neurotransmitters

Serotonin

inhibiting, susceptibility, Mann (1981)

Dopamine

amphetamines, antipsychotics

The role of hormonal mechanisms

Testosterone

action on brain areas, challenge hypothesis

Cortisol

mediating effect, anxiety, testosterone

▶ Lesson notes p.37

Understanding twin studies

There are two types of twin: *(draw stick people versions of them here)*

Twin type:

AKA:

Genes shared:

Twin type:

AKA:

Genes shared:

Dave is one half of a MZ twin pairing. He has an aggressive behaviour disorder.

Assuming aggressive behaviour is completely genetic, *what are the chances of his identical twin Arnold developing the disorder? Explain your answer.*

Arnold does NOT suffer from an aggressive behaviour disorder. Are Dave and Arnold concordant?

What is a concordance rate?

▶ Lesson notes p.38

Nature vs. Nurture

Trying to determine the role of genetic factors in aggression is essentially a question of **nature** and **nurture**.

Task: *Choose a different colour to shade in each row of the key. Then, shade in each study/point using this colour code to indicate which viewpoint this could be used to argue for. In your notes, explain how/why they support this viewpoint.*

KEY:

Nature

Nurture

Both Nature and Nurture

One of the few studies to specifically assess aggressive behaviour using adult twin pairs found that nearly 50% of the variance in direct aggressive behaviour could be attributed to genetic factors (Coccaro *et al.*, 1997).

A study of over fourteen thousand adoptions in Denmark found that a significant number of adopted boys with criminal convictions had biological parents (particularly fathers) with criminal convictions (Hutchings and Mednick, 1975).

Most twin studies have focussed on criminal behaviour, rather than aggressive behaviour directly.

Caspi *et al.* (2002) studied 500 male children. The researchers discovered a variant of the gene associated with high levels of the gene responsible for producing the protein MAOA. Those with low levels of MAOA were significantly more likely to grow up to exhibit antisocial behaviour but *only* if they had been maltreated as children.

In a replication of Bandura *et al.*'s Bobo doll study, twin pairs were encouraged to act aggressively towards the doll by being exposed to an adult model who also behaved aggressively towards it. Researchers found no difference in correlations between MZ and DZ twin pairs (Plomin *et al.*, 1981).

▶ Lesson notes p.38

Evolutionary explanations of behaviour

Brian was a loving husband to his wife, and doting father to his daughter Grace. He always spent a lot of time with her, bought her gifts and worked hard to make sure that she had everything she needed. When Grace fell ill and needed a kidney transplant, it emerged that Brian could not be the donor because they were not a genetic match. Brian learnt that he could not be Grace's father. Brian was absolutely enraged, divorced his wife and refused to pay any maintenance money to help with the upbringing of Grace.

- *Explain why Brian's behaviour might be viewed as an evolved and adaptive response. Try and use the following key terms in your answer:* ***cuckoldry, reproductive cost, investment.***

When Simon and Clare first started their relationship Simon was romantic, gentle and consistently told Clare how beautiful she was and how much he enjoyed spending time with her. Once they had been in their relationship for a year his behaviour started to change. Simon would always make fun of her, make her feel stupid, and make derogatory comments about her weight.

- *Explain why Simon's behaviour might be viewed as an evolved and adaptive response. Try and use the following key terms in your answer:* ***sexual jealousy, insults, self-esteem, mate retention.***

Amish is in a relationship with Jaspreet but his behaviour towards her can sometimes be strange. For example, he calls her several times a day and pretends he does this because he misses her, but actually he wants to know where she is and what she is doing. Occasionally, Amish will tell Jaspreet that he won't be home until late but will call home unexpectedly to see what she is up to.

- *Explain why Amish's behaviour might be viewed as an evolved and adaptive response. Try and use the following key terms in your answer:* ***sexual jealousy, mate retention, direct guarding, sexual autonomy.***

Andrew is an extremely jealous boyfriend. When he and Jenni (his partner) go out in the evenings, he will often shout at other males who look at her and threaten to hit them. He also threatens Jenni that he will stop buying her clothes and break up with her if she talks to other guys in the pub. She knows that if he sees her smiling or laughing around another male that he will be extremely angry and make threats against her.

- *Explain why Andrew's behaviour might be viewed as an evolved and adaptive response. Try and use the following key terms in your answer:* ***sexual jealousy, mate retention, negative inducements, infidelity.***

▶ Lesson notes p.39

Reductionism

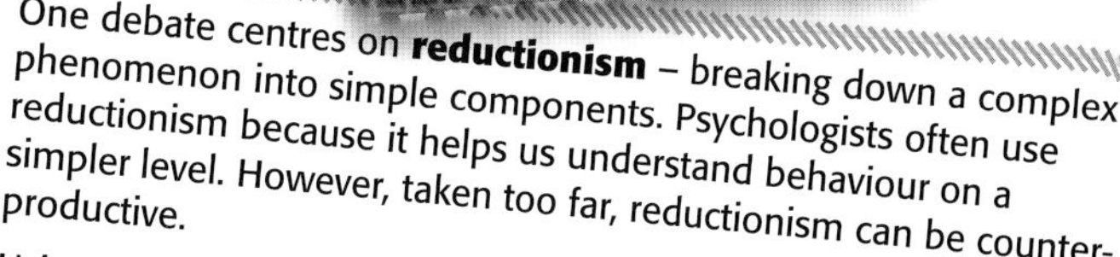

In order to get the highest marks in A2 Psychology, your essays must contain **synoptic elements**. One way in which you can do this is to link your knowledge and analysis of a topic to a **psychological debate**.

One debate centres on **reductionism** – breaking down a complex phenomenon into simple components. Psychologists often use reductionism because it helps us understand behaviour on a simpler level. However, taken too far, reductionism can be counter-productive.

Using the speech bubbles below, discuss reductionism in the **evolutionary explanations of aggressive group display**.

In what way are these evolutionary explanations reductionist – that is, what do they reduce aggressive behaviour to?

Evolutionary explanations of aggressive group display are reductionist because....

How is this reductionism useful in this case?

It could be argued this reductionism is useful because....

As a result of reductionism, what important factors/variables might these explanations ignore?

However, one problem with reductionism is that....

▶ Lesson notes p.39

Reading between the (head)lines

For each headline, rate the truthfulness of each story: 1 = false, no element of truth, 10 = truthful statement. Be sure to include at least one piece of research evidence to support your judgement.

Cinema circular

Showing sad films boosts sales of comfort food.

Related study:

Truthfulness of headline: 1 2 3 4 5 6 7 8 9 10

Reasons for judgement made:

Related study:

Education edition

Students of a higher socio-economic group are more likely to diet.

Truthfulness: 1 2 3 4 5 6 7 8 9 10

Reasons for judgement made:

Parenting periodical

Mommy and Daddy's diet dictates junior's dinner decisions.

Related study:

Reasons for judgement made:

Truthfulness: 1 2 3 4 5 6 7 8 9 10

▶ Lesson notes p.40

Daisy's diet club

Daisy runs a diet club. Each Monday her members weigh themselves after a week of restricted eating.

She finds a lot of her members struggle to stick to their eating programmes (she doesn't like to call them diets).

To help her members stick to their eating regimes and adopt a healthier eating lifestyle she designed a leaflet.

To help Daisy everyone should choose one statement and explain the science behind Daisy's diet tip.

Some of you could choose two statements to explain using research findings.

A few people could choose three or more statements to explain.

Hello Ladies and Gents, welcome to new members and warm embraces for long-standing clients. We all know how hard it can be sticking to our eating regimes, so I thought I'd gather together some handy tips to help you stay on the straight and narrow and avoid temptation. I've based each tip on psychological research to give you a brainy boost to eating healthily.

Reduce eating boredom by concentrating on the details of your dinner. Monday = Rocket salad (rather than just salad), Tuesday = Three bean salad (instead of just thinking 'salad' again), etc.

If you really want chocolate, don't deny yourself, just take a little nip occasionally.

Don't write off the whole week if you break your eating regime on one day. A biscuit with a cup of tea does not mean eat the whole pack as the day has been 'ruined'.

STOP, before you eat. Ask yourself 'how hungry am I?' Only eat if you score over 7 on a scale of 1 to 10. 1 = Not hungry, just bored... 10 = Terrible tummy rumbles!

Remember, there are no forbidden foods, just limited portions. Denying yourself cake means you spend all day thinking cake, cake, CAKE!

Change your thinking; you are not dieting, you are adopting a healthy lifestyle.

Extension

Practise your higher order thinking skills by ordering Daisy's diet tips from most to least successful. Give reasons for the choices you make.

▶ Lesson notes p.40

Switching eating on and off

Homeostasis

The body's tendency to maintain a relatively constant internal state. Mechanisms detect internal states and correct them, restoring the body's internal environment to its optimal state.

The body has two separate systems, one for turning on eating and one for switching it off. Among humans, glucose levels probably play the most important role in producing feelings of hunger. These feelings increase as glucose levels decrease.

Cut out the following strips and decide whether they are related to turning eating on (creating hungry feeling), or are responsible for switching eating off (feeling full). Then stick them in order to represent the control of hunger. Use the arrows to help you represent this mechanism.

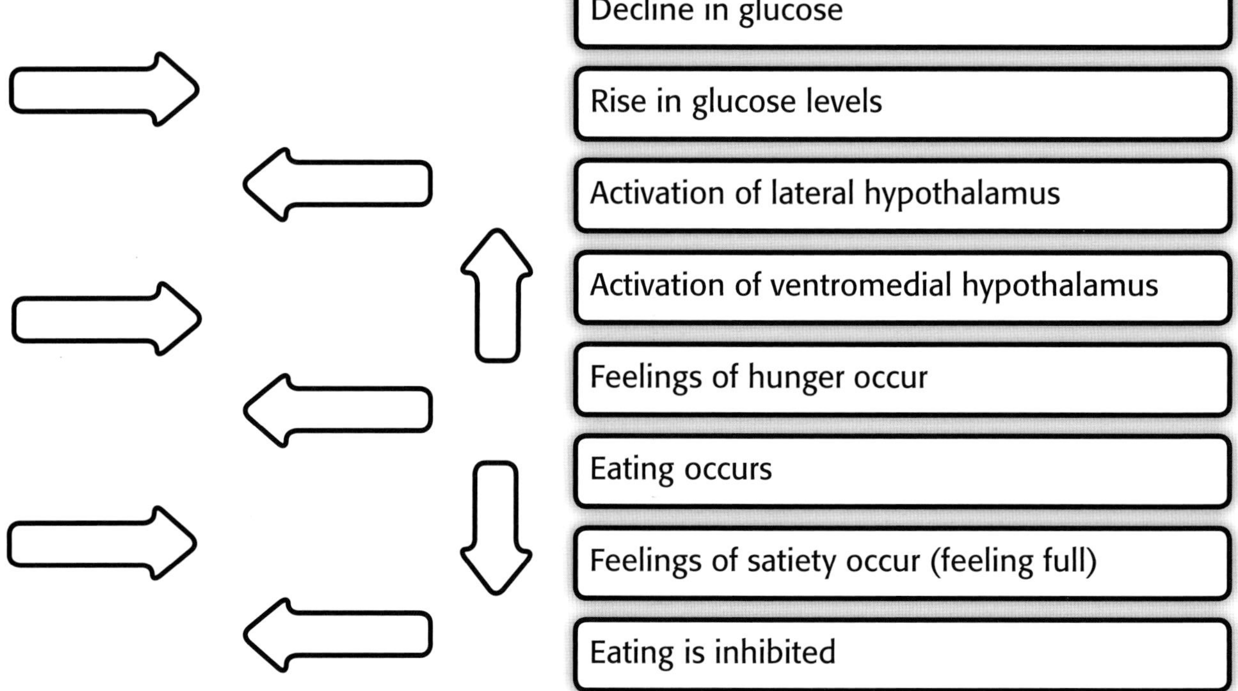

Now give two critical points for the control of eating and satiation mechanism you built above. Each criticism should be about 50 words in length. Use the example below as a guide to ensure you give a fully elaborated response.

Hunger and eating may not be under purely neural control.

Lutter *et al.* (2008) found the body produces extra quantities of the hormone ghrelin when stress is experienced. This hormone reduces depressive and anxious behaviours but also boosts appetite, leading to increased comfort eating.

This finding suggests the control of hunger and eating is more complex than the interaction between the lateral hypothalamus and ventromedial hypothalamus. Taking a reductionist approach may make a behaviour easier to investigate but it is at the risk of fully understanding a complex bodily process, which may mean potentially successful treatments for weight problems may not be developed.

▶ Lesson notes p.40

Outlining evolutionary explanations

Give a brief outline of **Preference for meat** as an explanation of our eating behaviour.

Use as many of the following key words as possible.

meat and organs	plant decline	energy source	brain growth
intelligence	amino acids	EEA	nutrients

Read the outline of **Taste aversion**.

Identify as many key words as possible that you could include if you were asked to produce an outline of this theory.

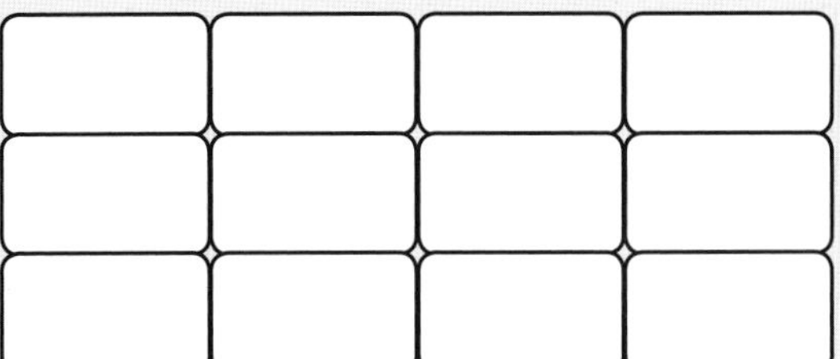

Humans and animals quickly learn to avoid certain tastes. Farmers trying to poison rats found rats would take a small bite of any food they encounter but should it make them ill, due to the poison inside, they rapidly learnt (classical conditioning) to avoid that food.

It seems we can avoid a food on the basis of taste and smell. We quickly form a dislike of foods that have an unpleasant taste or smell.

Avoiding these foods would have been beneficial to our ancestors in the EEA. If they survived eating a poisonous food, they would not make the same mistake by eating that food again. Taste aversion can be learnt up to 24 hours after eating. This is useful as there may be a delayed reaction after eating a poisonous food.

Recent research (Sandell and Breslin, 2006) supports the assumption that bitter taste evolved as a defence mechanism to detect potentially harmful toxins in plants. Participants who possessed the bitter taste receptor gene rated vegetables containing glucosinolate as 60% more bitter than those with the insensitive version of the gene. Glucosinolates are well known for their toxic effect at high doses. Therefore, it makes sense that the ability to detect glucosinolates would provide an evolutionary advantage to our ancestors, enabling them to avoid eating potentially toxic plants.

▶ Lesson notes p.40

Evolving food preferences

Hopefully you are now familiar with some of the principles of evolutionary explanations of behaviour. **Handout 21** 'Misunderstood monsters' should help with this.

Now try and use those same principles to explain our human food preferences below. Try and use the following key terms when you feel they are appropriate: **EEA, adaptive, natural selection, current environment, maladaptive, genome lag.**

Why is all nice food bad for you?

Let's be honest, we all crave fatty and calorific food! Next time you binge on fast food or chocolate you could have a ready-made excuse, 'It was evolution what dunnit!' Explain why…

Who'd be a veggie?

Many us of find the idea of vegetarianism quite alien and very much enjoy our carnivorous nature. How can evolution explain this?

▶ Lesson notes p.41

Has body image changed...?

A recent study by Rubenstein and Caballero (2000) used the height and weight figures of past Miss Americas to calculate a measure, called body mass index, and concluded that it has generally fallen over the years. BMI is weight divided by the square of height. In the 1920s, contestants had BMIs in the range now considered normal, which is 20 to 25, the researchers said. But an increasing number of winners since then have had BMIs under 18.5, which is the World Health Organisation's standard for undernutrition.

The data (from http://www.pbs.org/wgbh/amex/missamerica/sfeature/sf_list.html) is provided for you on • • • • • • • ••• •, to make your own calculations and conclusions.

As of 2002, 75 young women have won the title of Miss America. Averaging all the winners' vital statistics, the composite winner is 20 years and 3 months old; her average weight is just over 121 pounds; her height is 5 feet 6½ inches.

The 1925 winner of the Miss America beauty pageant, Fay Lanphier

Miss America 2002 was won by Katie Harman

▶ Lesson notes p.42

Statistics for Miss America pageant winners, 1921 to 2002

Year	Finalist	Age	Height (ft/ins)	Weight (lb)	Measurements
1921	Margaret	16	5'1"	108	30-25-32
1922/3	Mary	16	5'7"	140	35-26-36
1924	Ruth	18	5'6"	137	34-25-34
1925	Fay	19	5'6"	138	34-26-37
1926	Norma	18	5'4"	118	33-25-34
1927	Lois	17	5'5"	115	33-25-34
1933	Marian B	15	5'4"	112	32-26-37
1935	Henrietta	17	5'6"	120	33-23-35
1936	Rose	22	5'6"	114	34-23-34
1937	Bette	17	5'6"	120	32-26-36
1938	Marilyn M	20	5'7"	128	34-26-36
1939	Patricia	19	5'7"	126	36-25-34
1940	Frances	19	5'9"	120	34-23-35
1941	Rosemary	18	5'5"	120	34-24-36
1942	Jo-Carroll	18	5'5"	118	34-22-34
1943	Jean	19	5'8"	130	36-23-35
1944	Venus	19	5'7"	125	36-25-37
1945	Bess	21	5'10"	135	35-25-35
1946	Marilyn B	21	5'8"	123	35-25-36
1947	Barbara Jo	21	5'7"	130	35-25-35
1948	Bebe	18	5'9"	140	37-27-36
1949	Jacque	18	5'3"	106	34-22-34
1951	Yolande	18	5'5"	119	35-24-35
1952	Colleen	25	5'10"	143	36-24-36
1953	Neva Jane	19	5'6"	118	35-23-35
1954	Evelyn	20	5'8"	132	37-24-36
1955	Lee	19	5'8"	124	34-22-35
1956	Sharon	18	5'6"	116	35-23-35
1957	Marian M	19	5'5"	120	35-23-35
1958	Marilyn v. D	20	5'8"	130	35-25-36
1959	Mary Ann	21	5'5"	114	34-22-35
1960	Lynda	20	5'7"	120	36-24-36
1961	Nancy	18	5'6"	116	35-22-35
1962	Maria	19	5'5"	118	35-24-35
1963	Jacquelyn	20	5'5"	115	36-22-26
1964	Donna	21	5'6"	124	35-23-35
1965	Vonda Kay	21	5'6"	124	36-24-36
1966	Deborah	19	5'7"	115	36-23-36
1967	Jane	19	5'6"	116	36-24-36
1968	Debra B	20	5'9"	135	26-24-36
1969	Judith	18	5'7"	125	36-24-36
1970	Pam	21	5'5"	110	34-21-34
1971	Phyllis	21	5'8"	121	36-23-36
1972	Laurel Lea	22	5'7"	118	36-24-36
1973	Terry	23	5'8"	120	36-25-36
1974	Rebecca	23	5'9"	125	36-24-36
1975	Shirley	21	5'8"	119	36-23-36
1976	Tawny	18	5'10"	128	36-24-36
1977	Dorothy	20	5'7"	120	35-23-35
1978	Susan Pe	23	5'5"	105	34-24-35
1979	Kylene	22	5'4"	108	35-24-35
1980	Cheryl	22	5'7"	114	35-23-36
1981	Susan Po	21	5'4"	110	35-24-35
1982	Elizabeth Ward	20	5'9"	129	36-24-36
1983	Debra M	25	5'7"	115	35-22-35
1984	Vanessa	20	5'6"	110	34-24-34
1984	Suzette	20	5'3"	100	33-22-33
1985	Sharlene	20	5'8"	120	35-25-36
1986	Susan A	21	5'9"	114	35-22-35
1987	Kellye	21	5'8"	116	Statistics no longer given
1988	Kaye Lani	24	5'10"	131	
1989	Gretchen	22	5'3"	108	
1990	Debbye	23	5'8"	118	
1991	Majorie	25	5'6"	110	
1998	Kate	21	5'11"	145	
1999	Nicole	24	5'9"	133	
2001	Angela	24	5'4"	118	
2002	Katie	21	5'3"	110	

Missing years: no data on height/weight

▶ Lesson notes p.42

Collective memory

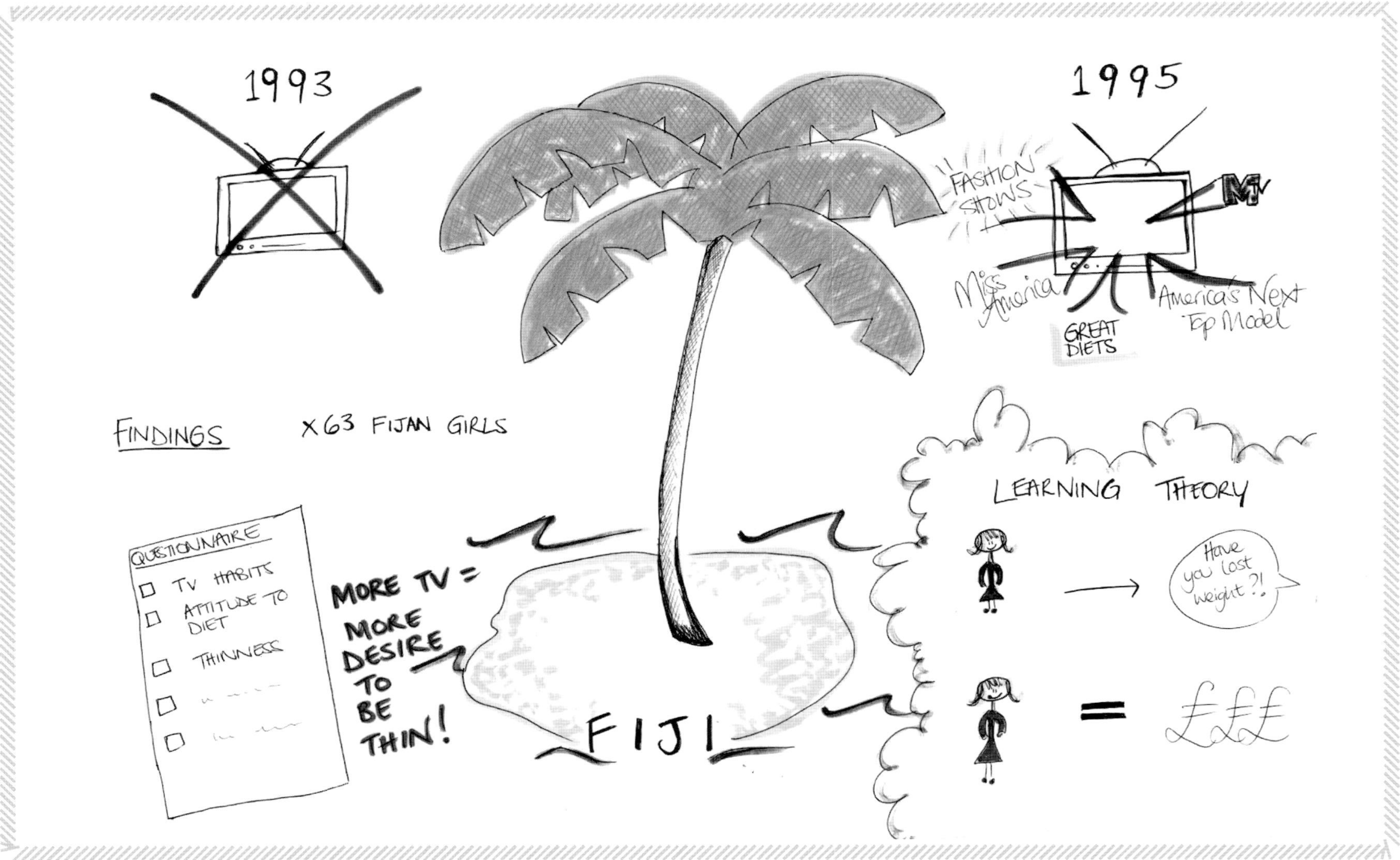

1993

1995

FASHION SHOWS

Miss America

GREAT DIETS

America's Next Top Model

FINDINGS X63 FIJAN GIRLS

QUESTIONNAIRE
- ☐ TV HABITS
- ☐ ATTITUDE TO DIET
- ☐ THINNESS
- ☐
- ☐

MORE TV = MORE DESIRE TO BE THIN!

FIJI

LEARNING THEORY

→ Have you lost weight?!

= £££

▶ Lesson notes p.42

AFFH connections

Weight loss	⟷	Physiological response
Extreme weight loss (e.g. famine)	⟷	Physiological response to normal weight loss
AN symptom - hyperactivity	⟷	Migration
AN symptom – denial of starvation	⟷	Survival

▶ Lesson notes p.43

Bulimia – a vicious cognitive circle

Cooper *et al.* (2004) put forward a **cognitive model** of bulimia nervosa (BN). The development of bulimia is usually a result of early trauma:

- As a result of the early trauma, they conclude they are worthless/unlovable.
- As they grow older they are exposed to criticisms about their weight and shape (either directly through friends/family, or indirectly via media representations of the 'ideal' shape).
- Bulimics learn that fat = bad, and thin = good and thus start to diet.
- Bulimics believe that by losing weight they will overcome the bad thoughts about themselves.

For example, they may have the cognition 'If I lose weight, people will like me'.

Following the **development of BN**, Cooper *et al.* believe that the **maintenance of BN** occurs due to a kind of 'vicious circle' of thoughts. This is displayed below. . . .

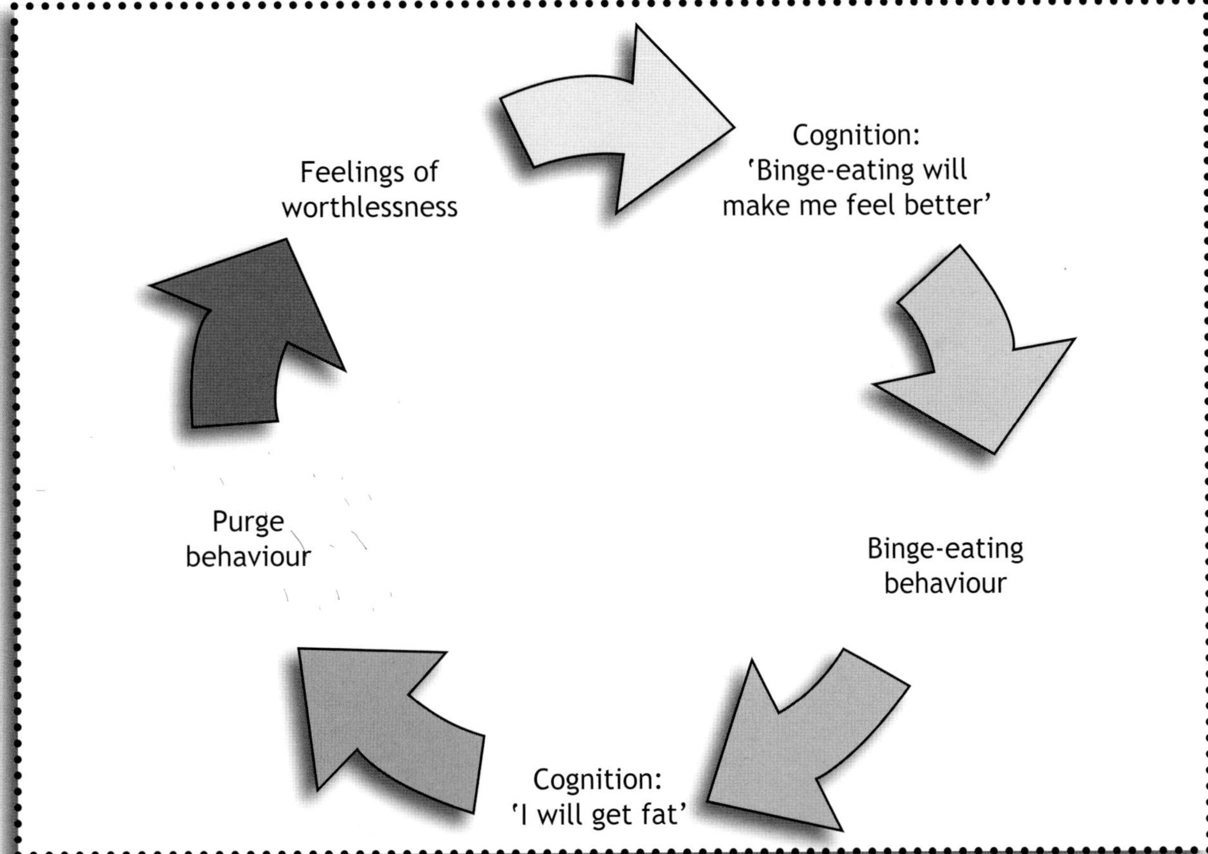

Task

- Explain what is going on in the 'vicious circle' diagram above, i.e. what does it suggest about why individuals with BN continue to binge-eat and purge?
- In your explanation, ensure you show understanding of key words such as **cognition**, **binge-eating**, **purge behaviour** and **vicious circle.**

▶ Lesson notes p.43

Translation

Neural explanations of bulimia nervosa (BN)

Serotonin

Bulimia has been linked to imbalances in the neurotransmitter **serotonin**. Serotonin plays an important role in controlling anxiety levels as well as perceptions of hunger and appetite. A study by Kaye *et al.* (2001) compared levels of the **neurotransmitters** serotonin, dopamine and noradrenaline in recovered bulimics and a control group of people who had never experienced bulimia. Levels of **dopamine** and **noradrenaline** were the same in both groups, but levels of serotonin were abnormal in recovered bulimics.

Low levels of serotonin can result in **depression**, while high levels can result in **anxiety**. Binge-eating may increase serotonin levels, which relieves feelings of depression and restores well-being. However, binge-eating may raise serotonin levels too high, leading to intense feelings of anxiety. The bulimic tends to associate these anxious feelings with eating and weight gain. To counter these feelings and to prevent weight gain, they purge. Purging reduces anxiety levels, but may lower serotonin levels too much, causing depression, and starting the cycle over again.

Task

The average onset for bulimia is 18 years of age. However, it can occur in children as young as 9. For these children it must be very difficult to make sense of the experience and the idea that the condition might be biologically caused may bring some comfort.

Your task is to *translate* the above information for a child of 12 years of age who is suffering from BN.

- Ensure it is written in a style of language that a normal 12 year old could understand.
- You may need to look up some of the key words and rewrite them in simpler terms, e.g. neurotransmitter.
- You may consider drawing a simple flow chart or diagram, especially for the second paragraph, which will be quite difficult for a child to follow.

By doing this, you are far more likely to make sense of the explanation yourself, and far more likely to remember the gist of it at the end of the lesson.

▶ Lesson notes p.43

Burger evaluations

The 'burger technique' (below) is a way for you to structure an evaluation paragraph where you use a study to support or undermine a theory/explanation. The important point of the process is the bottom of the burger where you explain how and why that study is relevant. This is where you can really illustrate your understanding of a) What the theory/explanation would predict, and b) whether or not we should accept that theory based on the research evidence.

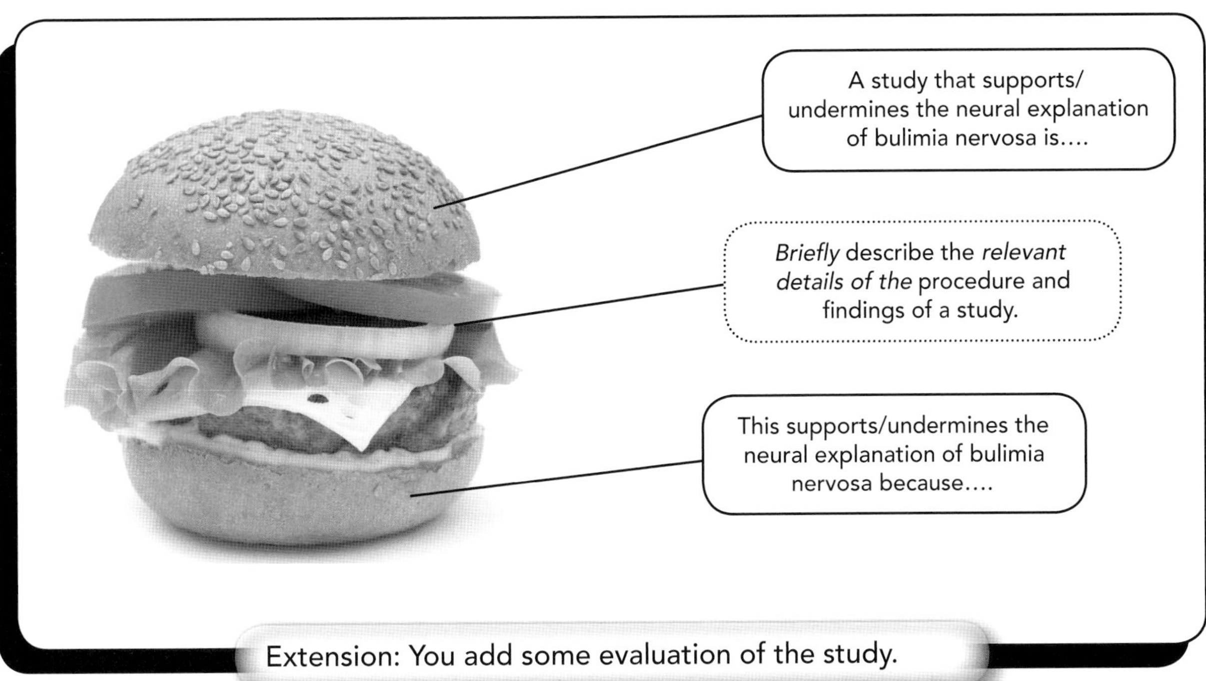

Use the studies below to evaluate the neural explanation of bulimia nervosa using the burger technique....

Walsh et al. (2000)

This study treated 22 patients with BN who had not responded to a course of cognitive behavioural therapy. Each patient was given a course of fluoxetine or a placebo (a drug which has no biological effect). Fluoxetine is a drug that raises levels of serotonin in the brain. Significant improvements were found in the fluoxetine group, particularly in terms of decreased incidence of binge-eating and purging.

Frank et al. (2002)

PET scans allow psychologists to look at activity level of brain areas. Frank *et al.* (2002) have shown with PET scans that there are fewer serotonin receptors in the brains of people with eating disorders. In addition, they have also shown that those that have recovered from eating disorders *also* show fewer serotonin receptors in the brain.

▶ Lesson notes p.44

Personality characteristics questionnaire

The items below enquire about what kind of person you think you are. Each item consists of a pair of characteristics, with the letters A-E in between. For example:

Not at all artistic A....B....C....D....E Very artistic

Each pair describes contradictory characteristics – that is, you cannot be both at the same time. The letters form a scale between two extremes. You are to choose a letter that describes where you fall on the scale. For example, if you think that you have no artistic ability, you would choose A. If you are only medium, you might choose C, and so forth. Method for scoring is given on **Handout 82**.

1 Not at all aggressive	A.......B.......C.......D.......E	Very aggressive
2 Not at all independent	A.......B.......C.......D.......E	Very independent
3 Not at all emotional	A.......B.......C.......D.......E	Very emotional
4 Very submissive	A.......B.......C.......D.......E	Very dominant
5 Not at all excitable in a major crisis	A.......B.......C.......D.......E	Very excitable in a major crisis
6 Very passive	A.......B.......C.......D.......E	Very active
7 Not at all able to devote self completely to others	A.......B.......C.......D.......E	Able to devote self completely to others
8 Very rough	A.......B.......C.......D.......E	Very gentle
9 Not at all helpful to others	A.......B.......C.......D.......E	Very helpful to others
10 Not at all competitive	A.......B.......C.......D.......E	Very competitive
11 Very home oriented	A.......B.......C.......D.......E	Very worldly
12 Not at all kind	A.......B.......C.......D.......E	Very kind
13 Indifferent to others' approval	A.......B.......C.......D.......E	Highly needful of others' approval
14 Feelings not easily hurt	A.......B.......C.......D.......E	Feelings easily hurt
15 Not at all aware of feelings of others	A.......B.......C.......D.......E	Very aware of feelings of others
16 Can make decisions easily	A.......B.......C.......D.......E	Has difficulty making decisions
17 Gives up very easily	A.......B.......C.......D.......E	Never gives up easily
18 Never cries	A.......B.......C.......D.......E	Cries very easily
19 Not at all self-confident	A.......B.......C.......D.......E	Very self-confident
20 Feels very inferior	A.......B.......C.......D.......E	Feels very superior
21 Not at all understanding of others	A.......B.......C.......D.......E	Very understanding of others
22 Very cold in relations with others	A.......B.......C.......D.......E	Very warm in relations with others
23 Very little need for security	A.......B.......C.......D.......E	Very strong need for security
24 Goes to pieces under pressure	A.......B.......C.......D.......E	Stands up well under pressure

▶ Lesson notes p.45

Scoring your questionnaire

Ring the answers you gave and then add up the scores in the boxes below:

Masculinity

Question 2	A=1	B=2	C=3	D=4	E=5
Question 6	A=1	B=2	C=3	D=4	E=5
Question 10	A=1	B=2	C=3	D=4	E=5
Question 16	A=5	B=4	C=3	D=2	E=1
Question 17	A=1	B=2	C=3	D=4	E=5
Question 19	A=1	B=2	C=3	D=4	E=5
Question 20	A=1	B=2	C=3	D=4	E=5
Question 24	A=1	B=2	C=3	D=4	E=5

Femininity

Question 3	A=1	B=2	C=3	D=4	E=5
Question 7	A=5	B=4	C=3	D=2	E=1
Question 8	A=1	B=2	C=3	D=4	E=5
Question 9	A=5	B=4	C=3	D=2	E=1
Question 12	A=1	B=2	C=3	D=4	E=5
Question 15	A=1	B=2	C=3	D=4	E=5
Question 21	A=1	B=2	C=3	D=4	E=5
Question 22	A=1	B=2	C=3	D=4	E=5

Masculinity–femininity score

Question 1	A=1	B=2	C=3	D=4	E=5
Question 4	A=1	B=2	C=3	D=4	E=5
Question 5	A=5	B=4	C=3	D=2	E=1
Question 11	A=1	B=2	C=3	D=4	E=5
Question 13	A=5	B=4	C=3	D=2	E=1
Question 14	A=5	B=4	C=3	D=2	E=1
Question 18	A=5	B=4	C=3	D=2	E=1
Question 23	A=5	B=4	C=3	D=2	E=1

Total masculinity score	=
Total femininity score	=
Total masculinity–femininity score	=

Extension:

Using your knowledge of methodology, evaluate the validity of this questionnaire in measuring gender-related personality characteristics.

▶ Lesson notes p.45

Spot the deliberate mistakes

In the following passage about **the role of genes in gender development** there are 10 deliberate mistakes, see if you can spot them and correct them. . . .

Each person has 25 pairs of chromosomes (in each cell of the body). Each of these chromosomes carries hundreds of genes containing instructions about physical and behavioural characteristics such as eye colour and predisposition to certain mental illnesses.

One pair of chromosomes is called the sex chromosomes because they determine an individual's gender. In the case of a male this pair is called XX, because both chromosomes are shaped like X's. The female chromosome pair is described as XY. The Y chromosome carries very little genetic material although it does determine the sex of a child.

There is usually a direct link between an individual's chromosomal sex (XX and XY) and their internal genitalia (vagina or penis) and external genitalia (ovaries or testes). During prenatal development all individuals start out the same – a few weeks after conception both male and female embryos have external genitalia that look essentially masculine. When the foetus is about three months old, if it is to develop as a male, the testes normally produce the male hormone oestrogen, which causes male external genitalia to develop.

Genetic transmission explains how individuals acquire their sex. It may also explain some aspects of gender (a person's sense of whether they are male or female) because of the link between genes, genitalia and hormones.

Chromosomes determine a person's sex but most gender development is actually governed by hormones. These are produced prenatally (e.g. testosterone as described above) and in childhood (a surge of hormones in puberty leads to primary sexual characteristics such as pubic hair). Hormones influence the development of genitalia and/or affect the development of the brain, both of which influence gender development.

▶ Lesson notes p.45

Evolving gender roles

Think about some of the evolutionary terms and principles you used on **Handout 21**, 'Misunderstood monsters'. Try and use those same principles in explaining **gender roles** – the different attitudes, interests and behaviours that members of each sex adopt.

Here are some key terms you might try to use:
EEA, survival, adaptive, natural selection, sexual selection, reproductive strategies, reproductive success, genome lag, current environment, evolutionary advantage.

Use your textbook or the Internet if you need to.

Division of labour

Men tend to believe they should take on roles that make them the 'bread-winner' and often like to be the main source of income for the family. The traditional image of man might be the 'hunter'. Although perhaps society is changing, women have traditionally taken more of a domestic role, for example cooking, cleaning, etc.

How might evolution explain this behaviour?

Mating choice

Although it might be somewhat of a generalisation, research has indicated that men tend to look for women who are physically attractive (for example, smooth skin, glossy hair, red lips and thin waist - all indicators of youth and health). In contrast, women seem to be more concerned in finding a partner who has resources such as wealth and power.

How could evolution explain these mate choice preferences?

Cognitive style

Most people would argue that women tend to be better at **empathising** (understanding what other people think and feel) and are more focussed on relationships. Compare this to men who seem to have more success than women in **systematising** - for example, understanding and building machines, systems, etc. In addition, rather than being focussed on relationships, men can be more defensive and protective than women.

How could evolution explain these different cognitive styles?

▶ Lesson notes p.46

The boy who was raised a girl 1

What accident occurred to David Reimer in his first year of life?

Why were his parents concerned about his future happiness?

Briefly outline details of John Money's theory of gender identity and development.

John Money suggested that Reimer's sex should be 'reassigned' and he should be raised as a girl ('Brenda'). What psychological justification did he give for this?

Outline some of Reimer's experiences and case details from when he was a young child.

▶ Lesson notes p.46

The boy who was raised a girl 2

Outline some of Reimer's experiences and case details from when he was an older child.

Outline some of Reimer's experiences and case details from when he was an adolescent.

What happened after Reimer learnt the truth about his gender reassignment?

What would you conclude about gender development from this case study? What are the problems with generalising the conclusions?

Comment on the ethics of Money's study, and the conflict between science and ethics.

▶ Lesson notes p.46

Gender constancy theory

Kohlberg's (1966) concept of **gender constancy** derives from Piaget's suggestion that young children cannot distinguish between appearance and reality (which is related to **conservation skills**).

Kohlberg's gender constancy theory holds that changes in gender thinking are solely the outcome of maturational changes in a child's cognitive abilities as the child gets older. Children naturally progress from one stage to the next as they mature.

Task: *Illustrate the limitations children have in their gender thinking at each stage using the cartoon grid below. You could use stick people, speech marks and speech bubbles to do this.*

Stage 1: Gender labelling (2-3½ years)

Stage 2: Gender stability (3½ - 4½ yrs)	Stage 3: Gender consistency

▶ Lesson notes p.47

The story of X – 1

'X' first appeared in 'Ms.' as a 'Story for Free Children' in 1972. Since then, the magazine say they have had more requests for reprints of 'X' than for anything else they have ever published. 'X' was praised in psychiatric journals and has appeared in hardcover (Daughters Publishing Company). This new excerpt was adapted by the author for 'Ms.' from the complete, new version published by Stonesong Press ($4.95, paperback).

Once upon a time, a baby named X was born. It was named X so that nobody could tell whether it was a boy or a girl. Its parents could tell, but they couldn't tell anyone else, not even Baby X – at least not until much later. It was all part of a Secret Scientific Xperiment – Project Baby X. The smartest scientists worked out the secret details of the Xperiment, and wrote the *Official Instruction Manual*, in a secret code, for Baby X's parents, whoever they were.

These parents had to be selected very carefully. Thousands of people volunteered, but almost everybody failed because they wanted a boy or a girl, and not a Baby X. Finally, the scientists found the Joneses, who really wanted to raise an X more than any other kind of baby.

The day the Joneses brought their baby home, friends and relatives came to see it. The first thing they asked was what kind of baby X was. When the Joneses said, 'It's an X!' nobody knew what to say. They couldn't say, 'Look at her cute little dimples!' On the other hand they couldn't say, 'Look at his husky little biceps!' The relatives all felt embarrassed about having an X in the family.

The *Official Instruction Manual* had warned the new parents that this would happen, so they didn't fret about it. Besides, they were too busy learning how to bring up Baby X.

Ms and Mr Jones had to be Xtra careful. If they kept bouncing it up in the air and saying how *strong* and *active* it was, they'd be treating it more like a boy than an X. But if all they did was cuddle it and kiss it and tell it how *sweet* and *dainty* it was, they'd be treating it more like a girl than an X. In the *Official Instruction Manual*, the scientists prescribed: 'plenty of bouncing and plenty of cuddling, *both*. X ought to be strong and sweet and active. Forget about dainty altogether.'

There were other problems too, like toys and clothes. Everything was in sections marked BOYS or GIRLS. Mr and Ms Jones consulted the *Official Instruction Manual*. It said firmly: 'Buy plenty of everything!' So they bought all kinds of toys. Likewise it said. 'If X gets dirty climbing rocks, never say, 'Nice little Xes don't get dirty climbing rocks. Or if X falls down and cries, never say, 'Brave little Xes don't cry.' Because, of course, nice little Xes do get dirty and brave little Xes do cry. No matter how dirty X gets, or how hard it cries, don't worry. It's all part of the experiment.'

Once a little girl grabbed X's shovel in the sandbox, and zonked X on the head with it. 'Now, now Tracy,' the mother began to scold, 'little girls mustn't hit little-' and she turned to ask X, 'Are you a little boy or a little girl, dear?' 'I'm a little X,' said X. 'Little girls mustn't hit little Xes, either! What good's hitting anyway?'

Then it was time for X to start school. The Joneses were really worried about this, because school was even more full of rules for boys and girls, and there were no rules for Xes. Teachers would tell boys to form a line, and girls to form another line.

The Joneses spent weeks consulting their *Instruction Manual*. X's mother had to teach X how to throw and catch a ball properly, and X's father had to teach X what to serve at a doll's tea party. X's teachers promised that the class could line up alphabetically, but nobody could help X with the biggest problem of all – Other Children. What would the other children think?

▶ Lesson notes p.48

The story of X – 2

(continued from **Handout 88**)

You couldn't tell what X was by its overalls or hairstyle. The children tried to find out by asking, 'Who's your favourite sports star?' X had two favourites: a girl jockey and a boy archery champion.

After school, X wanted to play with Other Children. 'How about shooting baskets in the gym?' X asked the girls. 'Boy, is *he* weird,' whispered Jim to Joe.

'How about weaving some baskets in the arts and crafts room?' X asked the boys. 'Boy, is *she* weird,' whispered Susie to Peggy.

Ms and Mr Jones asked X how things had gone at school. 'The other children hate me', X whispered.

Once more the Joneses reached for their *Instruction Manual*. 'What did you Xpect?' it said. 'Other Children have to obey silly boy-girl rules, because their parents have taught them to. Lucky X – you don't have any rules at all!'

The next morning, X won the spelling bee at school, and the relay race, and almost won the baking contest. One of the Other Children said, 'X doesn't care about winning. X just thinks it's fun playing boys' *and* girls' stuff. X is having twice as much fun as we are!'

From then on, some funny things began to happen. Susie refused to wear pink dresses to school – she wanted overalls like X's. And the twins, Joe and Peggy, decided to share everything.

Peggy used Joe's hockey skates and took half his newspaper route. Joe used Peggy's needlepoint kit and took some of her baby-sitting jobs. Peggy ran the lawnmower and Joe ran the vacuum cleaner. Their parents didn't care that Peggy mowed the lawn better, and that Joe vacuumed the carpet better. They were furious. It's all that little X's fault, they agreed. 'X doesn't know what it is so it wants to mix everybody else up too!'

Peggy and Joe were forbidden to play with X anymore. But it was too late: the Other Children stayed mixed up and happy and free and refused to go back to they way they'd been before X.

The parents held an emergency meeting. They told the principal X was a 'bad influence' and should take an Xamination to find out if it was a girl or a boy and start obeying all the old rules.

The principal was very upset – X was an Xcellent student and set a fine Xample! Reluctantly, he notified the Joneses who consulted their *Manual*. 'Sooner or later,' it said, 'X will have to be Xamined by an impartial team of Xperts. This may be the only way any of us will know for sure whether X is mixed up – or everyone else is.'

The next day, X reported to the school health office. Inside, the Xperts had set up their famous testing machine. There were buzzes, the Xpert's voices and X's voice, answering their questions.

At last, the door opened. 'What happened?' everyone began shouting. 'Young X,' said the Xpert, 'is just about the *least* mixed-up child we've ever examined!' The parents were angry and bewildered – how could X have passed. 'We still want to know what X is!' said one parent. 'Don't worry,' said the Xperts. 'You'll all know one of these days. And you won't need us to tell you.' Peggy and Joe realised at once. 'By the time it matters which sex X is, it won't be a secret anymore!'

The Joneses, scientists and Other Children were very happy. Even the parents promised not to make any trouble.

Later that day, X's friends found X playing with a tiny baby they had never seen before. 'How do you like our new baby?' X asked. 'It's got cute dimples,' said Joe. 'And husky biceps,' said Susie. 'What kind of baby is it?' asked Peggy.

X frowned at them. 'Can't you tell? *It's a Y!*'

▶ Lesson notes p.48

Do TV shows make teenagers sexist?

Rivadeneyra and Lebo (2008) investigated the relationship between TV use and gender role attitudes and behaviour in dating. The researchers surveyed 215 students in 14 ninth-grade classes in Midwest America (mean age 14.96).

The participants who agreed to take part indicated their current dating experience (e.g. age of first date, number of partners, etc.) as well as answering a range of other questions.

To investigate TV habits they were asked to complete the Television Exposure Scale (Rivadeneyra and Ward, 2005). This contained a list of 126 soap operas and primetime TV programmes that were on in America at that time. Participants had to indicate on a 5-point Likert scale how frequently they watched each of the programmes in the last month. Participants' viewing hours were calculated by multiplying the frequency that the program was viewed along with the length of the program.

The programmes on the list were categorised into five genres: soap operas, romantic reality shows (e.g. Beauty and the Geek), non-romantic reality shows (e.g. Fear Factor), romantic dramas (e.g. The O.C.) and non-romantic dramas (e.g. Law and Order).

Participants were also asked to complete the Perceived Realism on Television Scale (Rivadeneyra and Ward, 2005). This was also measured on a 5-point Likert scale with 28 questions. For example, 'Friendships between characters on TV are just like real friendships'.

Dating role attitudes were assessed using a new survey created for this study. The scale consisted of 20 questions that indicate dating behaviours (e.g. 'Initiates date', 'Initiates sexual interaction such as a kiss good night at the end of a date'). Participants were asked to indicate on a 5-point Likert scale whether males or females should perform each behaviour (1 = only males, 2 = more males, 3 = equal amounts, 4 = more females, 5 = only females).

The relationships between these variables were investigated using correlational analyses. It was found that watching romantic TV was associated with more traditional gender role attitudes in dating situations. However, watching non-romantic dramas and thinking TV was realistic, was related to less traditional role attitudes. In addition, watching soap operas was related to a younger age of dating initiation and a greater number of dating partners.

1. Write a list of the co-variables used in this study. Briefly explain how these co-variables were operationalised.
2. Explain why correlational analyses were used.
3. Write a conclusion for this study in about three sentences.
4. How does this study relate to the theories of gender you have studied so far? *E.g. does it support or contradict? Why?*
5. This is a correlational study and used self-report techniques. Using this information, make two separate evaluations of this study.

Lesson notes p.49

Study deconstruction

Aim:

Research method:

Independent variable(s):

Dependent variable(s):

Key results/findings:

Buss (1989)

...explored what males and females looked for in a marriage partner across 37 different cultures. Use your textbooks or Internet to complete this study deconstruction sheet.

Key conclusions:

Evaluation of methodology:

Link to reductionism debate an issue or debate:

Link to an approach:

▶ Lesson notes p.49

Psychometric word wall

Three theories are represented in the word wall below: Spearman's (1927) two-factor theory, Cattell's (1943) multifactor theory and Guilford's (1977) 'structure of intellect theory'. Colour code each brick to identify the theory the key word belongs to.

general factor	*crystallised*	*independent abilities*	*s*
operations	*fluid*	*general intelligence*	*Gc*
components	*contents*	*g*	*investment*
specific abilities	*Gf*	*products*	*multi factor*

Now choose two of the theories to explain using the word bricks and other key words you have identified from reading your textbook (page 116 *A2 Complete Companion*).

In exam essays you could be asked to outline one or more theories. Therefore it may be helpful to produce a revision summary for two explanations.

My 200-word summary will be of

Additional key words identified from textbook reading:

Reasons I have chosen to focus on this theory:

My 200-word summary will be of

Additional key words identified from textbook reading:

Reasons I have chosen to focus on this theory:

▶ Lesson notes p.51

Exploding the evaluation: Triarchic theory of intelligence

(AO1) Metacomponents...

(AO1) Performance components...

Berg & Sternberg (1985) provide evidence consistent with both the predictions of the triarchic theory and the generally acknowledged decline in cognitive abilities associated with aging. They found younger participants were superior in most of the **metacomponents** and **performance components** associated with intelligence. Older adults had more difficulty defining the problems to be solved, managing their attention to solve those problems and monitoring the effectiveness of any solutions.

(AO2) However, Cunningham & Tomer (1991) suggest knowledge components (based on experience) do not necessarily decline with age, especially if exercised by an old person trying to cope with new situations. This suggests that...

(AO3) If research only uses participants from a certain age range (e.g. 18–35 year olds) the results may not give a true understanding of intelligence because...

(AO1) An example of using practical intelligence would be...

The triarchic theory seems applicable to both school and university study. Sternberg *et al.* (1999) showed teaching triarchically tends to result in significant improvements in academic achievement. Williams *et al.* (2002) assessed the impact of the Practical Intelligence for Schools (PIFS) intervention in which all three types of intelligence were emphasised. Where PIFS was used as a major part of the curriculum, significant improvements in practical intelligence were obtained.

(AO1) The three types of intelligence are...

(AO3) Sternberg's theory is criticised as there is, as yet, no published test of triarchic abilities. This makes testing the theory difficult because...

(AO3) Gottfredson (2003) claims Sternberg's theory has failed to provide sufficient evidence to support his assertion that practical intelligence is distinct from general intelligence *(g),* nor that it equals or *exceeds g* in its ability to predict academic achievement and everyday success.

(AO1) Spearman's (1927) two-factor theory *describes g* as...

(AO3) Testing intelligence is difficult as researchers must be careful how they define and measure intelligence to reduce the risk of cultural bias...

▶ Lesson notes p.51

Multiple intelligence mix up

Match the multiple intelligence description to the type of intelligence identified by Gardner (1983/99)

Description	Intelligence	Description
Language skills such as the ability to learn languages and express oneself.	Bodily-kinaesthetic intelligence	Numerical skills such as the ability to carry out mathematical operations and investigate issues scientifically.
Skills such as playing an instrument or composing music.	Interpersonal intelligence	Using the body, for example using mental abilities to coordinate bodily movements.
Understanding and relating to others, for example understanding the intentions and motivations of others.	Intrapersonal intelligence	Understanding relationships in space, for example being able to transform mental images onto paper or to read a map.
Showing an expertise in the recognition and classification of the different species of flora and fauna that form the natural environment.	Linguistic intelligence	Understanding oneself, including an appreciation of feelings, fears and motivations.
	Logical-mathematical intelligence	
	Musical intelligence	
	Natural intelligence	
	Spatial intelligence	

Multiple intelligence mastermind

The questions below require you to access different thinking skills.
Try to answer as many as possible in the time set by your teacher.
Challenge yourself by choosing at least one question you find difficult to answer.

- Describe two revision activities based on two of the above types of intelligence.
- Do you think staying in education beyond GCSE improves certain types of intelligence, if so which ones and why?
- Mozart could write music before he could read. Are cases of exceptional talent strong support for Gardner's theory of multiple intelligences? Why?
- Gardner himself was a serious pianist. Do you think this influenced his theory. If so, how?
- Could certain physical areas of the brain be responsible for different types of intelligence? Can you give an example?
- Are some of the abilities Gardner describes simply talents rather than distinct forms of intelligence? Provide some evidence for your view.
- Can you identify two people each showing exceptional ability in one type of intelligence?
- What would Gardner think of IQ tests that give a single measure, such as a score, for intelligence?
- There is little psychometric or empirical evidence to support Gardner's theory yet many people apply his ideas to their own and others' learning. Why do you think Gardner's work is popular in educational settings?

▶ Lesson notes p.51

Sea lion training

Classical and operant conditioning have long been used by animal trainers to teach animals to produce the desired behaviour on command.

Use your knowledge of classical conditioning to help Shawn train the safari park sea lion to associate fish with a certain bucket.

Unconditioned stimulus UCS

FOCUS Unconditioned response UCR

Artificial (neural) stimulus NS

Conditioned stimulus CS

Conditioned response CR FOCUS

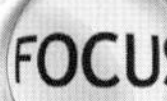

Extension: in your explanation try to include a time schedule to produce maximum learning.

Consider the following phenomena and explain how you will deal with them in your sea lion training.

- The CR (conditioned response) can quickly become **extinct** if food does not follow the presentation of the CS (conditioned stimulus). This is because the bucket (in this case) predicts the arrival of food, if food does not arrive, the association is no longer useful.
- Should a stimulus appear that is similar, but not identical to the CS (conditioned stimulus), the animal will elicit the CR (conditioned response). This is known as **stimulus generalisation**.
- If during the conditioning procedure other similar stimuli are presented without being followed by the UCS (unconditioned stimulus), then eventually the animal will only respond to the CS (conditioned stimuli). The animal has learnt to discriminate between CS and other stimuli. This process is known as **stimulus discrimination**.

Now Shawn has successfully taught the sea lion to associate food with a certain bucket, he can begin training him to perform tricks for the safari park audience. With the bucket present, Shawn's sea lion knows food is present. Desirable aspects of his behaviour can be reinforced, leading to tricks being developed and performed on command.

The type of reinforcement Shawn should use is: because:	Shawn should carry out this type of reinforcement by:	The reinforcement schedule Shawn should use is: because:

▶ Lesson notes p.52

Helping hands

5-digit description of classical conditioning

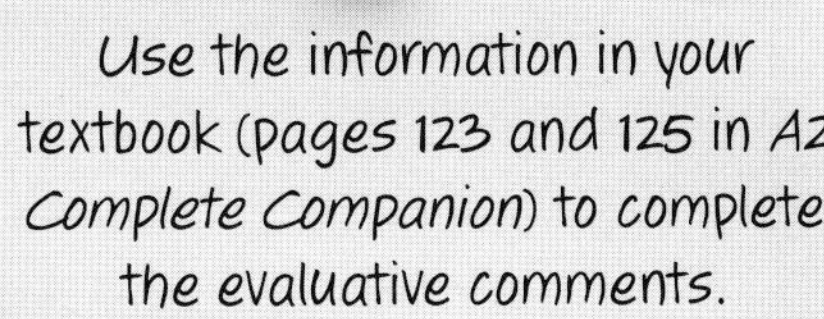

Use the information in your textbook (pages 123 and 125 in *A2 Complete Companion*) to complete the evaluative comments.

5-digit description of operant conditioning

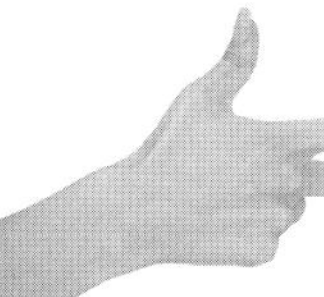

Point: The effectiveness of operant conditioning varies from one species to another depending on the innate abilities of the species.

Point upheld by...

Point: Different species differ in terms of their motives, cognitive abilities and the degree to which their life depends on learning. We must therefore be cautious about generalising classical conditioning research from one species to the next.

Support for this point: for example...

Criticism of the point: however, from the evolutionary perspective we should be able to generalise because all animals share the same building blocks.

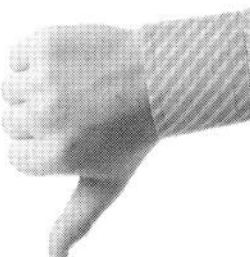

Extension:
Both classical and operant conditioning could be seen as reductionist approaches to describing the learning process.
What are the advantages and disadvantages of adopting such an approach for: research studies, application to and use in real life, contributing to our understanding of learning?

▶ Lesson notes p.52

Making predictions

Animals in captivity often receive food in the presence of humans.

Relevant notes from textbook

If humans must be present when food is given then combining their presence with another more appropriate stimuli will overshadow the human presence.

Principles of positive reinforcement training (PRT) can be used to train animals to cooperate voluntarily in veterinary procedures. This would be useful to the staff and the animal. Clay *et al.* (2009) found rhesus macaques who received positive reinforcement when in a laboratory environment showed a significant reduction in both the rate and duration of fearful cringing behaviour shown toward humans compared to a control group who received no such training.

Prediction: How will this affect their ability to feed in the wild?
(Hint: classical conditioning)

Prediction: What would be more appropriate stimuli to combine with humans?

Prediction: How could humans reduce their presence when providing food for the animals in their care?

Prediction: Why is it unwise to release animals into the wild who have become used to humans and food being present together?

Prediction: How could PRT help improve the ethical treatment of animals in scientific research?

Prediction: If PRT is used in veterinary procedures, what are the benefits for animals and medical staff?

▶ Lesson notes p.52

Cartoon critters

Self-recognition

Human babies can recognise themselves by the age of two, as can adult chimpanzees, bonobos and orang-utans. It seems the only other non-ape animals to possess this skill are bottle-nosed dolphins and killer whales.

Self-recognition research involves placing a mirror in an animal's enclosure. If the animal demonstrates they recognise the mirror's image is of themselves it is seen as a form of intelligence.

However, Plotnik *et al.* (2006) suggested that elephants also have self awareness...

Research validity:
Did the elephants really 'see' their own reflection with a cross on it?
Is there an alternative explanation for their behaviour?

▶ Lesson notes p.52

Colour coding

IDENTIFY WHETHER THE STATEMENT BELONGS TO:

Machiavellian Intelligence ■

Meat-sharing hypothesis ■

Developed by Whitten & Byrne in 1988

Developed by Stanford in 1999

The ability to plan and detect deception

Refers to the strategic sharing of meat

Forging alliances and encouraging mating

Refers to ability to subtly manipulate others

Diverting attention of others helps cheating

Natural ability restricted to the great apes

Cognitive ability needed to recall debts

Provides important source of saturated fats

Read each evaluative comment and make a judgement: does it provide strong support for the theory (green light), does it only give reasonable support (amber) or does the comment only provide weak commentary (red light). Be sure to explain the judgements you make and which theory the comments relate to.

Comment	Explanation of judgement:
Wason task (Cosmides 1989) found most people cannot solve an abstract relationship task but when the task is placed in a social context it is easily solved. This leads to the suggestion of a cheat detection mechanism.	
Hill & Kaplan (1988) found men of the Ache people, Paraguay did not share plant food and insect grubs beyond the immediate family. However, they did share meat with others.	
Wrangham (1975) suggests that meat sharing is not to forge alliances but to prevent the need to defend a kill from others or chase scavengers so saving themselves energy.	
Mitani & Watts (2001) found male chimpanzees in Uganda shared meat with each other more than with females. Forming alliances could be an important aspect of the social group.	

▶ Lesson notes p.53

Gut reactions

Read the statement then give your gut reaction in the box provided. Once all gut reactions have been made use your textbook (pages 132–133 in *A2 Complete Companion*) to find out about related evidence.

Use the PEE layout to ensure you make effective comments.

Comment

There is a genetic basis to intelligence. Bouchard & McGue (1981) estimated an average concordance rate (degree to which intelligence level was the same for two individuals) of IQ for DZ twins reared together of 60%, yet for MZ twins reared apart the concordance rate was much higher 75%.

Gut reaction (write anything you like, circle the area your reaction relates to)
Question, Ethical issue. Real-life experience, Agree/disagree, Comment on data, Nature/nurture, Other

Related research

Point (e.g. supporting the findings outlined above/ refuting evidence):	Evidence (research or issue that relates to the point made):	Expansion (explain the impact the evidence has on Bouchard & McGue's work):

Comment

Hill *et al.* (1999) divided children aged 6 to 15 years into two groups: the 'super-brights' with a mean IQ of 136 and the 'averages' with a mean IQ of 103. The gene IGF2R occurred in twice as many children in the high IQ group (36%) as in the average group (16%).

Gut reaction (write anything you like, circle the area your reaction relates to)
Question, Ethical issue. Real-life experience, Agree/disagree, Comment on data, Nature/nurture, Other

Related research

Point (e.g. supporting Hill *et al.*'s findings/criticising the research):	Evidence (research or issue that relates to the point made):	Expansion (explain the impact the evidence has on Hill *et al.*'s work):

▶ Lesson notes p.53

Organising information

Record key words in the middle section

In the second band summarise the main ideas related to the factor

The third band should display research evidence

In the outer band make a comment on the research evidence

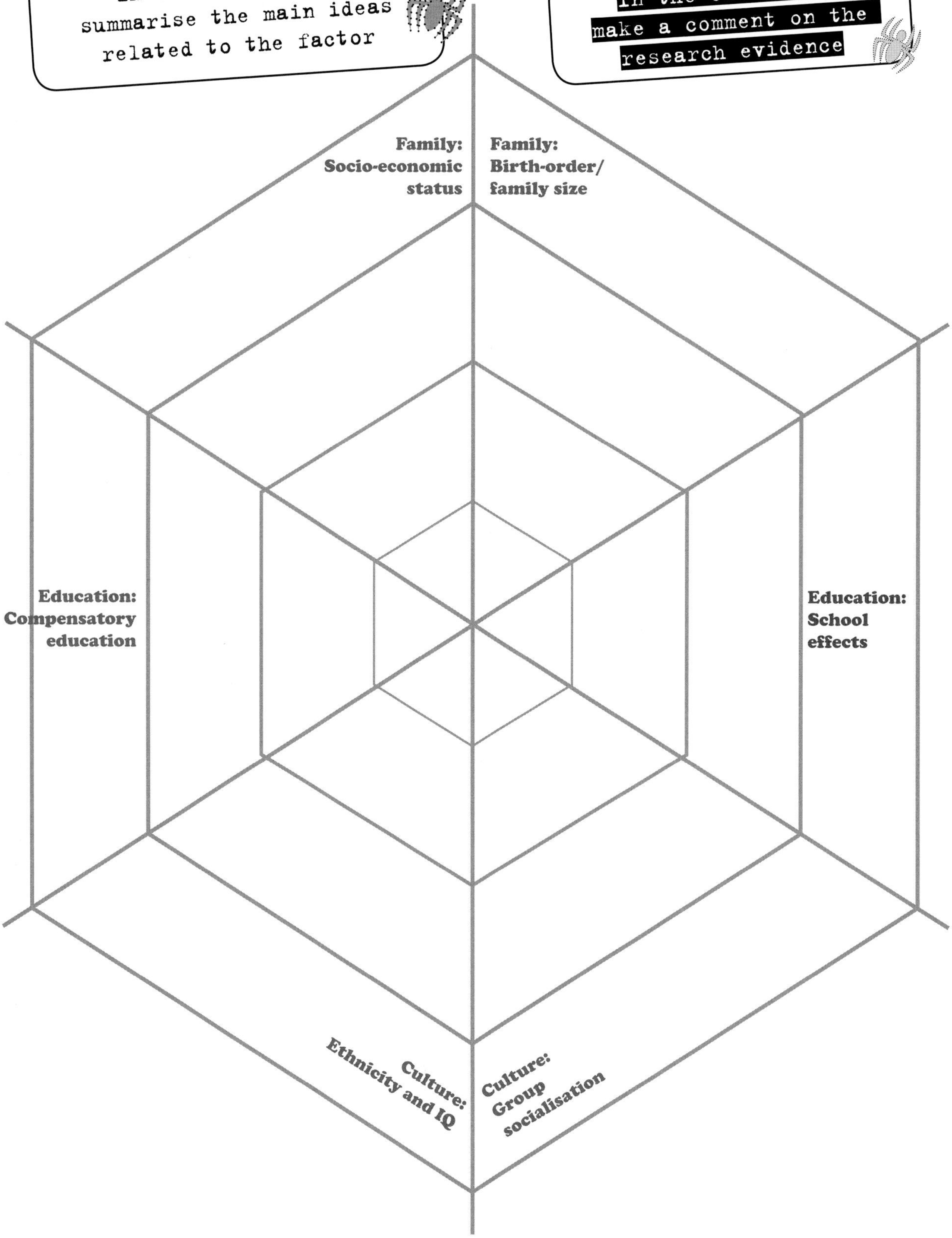

Family: Socio-economic status

Family: Birth-order/ family size

Education: Compensatory education

Education: School effects

Culture: Ethnicity and IQ

Culture: Group socialisation

▶ Lesson notes p.53

Piaget's postcards

Sender___________________

I know that…

To ___________________

I would like to know about…

From___________________

In answer to your request I can tell you…

Lost in post, found by___________________

I can add…

▶ Lesson notes p.54

Reading for meaning

The zone of proximal development (ZPD) is a key concept in Vygotsky's theory. It is defined as the distance between an individual's actual development level (as determined by independent problem solving) and the level of potential development (as determined through problem solving under adult guidance or in collaboration with more adult peers). 'What a child can do in cooperation today he can do alone tomorrow' (Vygotsky, 1934). Unlike Piaget, Vygotsky believed that learning or cognitive development does not take place in the area of current development (where the child already is), nor does it take place too far ahead of what the child can already do independently. In the former instance, nothing new would be learnt, in that the new challenges would be too far ahead from the child's current knowledge to be useful. A child's ZPD is the region where cognitive development takes place. The learner is aided by cultural influences (e.g. experts and language). At first learning is between people (social) and later it becomes internalised (individual).

Less important words here

Doodle any images that spring to mind
Can you represent Vygotsky's ideas in a diagram?

The three key points I must remember are...

▶ Lesson notes p.54

Bruner word web

- Connect related words with the same coloured ink.
- Be sure to explain why each word is connected.

Early childhood

Asking questions

Enactive

Key to knowledge

ACTION-BASED SKILLS

Image-based skills

Narrative thinking

Iconic

Adolescence

Spatial awareness

Using a diagram of a concept

Analytic thinking

Manipulating objects

Intuitive thinking

Middle childhood

Symbolic

Language-based skills

Visual recognition

Paradigmatic thinking

Extension

- *Choose at least one of the word webs you have created and use the words to produce an outline of one aspect of Bruner's theory of cognitive development.*

▶ Lesson notes p.55

Save or steal?

For each of the theorists, record two basic points relating to the application of their theory to education.

My basic Piaget points	My basic Vygotsky points	My basic Bruner points
1.	1.	1.
2.	2.	2.

Now record two basic points made by a neighbour.

My neighbour's Piaget points	My neighbour's Vygotsky points	My neighbour's Bruner points
1.	1.	1.
2.	2.	2.

Read the four points you have gathered for each theorist. You can only choose two points per theorist. Decide whether to **save** your points or **steal** a neighbour's ideas. Highlight the comments you wish to keep.

Working with your neighbour, produce two 50-word criticisms for each theorist.

Our Piaget criticisms	Our Vygotsky criticisms	Our Bruner criticisms
1.	1.	1.
2.	2.	2.

▶ Lesson notes p.55

Synoptic - i- tree

Starting with the branches on the left, record the problems of gender and cultural bias you can identify from simply reading about Kohlberg's theory.

Halfway through the lesson stop and add your new understanding of the problems Kohlberg's theory faces to the middle branches.

As a plenary add any final knowledge gained to the branches on the right.

At the end of the activity you should have comments relating to gender and cultural bias

halfway

start

plenary

▶ Lesson notes p.56

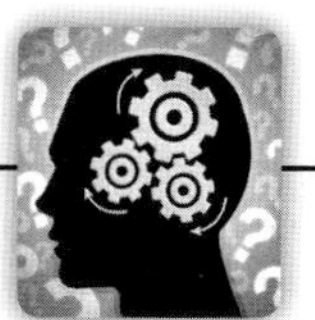

Levels of prosocial reasoning

Read the following scenario based on Eisenberg's prosocial stories. For each speech bubble identify the age of the speaker and the level of prosocial development they are functioning at.

If she ignored the puppy she knows she would be doing wrong. Animals need humans' help.

Age:

Level:

The police and the puppy's owners would see Ebony as a good person if she helped, so she should take the puppy to the police station.

Age:

Level:

Ebony was on her way to her friend's house to watch a film on DVD that she missed when it was released at the cinema. On the way she sees a puppy by the side of the road. The puppy seems scared and lost, no owner can be seen. Ebony knows the local police station is two streets away and she could take the puppy there. However, the police station is in the opposite direction to her friend's house. If she takes the puppy she will be late to her friend's house and miss the start of the film.

What should Ebony do? Why?

Level:

Age:

Ebony should carry on to her friend's house. She doesn't want to miss the start of the film or risk her friend being annoyed that she is late.

Ebony would feel bad if she ignored the puppy and left it at the side of the road so she should help and take it to the police station.

Age:

Level:

The puppy is lost and needs help so Ebony should help.

Level:

Age:

Complete the following sentences

Eisenberg disagreed with Kohlberg's theory of moral understanding...

Higher levels of prosocial development cannot be reached if empathy is lacking...

The development of theory of mind is an important aspect of prosocial development...

▶ Lesson notes p.56

Evaluation of sense of self studies

Point	Evidence	Expansion
Not all psychologists agree that infants are born with a rudimentary sense of self, or a basic ability to distinguish themselves from others.	Freudians such as Mahler *et al.* (1973) argue that at birth an infant has no sense of separateness from his/her mother.	These contrasting views represent the nature / nurture argument...

Point	Evidence	Expansion
Development of self-recognition may be, in part, dependent on the infant's attachment type, which may explain individual differences in the development of self-recognition.	Pipp *et al.* (1992) found faster development in securely attached infants and in babies raised to be independent (Borke *et al.* 2007).	These findings might explain cultural differences in the development of self-recognition because...

Point	Evidence	Expansion
Theory of mind (ToM) starts appearing at around three or four years of age. It is argued it is related to a biological pattern of maturation.	Baron-Cohen (1995) proposed a ToM module: a specific mechanism that matures in the brain around the age of four.	However, it may be unwise to ignore the impact of a child's environment...

Point	Evidence	Expansion
The mirror test investigates self-awareness in non-human animals. A smudge of ink is placed on the face and they are shown their reflection in a mirror, if the animal sees the reflection as themselves they attempt to wipe the smudge off their face.	Chimpanzees, bonobos and orang-utans can recognise their reflection in a mirror as can dolphins and killer whales. Recent research suggests that elephants can too.	The use of non-animals in research is a controversial issue because...

▶ Lesson notes p.57

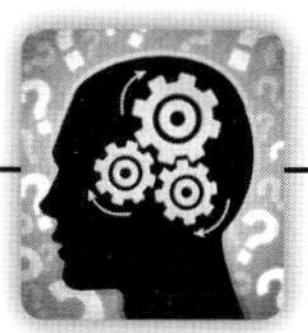

Building blocks

In your textbook (pages 154–155 *A2 Complete Companion*) read about research into children's understanding of others. Identify six key words from the passage and record them in the blocks below.

Now share your ideas with others in your class and record their words in the blocks below.

As a group, decide which words are the most relevant and must be included in any description of research into children's understanding of others. Use these words to write a 300-word description of the development of a child's understanding of others.

▶ Lesson notes p.57

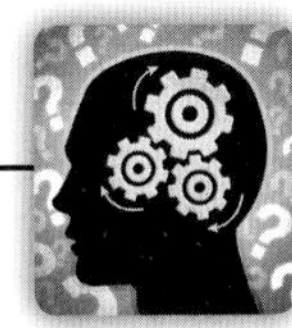

Stepping stones

Move from the bottom of the page to the top of the page by answering the question in a stepping stone. The next stone you choose must be touching the stone you have just answered.

Some stones may be easier than others: challenge yourself.

What do you think about current research into mirror neurons?

How can the nature/nurture debate been seen in mirror neuron research?

Why might reducing complex behaviour to the action of mirror neurons be problematic?

WHY MAY IT BE UNWISE TO GENERALISE FINDINGS FROM ANIMAL STUDIES TO HUMANS?

What criticisms have been made about the reality of mirror neurons?

What behaviours have mirror neurons been linked to?

How does the discovery of mirror neurons lend support to simulation theory?

What aspects of social cognition could mirror neurons be involved with?

Why don't we instinctively imitate all that we observe?

What is behaviour regulation?

WHY IS IMITATION IMPORTANT TO THE DEVELOPMENT OF LEARNING?

How many mirror neurons did Slack's (2007) research indentify?

What are intransitive actions?

When are mirror neurons activated?

What do mirror neurons allow us to do?

In what animal were mirror neurons first identified?

What brain areas seem to be associated with mirror neurons?

What does fMRI stand for?

What are mirror neurons?

Start here

▶ Lesson notes p.57

Matching clinical key terms

Delusions	For a significant portion of the time since the onset of the disturbance, one or more major areas of functioning such as work, interpersonal relations, or self-care are markedly below the level achieved prior to the onset.
Disorganised thinking	The reduction of, or inability to, persist in goal-directed behaviour (for example, sitting in the house for hours every day, doing nothing).
Affective flattening	These are unreal perceptions of the environment that are usually auditory (e.g. hearing voices) but may also be visual (seeing lights, objects or faces), olfactory (smelling things) or tactile (e.g. feeling that bugs are crawling on or under the skin).
Alogia	This refers to bizarre and abnormal motor movements. For example, holding the body in a rigid stance, moving in a frenzied way, peculiar facial movements, copying movements of others.
Social/occupational dysfunction	Bizarre beliefs that *seem* real to the person with schizophrenia, but they are not real. Sometimes these beliefs can be paranoid (i.e. persecutory) and sometimes involve themselves, e.g. inflated belief about their own importance.
Avolition	Poverty of speech, characterised by the lessening of speech fluency and productivity, this is thought to reflect slowed or blocked thoughts.
Hallucinations	A reduction in the range and intensity of emotional expression, including facial expression, voice tone, eye contact, and body language.
Catatonic behaviour	The feeling that thoughts have been inserted or withdrawn from the mind. In some cases the person may believe their thoughts are being broadcast so that others can hear them.

Tasks

- Match the schizophrenic clinical key terms to the definitions on the right.
- Highlight which of the characteristics you think are positive symptoms of schizophrenia and which are negative using different colours.

▶ Lesson notes p.58

It's not as clear cut as you think 1

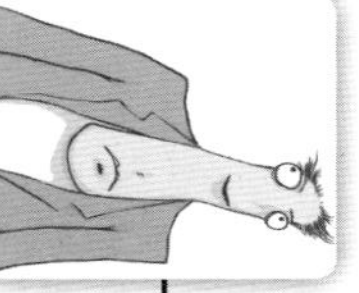

Schizophrenia

Bipolar disorder

Depression

▶ Lesson notes p.58

It's not as clear cut as you think 2

There is a tendency to think that the diagnosis of mental disorders is objective, clear cut and relatively simple. However, this is far from the case. Many disorders share symptoms with other disorders, which makes the jobs of psychiatrists and psychologists very difficult to determine who has a mental disorder and which mental disorder they have.

Tasks

1. Below is a list of symptoms that can occur in schizophrenia, bipolar disorder and/or depression. Write each of these symptoms into the appropriate place in the Venn diagram on **Handout 112**.
2. Use the Internet (be careful which sites you use) or your textbook to check and amend your answers. Were there any you were surprised about?
3. Looking at your Venn diagram, think about the difficulty of diagnosing mental disorders *reliably*. What problems might psychologists and psychiatrists face?
4. Comment on the issues this Venn diagram might raise for the *validity* of mental disorder diagnosis.

- Depressed mood most of the day, nearly every day
- Affective flattening
- Alogia (poverty of speech)
- Periods of mania (elevated mood)
- Psychomotor disturbances
- Insomnia or hypersomnia
- Subjective experience that thoughts are racing
- Inflated self-esteem and feelings/beliefs of grandiosity
- Delusions
- Inability to do everyday tasks
- Difficulty concentrating
- Feelings of worthlessness
- Excessive involvement in pleasurable activities
- Depressed mood most of the day, nearly every day without any periods of elevated mood (mania)
- Disorganised speech
- Hallucinations
- Significant weight loss or weight gain
- Recurrent thoughts of suicide
- Alternating moods between depression and mania

▶ Lesson notes p.58

Being synoptic – nature or nurture?

In order to get the highest marks in A2 Psychology, your essays must contain **synoptic elements**. One way in which you can do this is to link your knowledge and analysis of a topic to a **psychological debate**.

One debate centres on **nature vs. nurture** – do people become schizophrenic as a result of genetics/biology, or their environment and upbringing?

Using the speech bubbles below, discuss this debate using genetic evidence and evaluation of that evidence.

Outline the findings of a study that suggests that schizophrenia is genetic. Why do the results implicate the role of genes?

One study that indicates schizophrenia has a genetic basis found… This suggests…, because…

Outline an evaluation of the evidence presented above, or present evidence that supports the nurture argument.

However, it could be argued that…

What conclusion can be drawn in terms of the nature vs. nurture debate?

As such…

▶ Lesson notes p.59

Double binds – no win situation!

'You need to be more independent!'

Sarah kept annoying her mother by repeating everything she said.

After a few minutes of this her mother exclaimed, 'For goodness sake Sarah, would you like a smack?'

'If you loved me you would do this little thing for me'

When Josh arrived home from school she asked him to give her a hug.

When Josh gave her a hug she seemed to stiffen up and look away. She then broke away, turned round and said, 'I love you'.

All of the boxes above contain an example of what psychologists call **double binds**.

Double binds refer to contradictory messages and where an individual cannot 'win' in that situation. Bateson *et al.* (1956) suggests that children who received more of these messages from their parents are more likely to go on to develop schizophrenia.

Task:

In your notes, explain why each example might be considered a **double bind.**

▶ Lesson notes p.59

Connect 4

Nature vs. Nurture

Link...

Neurotransmitters...

Link...

Antipsychotic medication...

Link...

Ethics...

▶ Lesson notes p.60

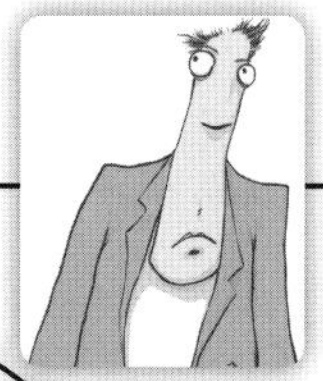

Storytime: 'The Magic shoes'

Twenty past six every Thursday was the time Dave dreaded the most. 'Are you ready?' his wife Sue would call up from the hallway while he tried to desperately think of an excuse to get out of their weekly salsa dancing class. 'Yes,' he'd inevitably gloomily reply.

On the drive to his local community centre Dave would imagine he was off down to the pub with his mates instead, before predictions of the insults dance instructor Hulio would have in store for him invaded his thoughts. 'Spaghetti arms' and 'Billy bow legs' had been last week's favourites.

As they entered the hall, Dave's stomach twisted into a knot at the sound of the salsa music blaring from Hulio's CD player. With a sigh he grabbed Sue's hand and walked towards his fate.

As the previous four weeks' classes had shown, try as he might, Dave was just a horrible dancer. He just couldn't seem to pick up the steps like everyone else, and even when he did manage a few, he was always a second behind. As he told himself for the millionth time that night 'you're doing this for Sue', he heard a loud 'Psssst!' behind him.

Turning around, Dave saw an unfamiliar face looking at him. 'I'm Clive,' the man said, 'I've been watching your moves.' Dave shifted from one foot to the other, embarrassed, not knowing where to look.

'No, don't worry – I want to tell you I think I might have something that will work for you,' Clive said, nodding down at his feet 'see these shoes? They're magic. I was just like you before I found them, but once I put them on I never looked back.' As he spoke, Clive broke into a spin before giving a perfect performance of the choreography Dave had tried – and failed – to pick up over the last month.

Dave's mouth fell open. 'I know, pretty magic ay?', said Clive, 'but do you know what the best part is? I'll let you buy them – £50.'

'Deal,' said Dave, looking behind him to check Sue was still chatting to her friend Anne. As Clive took Dave's money and handed over the shoes, he broke out into a huge grin, thinking smugly to himself, 'I can't believe he bought those fake shoes! That was the easiest money I've ever made'.

Dave couldn't wait to get home and try out his new shoes. As soon as he was sure Sue had fallen asleep that night, he got up and went down to living room. To his utter amazement he could remember the routine and not only that, he thought he was pretty good.

For the first time ever, Dave looked forward to twenty past six the next Thursday and couldn't wait to see Hulio's face when he started dancing.

The moment was just as good as Dave had hoped – gradually everyone around him stopped and stared as he swung Sue around with perfect timing and movement. 'I don't believe it,' said Hulio, open-mouthed.

Turning around to see the amazed faces around him, Dave caught sight of Clive at the back of the room. He wondered for a moment why Clive looked more surprised than everyone else but as the class all burst into applause suddenly it was only dancing – and how good he was – on Dave's mind.

By Alana Clogan (2009)

▶ Lesson notes p.60

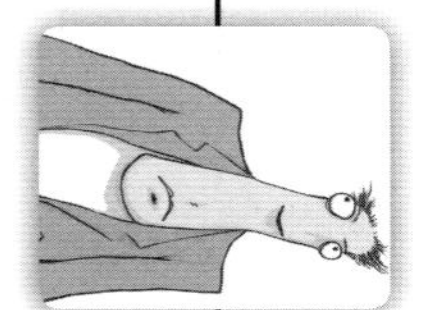

Evaluation and elaboration: CBT

In Unit 4, like all of your Psychology A level, you are expected to be able to evaluate aspects of psychology. In this case the handout requires you to evaluate **CBT as a psychological therapy of schizophrenia**. Many students miss out on evaluation marks because they do not elaborate their comments and evaluations in sufficient detail to get the full marks. To reach the highest marks your evaluations must be 'effective' and show evidence of synopticity.

Your task here is to match up the evaluation points from the left, further and further to the right in order to increase your evaluation marks (remember though that you may only have time for 2-3 evaluation points).

Rudimentary → Basic → Reasonable → Effective

Rudimentary

- One strength is that CBT has been supported by empirical research.
- Further support for CBT comes from studies that indicate patients receiving CBT recover to a greater extent than those taking medication alone.
- A problem with much of the research in this area is subject attrition.
- Another problem with CBT is that it is not suitable for some types of patient.

Basic

- For example, in Kingdon and Kirschen's (2006) study of 142 schizophrenic patients they found that many of the patients were deemed unsuitable for CBT because psychiatrists believed they would not fully engage with the therapy.
- For example, Gould *et al.* (2001) found that all seven studies in their meta-analysis reported a statistically significant decrease in the positive symptoms of schizophrenia post-treatment.
- For example, those receiving CBT as well as medication experience fewer hallucinations and delusions, a 25-50% reduction in recovery time (Drury *et al.* 1996), and lower drop-out rates and greater patient satisfaction (Kuipers *et al.* 1997).
- This refers to the problem of patients dropping out of the research sample or refusing to cooperate with the researcher midway through the study.

Reasonable

- This perhaps indicates that there is more to schizophrenia than abnormal levels of neurotransmitters and that there is also a need to address psychological abnormalities in thinking.
- However, most studies of the effectiveness of CBT have been conducted at the same time with antipsychotic medication.
- This results in a biased sample as it could be, for example, that researchers are most likely to lose data from the patients with the most severe expression of schizophrenia.
- In particular they found that older patients were deemed less suitable than younger patients.

Effective

- As a result, the outcome results of CBT studies perhaps show the therapy to be more effective than it actually is.
- Therefore it is very difficult to assess the effectiveness of CBT independent of biological therapies and unpick the variables involved in the recovery of schizophrenic patients.
- This presents a problem for the cognitive approach, since it suggests that maladaptive thinking is the cause of schizophrenia. As such a cognitive therapy should be effective and suitable for all those suffering from maladaptive thinking since it is the very origin of their problems.
- However, some could argue that the improved recovery measures are the result of a placebo effect, with patients improving because they expect to, rather than the actual action of CBT.

▶ Lesson notes p.60

Diagnosing depression

Depression is a mood disorder. Although depression and mania (bipolar disorder) are both key emotions, most people only suffer from depression (unipolar disorder). Depression is common: ranked first in the top ten causes of disability worldwide. Read the following statements and identify the depressive symptom portrayed.

Symptoms

Difficulties in sleeping (insomnia).	Loss of interest and pleasure in usual activities.	Shift in activity level, becoming lethargic/agitated.	Loss of energy and great fatigue.	Negative self-concept, feeling worthless or guilty.
Sad, depressed mood.	Difficulty in concentrating.	Recurrent thoughts of death or suicide.	Poor appetite and weight loss or increased appetite and weight gain.	

I just feel really empty, as if there is nothing inside of me: hollowed out.

I really am unlikeable. I have no friends, only people who tolerate me. It's understandable nobody wishes to be with me; I'm dull and talentless.

I'm tired all the time. Just can't seem to drag myself out of bed each morning.

I feel so trapped within myself, suicide seems like the only solution.

I don't seem to have any enthusiasm anymore.

Will I ever get to sleep? I roam around the house at night watching the hours pass.

Meal times are terrible, I stare at the food in front of me but cannot bring myself to eat.

I drum my fingers on surfaces, pace around the room, fidget in my chair. I can't seem to settle.

Thoughts trickle through my head. I find it hard to make a final decision.

The symptoms of depression can be grouped into four main domains:

Affective	Cognitive	Behavioural	Physical
depressed **mood**, sadness, feeling low	feeling guilty, **thinking** of self as worthless	**social** withdrawal, restlessness	Changes in **bodily** states, e.g. sleep, appetite

Assign each domain a colour then colour code the speech bubbles accordingly.

The exam could ask you to: 'Outline clinical characteristics of depression' (5 marks)

Extension task: Identify three characteristics of depression, give an example for each and state the domain.

▶ Lesson notes p.62

Developing depression discussions: biochemistry

Your PSYA4 Individual difference essay is marked out of 25 but 16 of these marks are for evaluation. Many students miss out on evaluation marks because they do not ***elaborate*** their comments sufficiently to get the full marks. Here is a brief guide to PSYA4 evaluation: Top band: Effective with coherent elaboration, Upper middle band: Reasonable elaboration, Lower middle band: Basic, only some evidence of elaboration, Bottom band: Rudimentary with material used ineffectually.

Your task here is to match up the evaluation points from the left, further and further to the right in order to increase your AO2 marks…

Rudimentary	Basic	Reasonable	Effective
One problem is that the effects of drugs are not immediate.	Delgano *et al.* (1990) suggest it is more likely that serotonin plays a *contributing* role in mood regulation as opposed to a *causal* role in depression.	If it were, all individuals should improve as a result of the drug.	In a way, this is like saying a lack of rash cream (corticosteroids) causes rashes, just because you observe that rash cream (corticosteroids) reduces a rash.
One problem is individual differences, drugs affect people in different ways.	Namely, is it serotonin that causes the symptoms of depression, or could it be that the symptoms of depression cause low levels of serotonin?	Low levels of neurotransmitter therefore cannot be the simple explanation for depression.	It may be that the drugs reduce depression by increasing the sensitivity of the receiving neurons, which takes some time to develop and explains how neurotransmitters affect depression.
There is also an issue linking cause and effect.	For example, not every depressed person is helped by taking serotonin-based drugs. This suggests that there are other causes for this disorder other than low serotonin activity.	Martin *et al.* (2001) compared the effects of antidepressant drugs with therapy using brain scanning and found patients showed the *same* changes in levels of serotonin.	This shows neurotransmitter levels such as serotonin *can* be caused by psychological factors such as mood, rather than just the other way around (i.e. serotonin causing changes in mood).
Some argue that while serotonin is a factor in depression, it does not cause the illness.	It normally takes several weeks before the effects of antidepressants on depression can be detected despite the fact that antidepressants raise the serotonin level immediately.	They support this saying it is a mistake to think depression is caused by decreased serotonin just because serotonin-based drugs reduce depression.	This is supported by the finding that some people who have low serotonin levels stay depression free, whereas others do not.

▶ Lesson notes p.62

Consideration continuums

It would help your essay writing if you could outline critical points for each explanation of depression to help you discuss explanations of depression. It may also be useful to consider one issue or debate relevant to these explanations.

Choose one psychological explanation of depression and complete each continuum. Be sure to give elaborated reasons for the position you adopt on each scale.

Six sentence summary of chosen psychological explanation

Psychological explanations of depression

Psychodynamic (Morning and melancholia),

Cognitive (Beck, learned helplessness, hopelessness),

Social-cultural (life events, social networks and skills).

Evidence to support the explanation

Little supporting evidence ⟷ Evidence provides strong support

Explanation of continuum position assigned

Psychological approach underlying the explanation

Considerable flaws with general approach ⟷ Considerable strengths with general approach

Explanation of continuum position assigned

▶ Lesson notes p.63

Cobweb commentary

Stick relevant comment here

Stick relevant comment here

Stick relevant comment here

Stick relevant comment here

To evaluate Beck's theory of depression, three important questions should be asked.

Does changing the way a person thinks reduce their depressive mood?

Do depressed people think differently to clinically normal people?

Does negative thinking occur before or after the onset (beginning) of depression?

Stick relevant comment here

Stick relevant comment here

Cut out the comment boxes below and stick them onto the correct web to build an elaborated evaluation of Beck's theory of depression. Make sure each comment adds a new layer of thought to the previous statement.

It is important to ask this question because Beck's theory is based on the assumption that depressed people ***do*** think differently, indeed this is the cause of their disorder.

It is important to ask this question because Beck believed negative thinking was the ***cause*** of depression so it should be found before the onset – otherwise negative thinking is only an ***effect*** of depression.

Cognitive-behavioural therapies have been shown to be very helpful in the alleviation of the symptoms of depression – thus supporting the idea that negative thinking is the cause.

Gotlib and Hammen (1992) reviewed hundreds of studies in this area and conclude there is **very** strong evidence for higher levels of negative thinking in depressed people.

It is important to ask this question because the answer would give a good indication of whether negative thinking is the cause of depression – if so, removing negative thinking should remove the mood.

Many of the studies are based on correlational data so are unable to determine cause and effect relationships. Unfortunately, there have been very few longitudinal studies – but those that there are have failed to show that cognitive vulnerability is a predictor of depression.

▶ Lesson notes p.63

123

Formulating evaluations

Using information in your textbook, decide what each image represents and explain the point in your own words.

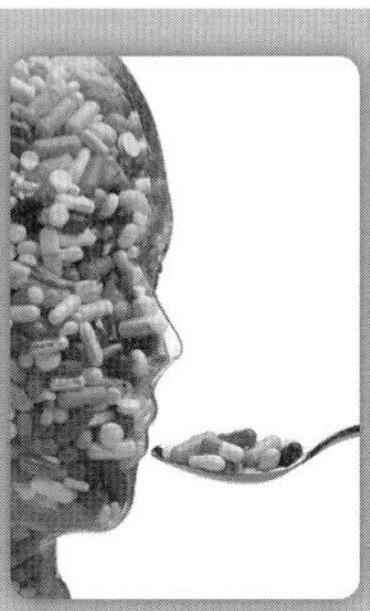

The point is...	Evidence relating to the point...	Expansion/evaluation...

The point is...	Evidence relating to the point...	Expansion/evaluation...

The point is...	Evidence relating to the point...	Expansion/evaluation...

The point is...	Evidence relating to the point...	Expansion/evaluation...

▶ Lesson notes p.63

Quick questions

Answer three questions shown below: one from the top row, one from the middle and one from the bottom.

Synoptic comments

How can I use knowledge of psychodynamic therapy for depression to comment on the free will/determinism debate?	**How can the use of psychodynamic therapies for depression be presented as an example of reductionism?**	In what way could the use of psychodynamic therapy contribute to the benefit of society?	What ethical concerns are associated with the use of psychodynamic therapy in general and as an alternative to biological treatments?

AO2: Evaluating

What does research evidence suggest about the usefulness of psychodynamic therapy as a treatment for depression?	Would this form of therapy be appropriate for all sufferers of depression?	Why are modern-day therapies (e.g. PIT/BDT) more suitable for patients compared to classical psychotherapy?	What factors influence the success of psychological therapy?

AO1: Outlining

Which three sentences do you feel are most relevant to your understanding of the psychodynamic therapy for depression?	If a GCSE student asked you about the therapy, which part are you most likely to explain? Which part would be most difficult to explain?	Can you summarise the therapy in four sentences?	What is the therapist's role in a psychoanalytic therapy session?

Now join with another student to build an essay response to the following question.

*Outline and evaluate **one** psychological therapy used in the treatment of depression. (25 marks)*

Use at least one of your quick question answers from the bottom line for the AO1 'outline' section.

Use at least two (you could even consider three) quick question answers from the AO2 Evaluation middle row.

Finish by using one synoptic comment from the top row.

▶ Lesson notes p.64

Suggesting solutions

Read the case study carefully. Decide on the therapy you feel would be most helpful to the client and that which would be least beneficial to the patient.

Make sure you explain your choices in detail and support your choice with research evidence.

Greta suffers from unipolar depression. She often experiences feelings of hopelessness and worries constantly that she is a burden to others; she feels guilty for having depression. This has affected her work, as she believes she cannot cope, some days she finds it difficult to even get up let alone travel to work. She reports losing interest in food and finds sleeping difficult. Previously Greta was in a relationship, which she describes as very controlling. Following the breakdown of this relationship Greta found herself staying at home more, avoiding friends and losing enthusiasm for life in general. Although she now realises her partner was very manipulative, she blames herself for how she was treated.

Following a discussion with her GP, Greta understands she needs to seek some form of help for her depression. She recognises her thought processes are affecting her emotionally and socially. Additionally, she is desperate to improve her energy levels and regain her appetite.

Therapy I would be most likely to suggest:

Reasons for choice:

Evidence to support choice:

Therapy I would be least likely to suggest:

Reasons for decision:

Evidence to support decision:

▶ Lesson notes p.64

Clinical characteristics crossword

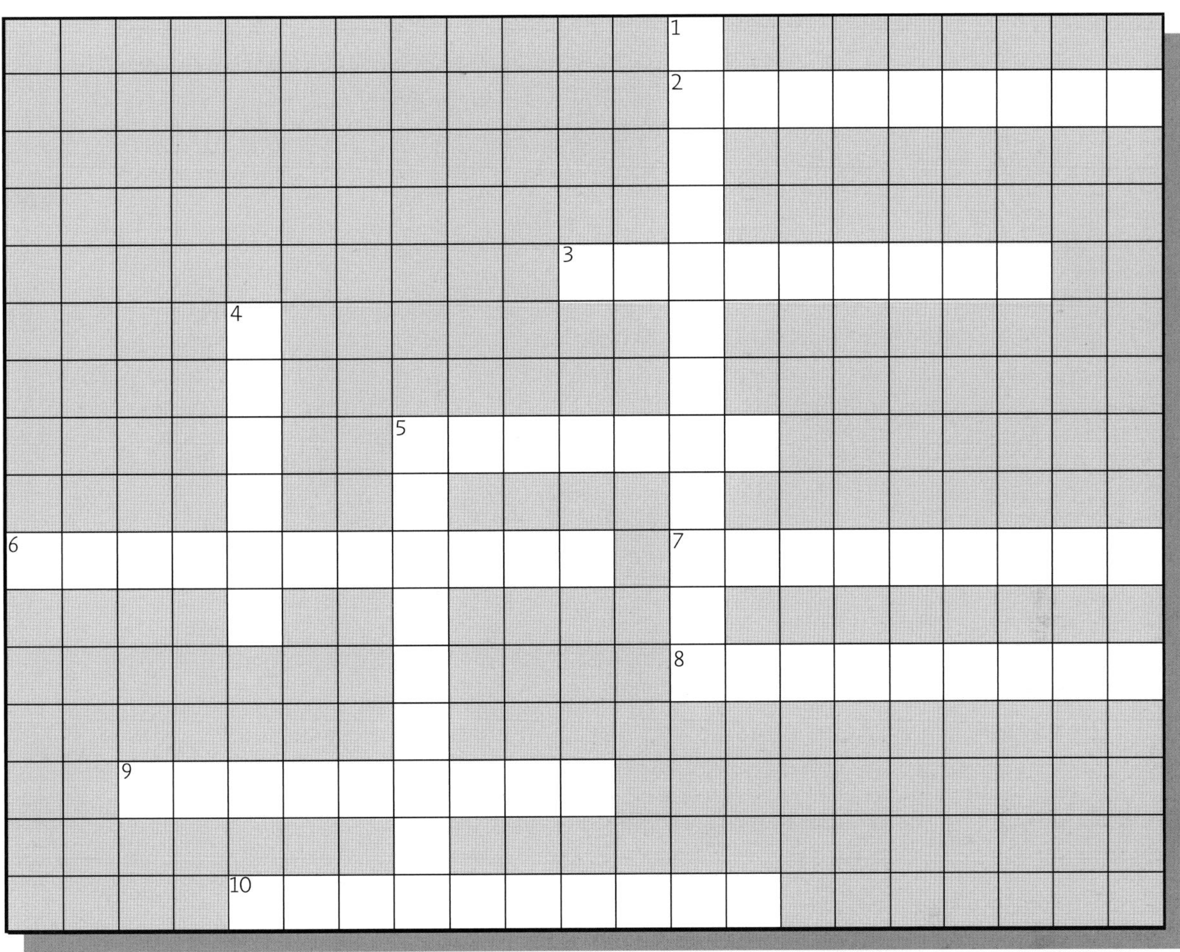

Down

1. A common symptom associated with phobias. Involves a pounding heart, difficulty breathing, dizziness and stomach upset. Plural. (5,7)

4. The type of phobia related to the more normal anxieties we feel when having to, for example, speak in public. (5)

5. This behaviour refers to when a sufferer deliberately keeps away from the phobic stimulus or prevents the situation from happening. (9)

Across

2. To be diagnosed a phobic, the anxiety is not better ___________for by another mental disorder, e.g. OCD. (9)

3. The fear of the phobic stimulus is exceeding normal and acceptable limits. (9)

5. Exposure to the phobic stimulus almost always provokes an ________ response. (7)

6. The fear of being trapped in a public place where escape is difficult or embarrassing. (11)

7. Sufferers recognise that their fear is unreasonable. However, this feature may be missing in _________. (8)

8. A type of phobia. Refers to fears of certain objects or situations. (8)

9. In individuals under 18 years of age the duration has to be at least ________ ________. (3,6)

10. The phobia ___________ significantly with the person's normal routine, relationships or occupation. (10)

▶ Lesson notes p.65

Prepotency and preparedness 1

- Evolutionary psychologists propose that phobias are related to 'ancient fears' such as fear of snakes, heights, storms, darkness, strangeness, separation and leaving the home range. Other things (such as leaves and stones), which were part of our ancestral environment but which posed no danger, have not become ancient fears. Things that are dangerous today (such as cars and electricity) rarely develop into phobias.
- The suggestion, therefore, is that we inherit a predisposition to have certain fears. There are a couple of possible options:
    - It may be that we actually inherit a predisposition to be afraid of certain classes of objects (these objects have **prepotency**). One suggestion is that we fear **strange** animals, i.e. those that are very different from the human form, such as texture of skin and number of limbs.
    - Or, we inherit a readiness (**preparedness**) to rapidly learn an association between (potentially life threatening) stimuli and fear.
- Bennet-Levy and Marteau (1984) attempted to investigate the first possibility – that we inherit a fear of animals that are discrepant to the human form or who have aversive stimulus configurations (e.g. sliminess).

Read the details of the study below, and then answer the discussion questions.

Aim

To investigate inherited and learned explanations for fear of animals.

Method

Participants are asked to rate 29 animals using a simple 3-point rating scale – see **Handout 128**. Using these scales, they are asked to rate each animal in terms of how fearful, harmful and strange they think it is. Strangeness may be rated in terms of ugliness/sliminess/speediness.

Analysis

The data generated from the questionnaire (see **Handout 128**) is used to calculate a correlation coefficient for two sets of data:

- A correlation coefficient for fearfulness and harmfulness.
- A correlation coefficient for fearfulness and strangeness.

Questions and discussion

- Which correlation coefficient would you expect to be larger if the prepotency explanation is supported? Why?
- Which correlation coefficient would you expect to be larger if the preparedness explanation is supported? Why?
- What do you conclude from your results (if you have used **Handout 128**)?
- What methodological problems might there be with the study?

▶ Lesson notes p.66

Prepotency and preparedness 2

For each animal listed below rate it on a scale of 1–3 for fearfulness, harmfulness and strangeness, where 3 is very fearful, very harmful or very strange. Circle your answer.

	Fearfulness			Harmfulness			Strangeness		
	Not afraid	Quite afraid	Very afraid	Not harmful	Quite harmful	Very harmful	Not strange	Quite strange	Very strange
Jellyfish	1	2	3	1	2	3	1	2	3
Squirrel	1	2	3	1	2	3	1	2	3
Ant	1	2	3	1	2	3	1	2	3
Seal	1	2	3	1	2	3	1	2	3
Lamb	1	2	3	1	2	3	1	2	3
Spaniel	1	2	3	1	2	3	1	2	3
Cat	1	2	3	1	2	3	1	2	3
Rabbit	1	2	3	1	2	3	1	2	3
Moth	1	2	3	1	2	3	1	2	3
Mouse	1	2	3	1	2	3	1	2	3
Hamster	1	2	3	1	2	3	1	2	3
Slug	1	2	3	1	2	3	1	2	3
Beetle	1	2	3	1	2	3	1	2	3
Butterfly	1	2	3	1	2	3	1	2	3
Rat	1	2	3	1	2	3	1	2	3
Chimp	1	2	3	1	2	3	1	2	3
Lizard	1	2	3	1	2	3	1	2	3
Tortoise	1	2	3	1	2	3	1	2	3
Blackbird	1	2	3	1	2	3	1	2	3
Caterpillar	1	2	3	1	2	3	1	2	3
Ladybird	1	2	3	1	2	3	1	2	3
Grasshopper	1	2	3	1	2	3	1	2	3
Robin	1	2	3	1	2	3	1	2	3
Frog	1	2	3	1	2	3	1	2	3
Spider	1	2	3	1	2	3	1	2	3
Crow	1	2	3	1	2	3	1	2	3
Grass snake	1	2	3	1	2	3	1	2	3
Worm	1	2	3	1	2	3	1	2	3
Cockroach	1	2	3	1	2	3	1	2	3

▶ Lesson notes p.66

Broken pieces

A major claim made against the behavioural explanation is the idea that phobias are *inherited* rather than *learnt*. ●

● As such, the argument made against this behavioural explanation is that it is too focussed on the role of nurture and therefore ignoring the evidence that nature also has an influence.

However, this explanation also struggles to explain some individual differences. For example, why one sibling might fear dogs but another does not, when they had both previously observed their mother being bitten by a dog. ●

● This supports the explanation because it verifies the suggestion that phobias occur when a person associates a previously neutral stimulus (e.g. dog) with a fear response, i.e. that phobias are learnt as a result of the environment.

One supporting argument for the conditioning explanation is that people with phobias can often recall a specific incident when their phobia appeared (Sue *et al*., 1994). ●

● Indeed, this would be better able to explain the fact that not all people who experience a traumatic event go on to develop a phobia related to it.

However, not everyone who has a phobia can recall an incident when it occurred. Although, on the other hand, it could be argued that these events did happen but have been forgotten (Ost, 1989). ●

● Bandura and Rosenthal (1966) showed that an observer who watched a model apparently experiencing pain every time a buzzer sounded, later demonstrated an emotional reaction to that sound.

One strength of the behavioural approach is that the role of social learning has been demonstrated experimentally. ●

● Another problem with this evidence is not everyone who has been bitten by a dog develops a phobia of a dog (Di Nardo *et al*., 1988). The principles of conditioning suggest that they should.

This appears to show that phobias can also be learnt via observation, and that direct experience of a traumatic event is not always necessary for the development of fear associations. ●

● For example, Seligman (1970) suggests that we are biologically prepared from birth to rapidly learn a fear association (phobia). Others suggest we inherit phobias of certain types of objects (*prepotent objects)*.

▶ Lesson notes p.67

Triplets

All the words below relate to chemotherapy (a biological therapy for phobic disorders).

For each set, select three words by writing their number on each line and explain how they are connected to each other. When you have finished, give each set a title.

1. Benzodiazepines	2. Arousal	3. Mood
4. Blocking reuptake	5. Blocking receptors	6. Adrenaline/ Noradrenanline
7. Serotonin	8. Central nervous system	9. GABA

Set A ____________ Title: ____________

Set B ____________ Title: ____________

Set C ____________ Title: ____________

▶ Lesson notes p.68

REBT revision cards

What does

stand for?

REBT revision card 1

Summarise in exactly 15 words, the rationale of REBT in treating phobic disorders.

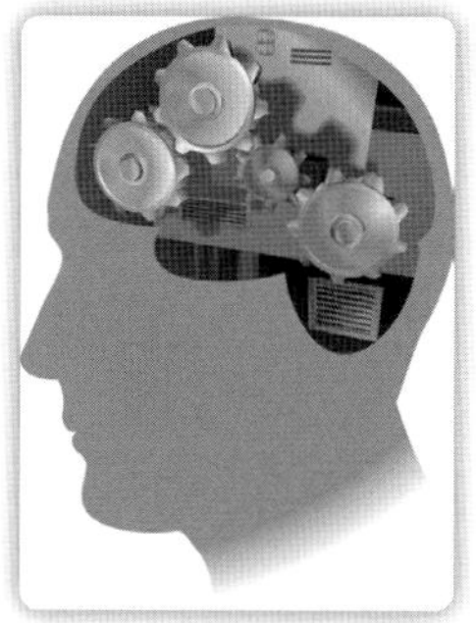

REBT revision card 2

How does Ellis (1957) think we should identify rational thoughts?

ABC

REBT revision card 3

Outline the three ways patients are encouraged to dispute their self-defeating beliefs.

REBT revision card 4

'Maria suffers from social phobia. She remembers when she was a lot younger being asked to give a presentation in front of her Yr 7 class but she kept stuttering on some of the words. She thought everyone would think she was stupid and useless and decided to avoid speaking in front of people ever since'

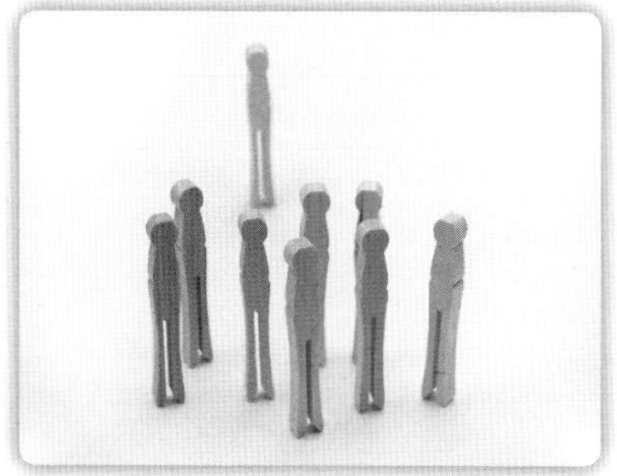

How would REBT identify problems in Maria's thinking, and treat her social phobia?

REBT revision card 5

▶ Lesson notes p.69

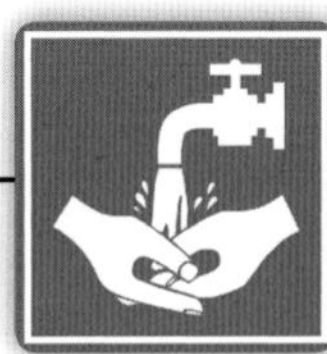

What is OCD?

Use your textbook (page 204 *A2 Complete Companion*) to identify the key points regarding obsessions.

Now identify the key points regarding compulsions

Similarities between obsessions and compulsions

Differences between obsessions and compulsions

▶ Lesson notes p.70

Biological breakdown

▶ Lesson notes p.70

Psychological explanations

ANSWERS

QUESTIONS

1. Which psychological approach is this handout dedicated to?

1.

Knowledge

2. Give three key words you must use when outlining this approach.

2.

Comprehension

3. Summarise, in one or two sentences, the main idea proposed by this approach.

3.

Application

4. What questions would you ask of the main psychologists working within this approach?

4.

Synthesis

5. How well would we understand the illness if the approach did not exist?

5.

Evaluation

6. How useful do you feel this explanation is for sufferers and/or medical professionals?

6.

▶ Lesson notes p.70

Target and challenge

Now you have read about the biological approach to treatment, see how many points you can recall from the text (page 210 *A2 Complete Companion*).

working alone

1.
2.
3.
4.
5.
6.
7.
8.

Target: make 5 points

Challenge: try to reach 8 points.

working in pairs

9.
10.
11.
12.
13.
14.
15.
16.

target

challenge

working with text

17.
18.
19.
20.
21.
22.
23.
24.

target

challenge

▶ Lesson notes p.71

Six hats analysis

Edward de Bono's 6 hats is a way of looking at an issue from a number of different perspectives.

Use this technique to consider a specific psychological approach to treating OCD.

White hat	What data is available regarding the use of this therapy with sufferers?
Red hat	What do you feel about the use of this therapy with sufferers of OCD? Does it seem like a useful form of treatment?
Black hat	What problems does the therapy face? Who disagrees with the use of this therapy with OCD sufferers? Are there any weaknesses with the therapy?
Yellow hat	What are the strengths of this therapy? Who supports the use of this therapy with OCD sufferers?
Green hat	How can this therapy be used in the real world to improve people's psychological well being?
Blue hat	How would this therapy be viewed by biological psychologists?

▶ Lesson notes p.71

The media and prosocial behaviour

Listed on the left are six ways in which the media can have a prosocial effect. Think about the four television programmes shown, and comment upon which of the explanations applies to each programme and why.

	Children in Need	Sesame Street	Blue Peter	Coronation Street
TV presents prosocial role models				
TV can discourage negative stereotyping				
TV can help us develop prosocial norms				
TV can be educational				
TV can encourage a sense of shared social values				
TV can encourage altruism				

▶ Lesson notes p.72

Dodgy conclusions

Dr Psychologist conducted a study on the link between exposure to media violence and aggression.

- *His sample was 50 boys aged 3-4 years old.*
- *25 watched a violent film clip 10 minutes long.*
- *25 watched a non-violent film clip 10 minutes long.*
- *He then made them run around for 10 minutes outside (distraction task).*
- *Afterwards, he left them in a room with balloons and a pair of scissors. Those who watched the violent clip were more likely to pop the balloons.*

He concluded: *'Violent TV causes aggression. For example, if a child watches violent TV, they are more likely to then be aggressive (e.g. hit another child). As such, violent TV will be banned for all those under the age of 16 to prevent this.*

What is wrong with this conclusion?

Problem	Explanation

▶ Lesson notes p.72

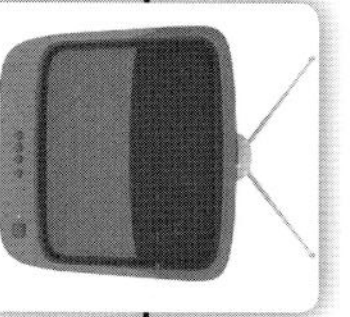

Elaboration ladders

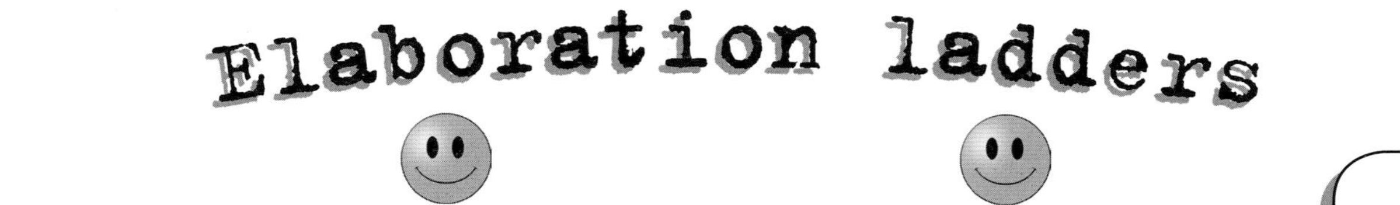

Ladder 1

One of the problems with experimental studies of video games and aggression is ecological validity.

Hint: Think about the ways in which experiments operationalised (measure) aggression.

Hint: Explain why this is a problem.

Ladder 2

Another problem with experimental studies is that they usually only investigate short-term effects of video games.

Hint: Explain what this means.

Hint: Explain why this is a problem.

Ladder 3

However, a positive aspect of experimental studies is that they can determine cause and effect relationships.

Hint: Think about the use of IV's and DV's.

Hint: Put this in the context of the study you are evaluating.

Hint: You could contrast the use of experiments with correlational studies.

Why does that matter?

How would that affect the results/validity?

Can I explain my point with an example?

Have I got evidence?

How could it be improved?

Have I got a counter argument?

How does this affect the main argument?

*Use the prompts above to help you **elaborate** the evaluative arguments on the bottom rung on the ladders.*

The more you elaborate your points (without repeating yourself), the more marks you get – hence the smiley face at the top!

▶ Lesson notes p.73

Exam practice: video games

A psychologist conducted a study with 50 12–13 year olds. The children were randomly allocated to play either a violent or non-violent video game. Exactly 24 hours after completing the game, their parents were asked to complete a survey about their child's aggressive behaviour after the experiment and an aggressive behaviour score was calculated for each child. The scores of the children from each condition were compared.

It was found that the group of children who had played the violent video game had higher aggressive behaviour scores than those who had played the non-violent video game.

Discuss the findings of this study in relation to research into media influence on aggression. *(15 marks)*

What do the results show?

How do the study findings relate to the theories you have been studying?

How do the results compare to other research studies?

Are there any methodological problems with the study described above?

▶ Lesson notes p.73

'Because I'm worth it!'

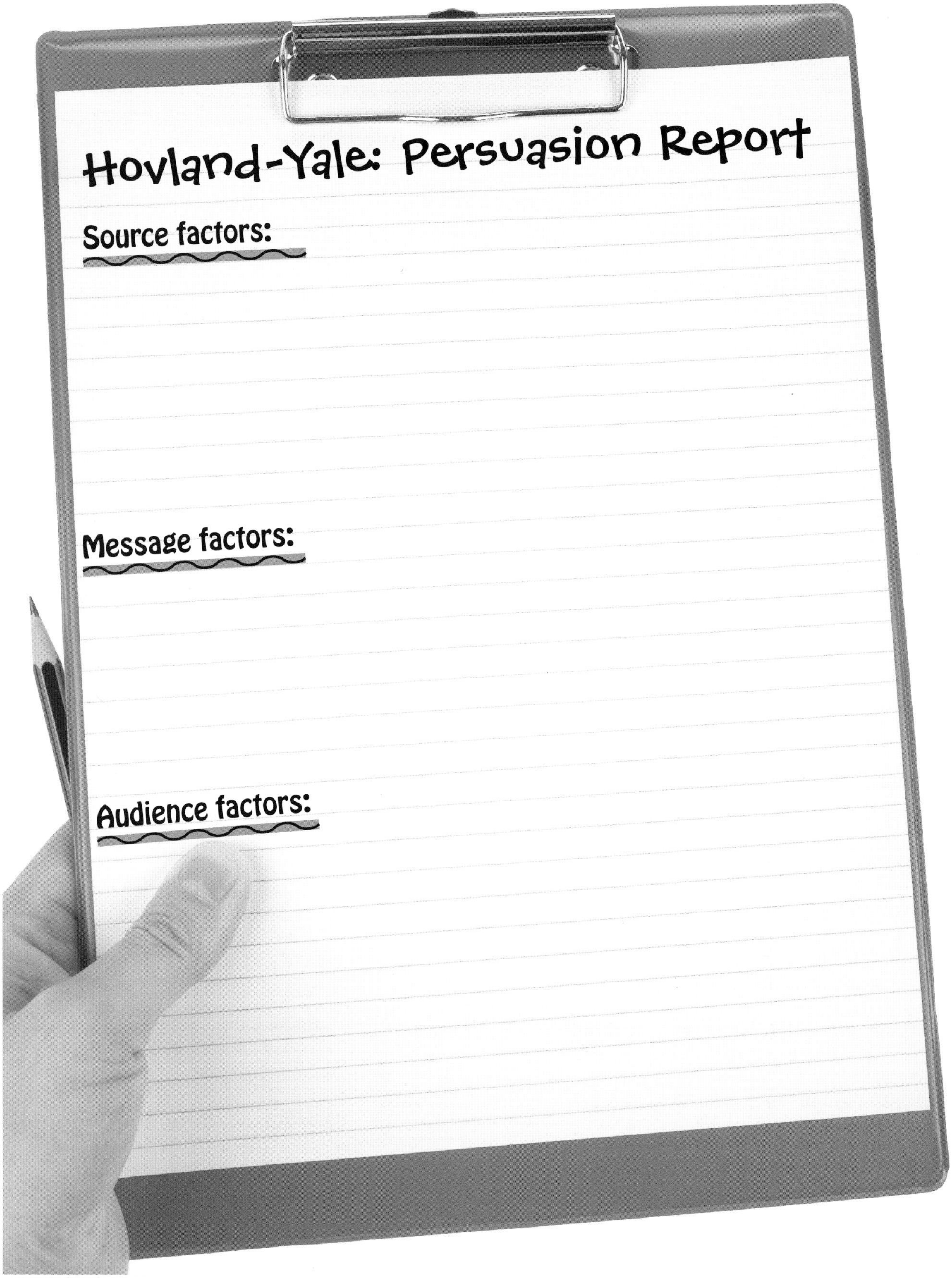

Hovland-Yale: Persuasion Report

Source factors:

Message factors:

Audience factors:

▶ Lesson notes p.74

Doing A02 - testing hypotheses

A good strategy for evaluating a theory is to test a hypothesis based on that theory.

Theory - an explanation of something:
The theory is that the moon is made of cheese.

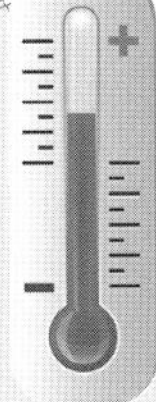

Hypothesis – a prediction based on the logic of the theory:
The theory would predict that at high temperatures, the moon would melt.

Evidence – research study conducted to test a hypothesis:
Clogan (2019) tested the above hypothesis. She flew to the moon with a research team and broke off fragments of the moon's surface. When tested under hot temperatures (up to 100°C) in the space station, no change was observed in the state of the matter.

Conclusion – what we learn as a result of the research:
As such, it is possible to conclude that the moon is NOT made of cheese. If it was, we would have expected it to melt and change from a solid to a liquid.

Over to you!

Use the above structure to help you evaluate cognitive dissonance or self-perception theory as explanations of the influence of attitudes on decision making.

Choose a study (e.g. Festinger and Carlsmith, 1959; Kleinjan *et al.*, 2009; Cooper and Fazio, 1984) and use the same process as above in order to *use evidence* to evaluate the theory.

For example: *Cognitive dissonance suggests that… As such, it would predict that… Research has found… Therefore…*

▶ Lesson notes p.74

Looking at the bigger picture

A CHALLENGE TO BEHAVIOURISM

Cognitive dissonance theory presents a challenge to the underlying behaviourist assumption that people's actions are governed by reward and punishment. Behaviourists would argue that anything associated with reward becomes more attractive, and anything associated with pain becomes undesirable.

Cognitive dissonance theory demonstrates that our behaviour transcends the effects of rewards and punishments and often contradicts them.

Tavris and Aaronson (2007) predicted that if people go through a great deal of pain, effort, or embarrassment to get something, they will be happier with that 'something' than if it came to them easily. To a behaviourist it would make no sense that someone would like doing something associated with pain. However, this all makes sense within the context of cognitive dissonance theory. The cognition that I am a sensible person is dissonant with the cognition that I am willing to put myself through a painful procedure to achieve something (e.g. to get fit). Therefore, I would distort my perceptions of the procedure in a positive way, trying to find good things about it and ignoring any bad aspects.

Cut out the key words and phrases below. Using the information above, reorganise them into a logical order or mindmap and stick them down onto A3 paper. Draw links and arrows between ones that you think are connected. Explain on those links and arrows *how and why* you think they are connected.

Using your A3 'bigger picture', write a summary on how cognitive dissonance theory undermines behaviourism in your own words. Use this sentence starter if you wish….. *'Cognitive dissonance theory undermines the main assumptions of behaviourism. This is because…'*

Behaviourism

Contradiction

Association

Cognitive dissonance

Rewards and punishments

Happiness

Pain, effort

Selective exposure to subsequent information

Undesirable

▶ Lesson notes p.75

Self-monitoring scale

Read the statements below and write next to them whether they are TRUE or FALSE in your case.

If you think the statement is mostly or usually true – answer TRUE.	If you think the statement is mostly or usually false – answer FALSE.

1. I can imitate the behaviour of others, e.g. doing impressions.
2. I wear my heart on my sleeve; I am not good at hiding how I feel.
3. When I'm with a group of people, I always make sure I do not do or say things that others would not like.
4. I can put on a show to impress and entertain people.
5. If I am uncertain of how to act in a situation, I look to other people to see how to behave.
6. I would probably make a very good actor/actress.
7. When choosing a book to read, movie to watch, etc., I do not usually seek the advice of friends.
8. If I am watching a comedy show or film, I am more likely to laugh if others are with me than if I am watching it alone.
9. I am rarely the centre of attention in large groups of people.
10. I act very differently and show different personalities depending on who I'm with.
11. I sometimes pretend to be having a good time, even if I am not.
12. I have sometimes changed what I say or do in order to make people like me.
13. I have never been good at improvisation, e.g. like in games such as charades.
14. I can tell convincing lies to people's faces (if for a good cause).
15. People might think that I like them when I don't, because I am able to 'act' friendly with them.

Something to think about:

- What was your self-monitoring score and what does this mean?
- According to the research, would you be more persuaded by the soft-sell or hard-sell persuasion approach?
- Why do you think this is? Do you agree?

▶ Lesson notes p.75

Connect 4

Identification/attraction...

Link...

Celebrity...

Link...

Parasocial relationships...

Link...

Anxious ambivalent attachment...

▶ Lesson notes p.76

Celebrity attitude scale

Score			
5	if you strongly agree with the statement	3	if you are neutral
4	if you agree	2	if you disagree and
		1	if you strongly disagree

1	If I were to meet my favourite celebrity in person, he/she would already somehow know that I am his/her biggest fan.	5 4 3 2 1
2	I share with my favourite celebrity a special bond that cannot be described in words.	5 4 3 2 1
3	I am obsessed by details of my favourite celebrity's life.	5 4 3 2 1
4	I would gladly die in order to save the life of my favourite celebrity.	5 4 3 2 1
5	My friends and I like to discuss what my favourite celebrity has done.	5 4 3 2 1
6	When something good happens to my favourite celebrity I feel like it happened to me.	5 4 3 2 1
7	My favourite celebrity and I have our own code so we can communicate with each other secretly (such as over the TV car or special words on the radio).	5 4 3 2 1
8	One of the main reasons I maintain an interest in my favourite celebrity is that doing so gives me a temporary escape from life's problems.	5 4 3 2 1
9	I have pictures and/or souvenirs of my favourite celebrity which I always keep in exactly the same place.	5 4 3 2 1
10	If my favourite celebrity endorsed a legal but possibly unsafe drug designed to make someone feel good, I would try it.	5 4 3 2 1
11	My favourite celebrity is practically perfect in every way.	5 4 3 2 1
12	The successes of my favourite celebrity are my successes also.	5 4 3 2 1
13	I enjoy watching, reading, or listening to my favourite celebrity because it means a good time.	5 4 3 2 1
14	I consider my favourite celebrity to be my soulmate.	5 4 3 2 1
15	I have frequent thoughts about my favourite celebrity, even when I don't want to.	5 4 3 2 1
16	When my favourite celebrity dies (or died) I will feel (or I felt) like dying too.	5 4 3 2 1
17	I love to talk with others who admire my favourite celebrity.	5 4 3 2 1
18	When something bad happens to my favourite celebrity I feel like it happened to me.	5 4 3 2 1
19	Learning the life story of my favourite celebrity is a lot of fun.	5 4 3 2 1
20	My favourite celebrity would immediately come to my rescue if I needed help.	5 4 3 2 1
21	I often feel compelled to learn the personal habits of my favourite celebrity.	5 4 3 2 1
22	If I were lucky enough to meet my favourite celebrity, and he/she asked me to do something illegal as a favour, I would like to probably do it.	5 4 3 2 1
23	It is enjoyable to be with others who like my favourite celebrity.	5 4 3 2 1
24	When my favourite celebrity fails or loses at something I feel like a failure myself.	5 4 3 2 1
25	If I walk through the door of my favourite celebrity's home without an invitation he or she would be happy to see me.	5 4 3 2 1
26	If my favourite celebrity saw me in a restaurant he/she would ask me to sit down and talk.	5 4 3 2 1
27	If my favourite celebrity found me sitting in his/her car he or she would be upset.	5 4 3 2 1
28	If someone gave me several thousand dollars to do with as I please, I would consider spending it on a personal possession (like a napkin or paper plate) once used by my favourite celebrity.	5 4 3 2 1
29	I like watching and hearing about my favourite celebrity when I am in a large group of people.	5 4 3 2 1
30	If my favourite celebrity was accused of committing a crime, that accusation would have to be false.	5 4 3 2 1
31	Keeping up with news about my favourite celebrity is an entertaining pastime.	5 4 3 2 1
32	News about my favourite celebrity is a pleasant break from a harsh world.	5 4 3 2 1
33	To know my favourite celebrity is to love him/her.	5 4 3 2 1
34	It would be great if my favourite celebrity and I were locked in a room for a few days.	5 4 3 2 1

▶ Lesson notes p.76

Profiling biological models of addiction

In A2 Psychology you are expected to be thinking about the wider issues in psychology, as well as how theories link to the concepts of 'How Science Works'. The following activity is designed to help you consider how you might do this with biological models of addiction. Mark the spot that corresponds with your opinion of this theory. *Don't forget to justify your analyses!*

Nature ⟷ Nurture

Justify...

Determinist ⟷ Free will

Justify...

Reductionist ⟷ Holist

Justify...

Powerful evidence ⟷ Weak evidence

Justify...

▶ Lesson notes p.77

Profiling cognitive models of addiction

In A2 Psychology you are expected to be thinking about the wider issues in psychology, as well as how theories link to the concepts of 'How Science Works'. The following activity is designed to help you consider how you might do this with cognitive models of addiction. Mark the spot that corresponds with your opinion of this theory. *Don't forget to justify your analyses!*

Nature ⟷ Nurture

Justify...

Determinist ⟷ Free will

Justify...

Reductionist ⟷ Holist

Justify...

Powerful evidence ⟷ Weak evidence

Justify...

▶ Lesson notes p.77

Fruit machine cognitions

Putting only a quid in bluffs the machine.

This 'fruity' isn't in a good mood.

I've a fair bit of money but I've had loads of near misses.

The law of averages says a big win is just around the corner!

How might the cognitive model of addiction explain this man's gambling behaviour?

Initiation

Maintenance

Relapse

Other factors

▶ Lesson notes p.78

Key word boxing

Revise your knowledge of behaviourism and learning by putting the following key words into their correct boxes (well... writing them on!). Then, use those key words to try and explain how addictions might be learnt.

Conditioned response | Vicarious reinforcement | Negative reinforcement

Unconditioned stimulus | Positive reinforcement | Conditioned stimulus

Observation | Unconditioned response | Rewards | Imitation

Operant conditioning

Addiction...

Addiction...

Classical conditioning

Social learning theory

Addiction...

▶ Lesson notes p.78

Don't gamble on the exam!

There are different types of questions that might come up on your exam and you must be ready for them all!

In one type of question you might be asked to apply your knowledge and understanding to a novel situation. It is worthwhile taking a couple of minutes to plan how to tackle this type of question. Use the example and planning sheet below to help you think about this.

Just like his granddad, Simon is addicted to gambling. When he was younger his granddad used to drag him into the betting shops and give him a couple of pounds to spend. Simon then started to go with his friends once he turned 18 and was soon spending all his time and money there. His friends would always ask his advice about different types of bets because he was the 'expert'. He also started visiting casinos and loved the feeling of a 'big win'. Most of the time he felt like he was close to the 'big win' but was actually losing a lot of money.

Discuss explanations for Simon's gambling addiction. *(15 marks)*

Explanation 1…

Evaluation…

Explanation 2…

Evaluation…

Moderating variables/links to issue, e.g. free will/determinism…

▶ Lesson notes p.78

Discussing self-esteem and addiction

Suggested starting point – Why have psychologists suggested self-esteem and addiction are linked?

What evidence is there to suggest that this is or isn't the case?

Does the evidence have any methodological flaws that undermine the arguments made so far?

Is there any further supporting or counter evidence?
Does the topic link in any way to the main psychological debates?

Overall, based on all the arguments, what is your conclusion?

▶ Lesson notes p.79

The dangers of ice cream

ICE CREAM CAUSES ADDICTION

A recent study conducted on Blackpool's beach front reveals that as ice cream sales go up, so does the use of slot machines and fruit machines. Also, as ice cream sales go up, so do cases of drowning. Clearly ice cream is a social menace, similar to class A drugs – the statistical evidence is staring us in the face. The government must ban ice cream now!

Please answer the following questions:

1. What variables have been measured in this study?
2. Which variables do you think would have been difficult to measure?
3. How do you think they were measured?
4. How would you describe the statistical relationship between ice cream and slot machines and fruit machines?
5. Why would it be a mistake to argue that ice cream causes use of fruit/slot machines or drowning?
6. Why would it be useful to do an experiment in this area?
7. Why would it be difficult to conduct an experiment like this?

Consistently, psychological research shows a clear positive correlation between media exposure and addictive behaviour, e.g. drug and substance abuse. The more a person is exposed to drug abuse on films, the more likely an individual is to exhibit addictive behaviour.

Given the issues raised in the questions at the top of this handout, write a 100–150-word analysis of the research outlined above. Think about including some of the following:

- How the results could be explained.
- The major weakness of correlational studies in the context of this research.
- The difficulty of measuring the variables (hence the use of correlation method).
- Potential hidden variable(s) that could explain the relationship between media exposure and addiction.
- The usefulness of conducting an experiment.
- The difficulty of conducting such studies.

▶ Lesson notes p.79

Models of prevention: TPB

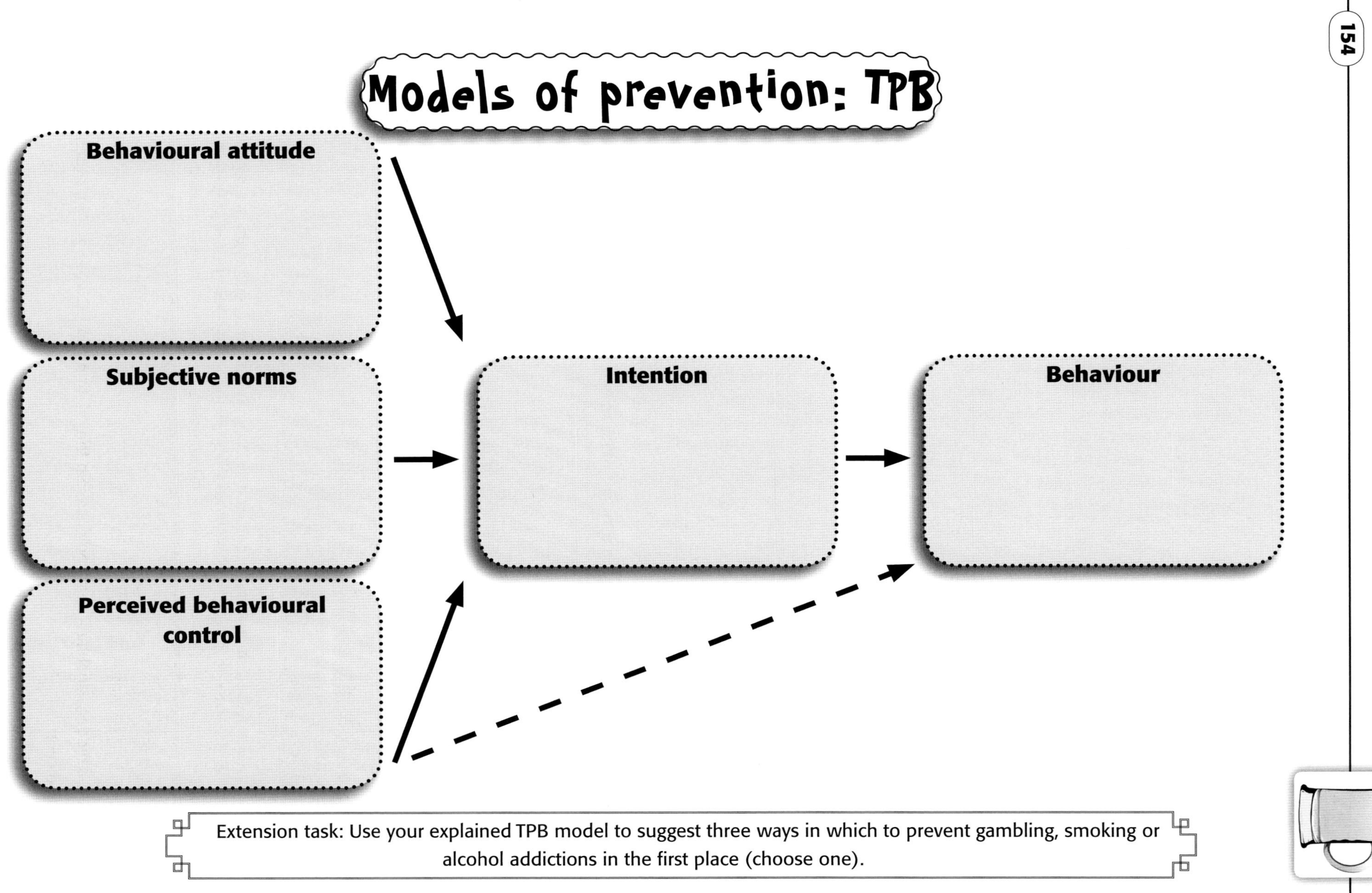

Extension task: Use your explained TPB model to suggest three ways in which to prevent gambling, smoking or alcohol addictions in the first place (choose one).

▶ Lesson notes p.80

Evaluation and elaboration: interventions

In Unit 4, like all of your Psychology A level, you are expected to be able to evaluate aspects of psychology. This handout requires you to evaluate **types of intervention – both biological and psychological.** Many students miss out on evaluation marks because they do not elaborate their comments and evaluations in sufficient detail to get the full marks. To reach the highest marks your evaluations must be 'effective' and show evidence of synopticity.

Your task here is to match up the evaluation points from the left, further and further to the right in order to increase your evaluation marks (remember though that you may only have time for 2-3 evaluation points in an essay).

Rudimentary →	Basic →	Reasonable →	Effective
There is significant support for CBT as an effective intervention strategy.	Although research has found reinforcement therapies to be effective in reducing addictive behaviour, such interventions do nothing to address the problem that led to the addiction in the first place.	This means that although a specific addictive behaviour might have been reduced, there is a possibility the person may simply engage in a different addictive behaviour instead.	The UK statistics authority showed that methadone was responsible for over 300 deaths in the UK in 2007.
It has been argued that psychological reinforcement interventions do not address the underlying problems.	Hollander *et al.* (2000) found that gamblers treated with SSRIs to increase serotonin levels showed significant improvements compared to a control group.	However, the reliability of this evidence might be questioned, since the sample size was very small (n = 10) and the study was short in duration (16 weeks).	Indeed a larger and longer study (Blanco *et al.*, 2002), involving 32 gamblers over six months failed to demonstrate any superiority for the drug treatment over a placebo.
The evidence suggests drug treatments for gamblers can work.	Ladouceur *et al.* (2001) randomly allocated 66 pathological gamblers to either a cognitive therapy group or a waiting list control group. Of those who completed the treatment, 86% no longer fulfilled the DSM criteria for pathological gambling.	Indeed the problem is so great that the unsupervised patients have created a black market, with users sometimes selling their doses for only £2.	As such, this supports the notion of free will, since the gamblers are in control of their own behaviour. If they can change their thought processes, they will be able to change their behaviour.
One issue with methadone treatments is the problem of substitute addiction.	Many drug addicts who are on the methadone programme become as reliant on methadone as they were on heroin.	They also found that after treatment, gamblers had a better perception of control over their problem and increased self-efficacy showing changes to their thinking.	A drug addict may, for example, turn to alcohol, but in most cases new addictions tend to be subtle, including compulsive spending or even developing dependent relationships.

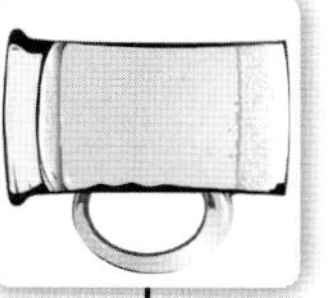

▶ Lesson notes p.80

Construct a conversation

Statements you may wish to use to help you debate whether paranormal psychology is a pseudoscience.

Defence: Paranormal psychology is a valid area of research.

Opposition: Paranormal psychology is a pseudoscience.

Lack of supporting evidence can be attributed to the presence of sceptics, which causes the phenomenon to disappear.

R. B. Rhine strove to maintain high standards in his research even reporting his assistants for cheating.

Insisting on rigorous control of research suggests a lack of belief.

It is not the remit of believers to prove the reality of a psi phenomenon. It is up to sceptics to disprove its existence.

The American Association for the Advancement of Science (AAAS) allowed the Parapsychological Association to become affiliated members in 1969. Surely this confirms its status as a science?

Scientific fraud is common throughout research. For example, Cyril Burt's work into the hereditability of intelligence has been questioned.

Fraud is common in paranormal research. For example, when carrying out Ganzfeld research Carl Sargent failed to follow protocol. Although he defended his practices, his departure from the research field was taken as confirmation of his dishonesty.

Hard science dictates that the believer, not the sceptic, should shoulder the burden of proof.

Scientific theories constantly change as a result of hypothesis testing. Psi phenomena have been explained in the same way for centuries.

Occam's razor is the principle of simplicity. If two competing explanations exist and all else is equal then the simpler of the two explanations should be accepted. In this case: 'psi phenomenon doesn't exist' should be accepted over 'sceptics make phenomenon jealous so they go away'.

You cannot investigate a theory's validity if a lack of evidence can always be blamed on the presence of a sceptic.

Many studies lack control and fail to be replicated. A lack of reliability casts doubt on original research findings.

Synoptic sideline

The debate about whether parapsychology is a science can be widened to consider whether all aspects of Psychology can be called a science. What about Humanistic Psychology with its emphasis on individual experience? Is Behaviourism a science because it only considers observable phenomena? Can Psychology only be a true science if it adopts a biological approach, taking empirical measurements? Can Freud's theory be studied scientifically?

Do you think Psychology can be called a science? Give two reasons to support your answer.

▶ Lesson notes p.82

Construct a commentary

GANZFELD STUDIES

Label the two images and explain why the Ganzfeld technique was developed.

Hyman (1985)

Reanalysed data = no evidence of psi. Lack of security and erroneous statistical analysis.

32% =

25% =

Hyman & Honorton (1986)
Autoganzfeld =

11 =

34% =

25% =

Space for extra info

Milton & Wiseman (1999)

Bem *et al.* (2001)

Risk of researcher bias

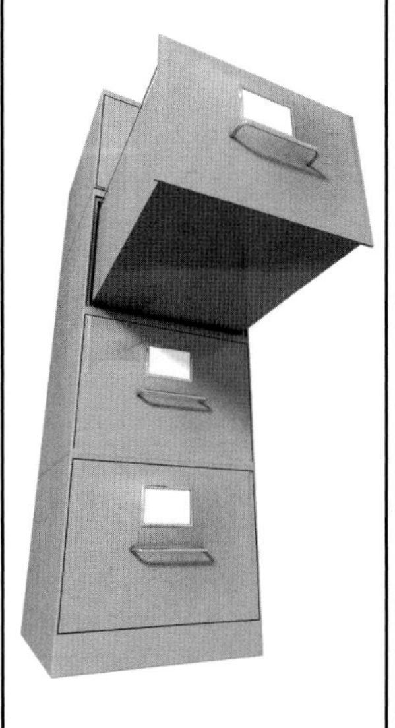

The psi assumption

▶ Lesson notes p.82

What makes a sheep a sheep?

Why do some people believe in anomalous phenomena (sheep) while others do not (goats).
Factors that underlie anomalous experience can be split into three categories:
cognitive □, personality □ and biological □.
Colour code each image according to the category it falls in to.

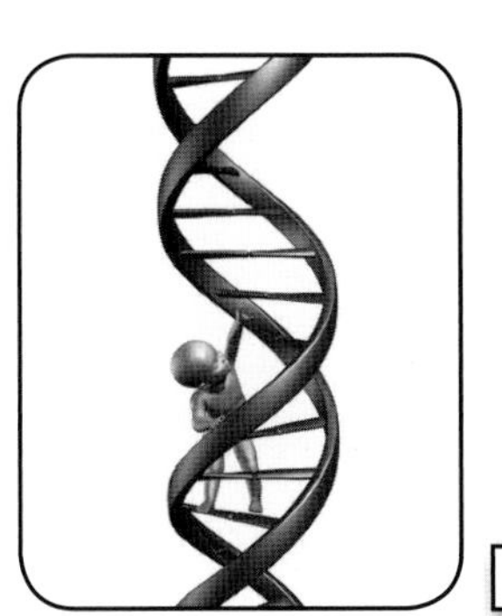

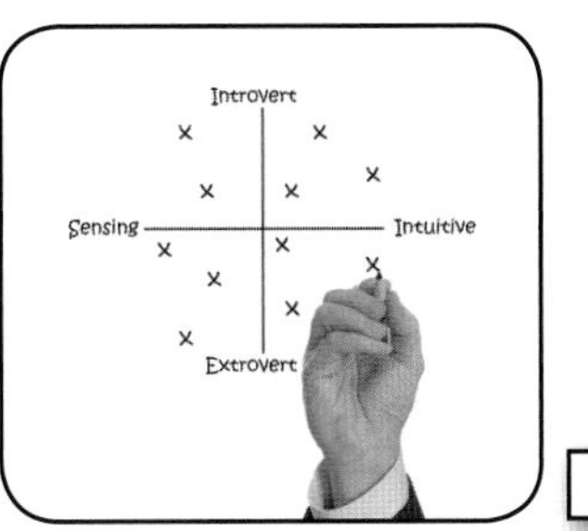

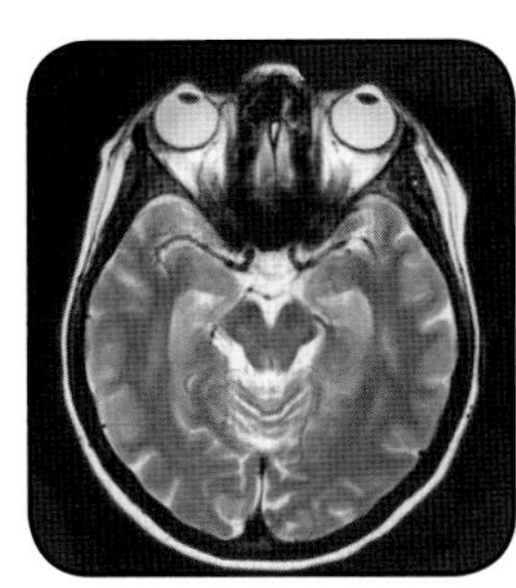

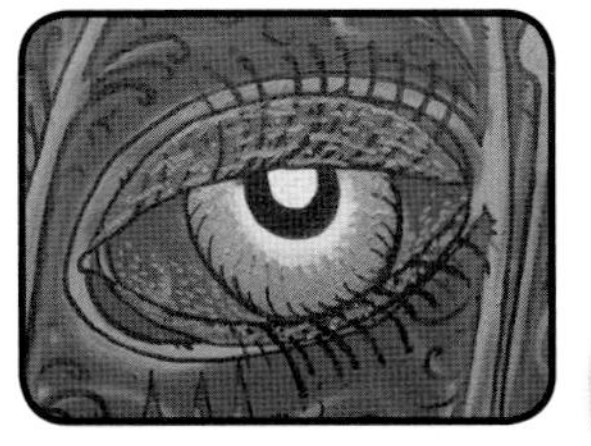

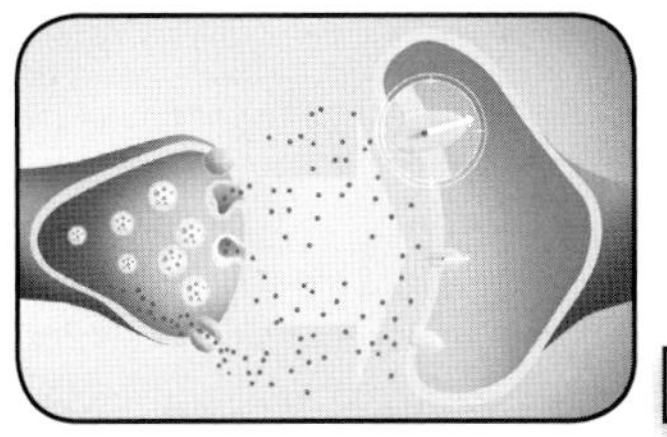

▶ Lesson notes p.82

Peer reviews

Answer the following question on a separate piece of paper:

Describe, in about 100 words, the functions of paranormal and related beliefs.

Now swap your work with another student and complete the forms below based on their response. Remember to be honest!

First function identified: ____________________

Belief type: paranormal or related (circle one)

Description given (leave blank if none given): ____________________

____

____

____

____

____

Is this description: flawed, basic, reasonable detail & generally accurate, detailed & accurate? (circle one)

Second function identified: ____________________

Belief type: paranormal or related (circle one)

Description given (leave blank if none given): ____________________

____

____

____

____

____

Is this description: flawed, basic, reasonable detail & generally accurate, detailed & accurate? (circle one)

Third function identified: ____________________

Belief type: paranormal or related (circle one)

Description given (leave blank if none given): ____________________

____

____

____

____

____

Is this description: flawed, basic, reasonable detail & generally accurate, detailed & accurate? (circle one)

▶ Lesson notes p.83

Teaching in teams

Your group is focussing on one of the following areas: deception, self-deception, superstition or coincidence.

TOPIC:

100-word summary:

Related research:

Key words:

Interesting point:

Links to other areas:

Be sure to record as details in NOTE form and in YOUR OWN WORDS as you will be using this sheet to teach others.

▶ Lesson notes p.83

Forming a considered opinion

OUTLINE

Write a brief summary of your chosen topic here.

EVIDENCE FOR

EVIDENCE AGAINST

MY OPINION IS . . .

▶ Lesson notes p.84

One minute wonder

You have to talk for one minute on the topic of out-of-body experiences or near-death experiences. Once you have decided on the points you wish to include, write a script of your speech. Time yourself and make any amendments to ensure you hit the 60-second target exactly.

Key points I wish to include are:

One minute wonder script:

Time taken to read script:

Amended script:

Time taken to read amended script:

▶ Lesson notes p.84

Planning a study

AIM:

PROCEDURE:

IV Operationalised (or covariable 1) =

DV Operationalised (or covariable 2) =

Research method =

Research design =

Sampling technique =

Experimental hypothesis =
Delete as appropriate.....
Non directional/Directional

Null hypothesis =

Stats test =

Delete as appropriate....

Looking for a difference / Looking for a relationship

Unrelated / Related data

Ordinal / Categorical data

Therefore use...

Spearman's Rho / Mann-Whitney / Chi-squared / Wilcoxon

▶ Lesson notes p.85

Story time

We all have our pet peeves, and despite generally being a very happy person, Sarah is no exception. The thing that winds her up more than anything else is carrier bags!

It seems that every time she goes shopping, her carrier bags always burst open, spilling everthing out onto the floor. The thing Sarah doesn't seem to realise, though, is that the bags break because she over fills them.

Just last week she went to the TESDA supermarket to do her food shopping. As usual, she tried to pack too much into her bag – 4 bottles of wine and 6 large plates from the homeware section. As she was walking home, the bag burst, breaking all of her shopping!

A couple of days later, Sarah went shopping at the Jean Louis department store. True to form, she bought a large vase, a gold clock and a couple of large plates and packed everything into the same bag. Just outside the shop the bag burst, causing more devastation.

Yesterday, taking out her rubbish, Sarah had an epiphany. As she took the TESDA value bin liner out of her kitchen bin and carried it outside. She realised the bag hadn't broken! She decided TESDA value bin liners must be the strongest type of bag and can hold the most before breaking. Sarah decided there and then that she would go shopping with these bin liners in the future.

1. What conclusion has Sarah arrived at?
2. Why might that conclusion be incorrect?
3. How could you reach a more valid conclusion? Why would that method be better?
4. Why would independent and dependent variables be particularly useful?
5. How could you operationalise these variables?

▶ Lesson notes p.85

Harlow's monkeys 1

Developmental psychologists have always been interested in why infants attach themselves to an adult caregiver - how and why does this attachment form with that particular adult? One theory put forward by learning theorists (a certain type of psychologist) was that babies learn to associate their caregivers with food, and so they come to love the adult figure who provides them with that food - hence an attachment is formed.

In order to test this hypothesis, Harlow (1959) conducted a series of experiments with rhesus monkeys. Harlow placed the monkeys in cages with two surrogate (substitute) mothers. One was made from wire and had a baby bottle fitted to 'her'; the other was made from a soft, cuddly cloth (but didn't have a bottle fitted). Harlow found that the babies spent most of their time clinging to the cloth mother, even though she provided no milk. They would cling to this cloth mother particularly when they were frightened. This semed to show that the infants did **not** attach with the adults because they provide food, but rather, because they provide contact comfort. As such, this study provides evidence against the learning theory explanation of attachment.

Use this information to help you complete Handout 166. This will help you think about the 'How Science Works' process and the deductive process in particular.

▶ Lesson notes p.85

Harlow's monkeys 2

What have psychologists noticed that all infants do?

How science works

1 Observe human behaviour.

2 Develop explanation/ hypothesis.

3 Test hypothesis.

4 Collect results.

????????

5 Draw conclusions.

What theories were developed about this behaviour?

What is Harlow's **hypothesis** for the study?

What was the IV in this study?

How was it ***operationalised***?

What was the DV in this study?

How was it ***operationalised***?

Results of the study:

What conclusions were drawn? Make reference to the original **theory** and **hypothesis** (step 2).

▶ Lesson notes p.85

167

Triplets

All the words below relate to means of establishing the value of any research.
For each set, select three words by writing their number on each line and explain how they are connected to each other.

1. funding	9. universities	17. rivalry
2. subjective	10. appropriate	18. responsible
3. prevent	11. findings	19. anonymity
4. grants	12. Medical Research Council	20. slow
5. expert	13. bias	21. review
6. objective	14. faulty	22. peer
7. journals	15. ideal	23. quality
8. incorrect	16. research ratings	24. results

Set A ___ ___ ___ ________________________________

____

____

____

Set B ___ ___ ___ ________________________________

____

____

____

Set C ___ ___ ___ ________________________________

____

____

____

Set D ___ ___ ___ ________________________________

____

____

____

Set E ___ ___ ___ ________________________________

____

____

____

Set F ___ ___ ___ ________________________________

____

____

____

▶ Lesson notes p.85

Do you know your methods?

Experiments	Sometimes the only way to study rare behaviours and experiences, e.g. effects of privation, treatments of schizophrenia.
Experiments (strength)	Separate groups of participants are used for each IV.
Experiments (weakness)	The main problem is social desirability: participants providing answers to portray themselves in a good light.
Field Experiment	Are sometimes so highly controlled they lack ecological validity.
Field Experiment (strength)	Good research method when ethical studies are not possible or practical.
Field Experiment (weakness)	Participants are not randomly allocated to the conditions of the experiment, which may reduce validity.
Natural Experiment	The most obvious psychological research method: Watch what people do.
Natural Experiment (strength)	A research method that always uses an IV and a DV.
Natural Experiment (weakness)	Can be easily repeated and allow fast collection of data.
Independent groups	An experiment that makes use of existing IVs.
Repeated measures	Cannot determine cause and effect relationships. May be affected by intervening variables, which can explain why variables are linked.
Self-report	Participants usually unaware they are in a study, so this removes experimenter effects.
Self-report (strength)	A research method that investigates the relationship between two variables (called covariables).
Self-report (weakness)	Are able to demonstrate cause and effect relationships.
Observations	Observers use these because there is so much available data to collect. As such, they only record certain instances of behaviour.
Behavioural categories	The use of questionnaires or interviews as a research method.
Correlations	More difficult to control extraneous variables.
Correlations (strength)	Each participant is tested on all the IVs.
Correlations (weakness)	An experiment where an IV is manipulated in a more natural environment.

▶ Lesson notes p.86

Validity word wall

Colour code each brick so that it relates to the correct key term displayed at the top of the wall. Use all bricks of one colour to write a definition of that key word. Each term has four related bricks.

External validity	Internal validity	External reliability	Internal reliability

Includes ecological, population and historical	Inter-interviewer reliability is important	Can be affected by observer bias
Check by making comparisons of findings	Inter-observer reliability should be checked	Can be affected by observer bias
Concurrent validity	Test–retest method	Representativeness

Measures what it intends to measure	Generalisable	Split-half method	Face validity

Consistency within itself	Can be applied to other situations	Consistency over occasions

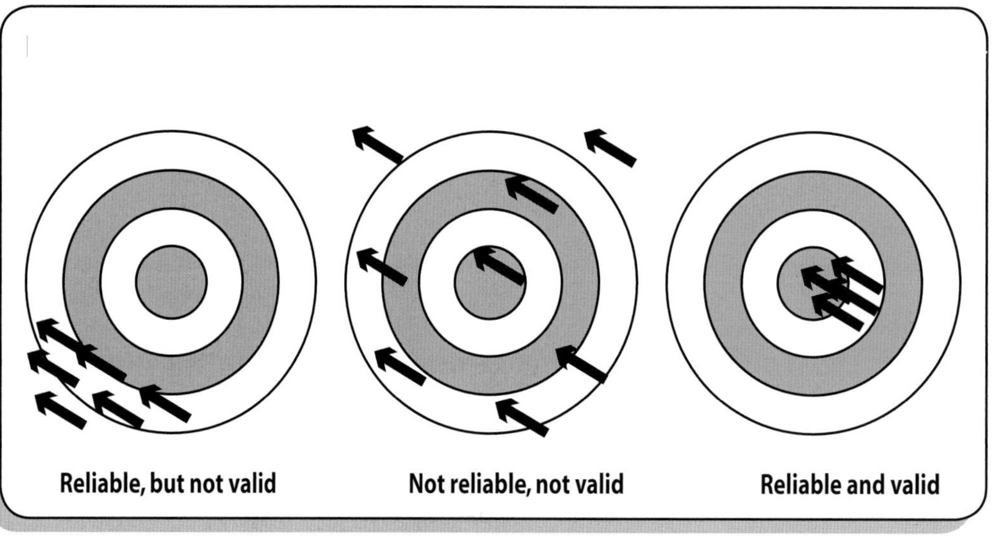

Reliable, but not valid

Not reliable, not valid

Reliable and valid

Use the words and target diagram to help choose at least one of the key words to define. Try to include what the term means, why it is important and how investigators can ensure their findings are valid or reliable.

▶ Lesson notes p.86

Sampling techniques

Strengths for the researcher

E.g. this technique did not take long to do. The researcher probably did not have access to a lot of sufferers so this was a quick way to gather his sample.

A researcher wishes to study patients with clinical depression. He contacted the chief psychologist of a local health care trust and arranged to test the patients treated at one centre.

Sample technique

Weaknesses for the researcher

Strengths for the university department:

A university department undertook a study of celebrity worship in adolescents, using a questionnaire. The questionnaire was given to a group of students in a local comprehensive school, selected by placing all the students' names in a container and drawing out 50 names.

Sample technique

Weaknesses for the university department:

Strengths for the psychology students:

A class of psychology students conduct a study on paranormal belief. They put a notice on the notice board in the sixth form common room asking for participants who have an hour to spare.

Sample technique

Weaknesses for the psychology students:

▶ Lesson notes p.86

Conforming to the code

The current BPS code of ethics and conduct (BPS, 2009) identifies four ethical principles and includes advice on how these should be dealt with.
Use your knowledge of psychological research from AS and A2 to complete each box shown below.

Respect for the dignity and worth of all persons. This refers to ...	Research example of this principle not being met...	**What should have been done?**
Competence means...	*Research example of this principle not being met...*	*Why is it important a researcher is competent?*
Psychologists have a responsibility to...	Research example of this principle not being met...	How did the researcher in the example you gave justify their procedure?
Psychologists should be honest and accurate. Integrity relates to...	Research example of this principle not being met...	Why is dishonesty in research dangerous?

▶ Lesson notes p.87

MATCH UP

Type of test used when the study has a non-directional hypothesis

Term for data that could not have arisen by chance, or is extremely unlikely to have arisen by chance

Accepting a null hypothesis that is actually not true

Calculation that allows conclusions to be drawn based on the probability that a particular pattern of results could have arisen by chance

Value a test statistic must reach in order for the null hypothesis to be rejected

Data that is measured using units of equal intervals, for example number of correct answers on an IQ test

Inferential statistics

Significant

Nominal level

Ordinal level

Interval level

Ratio level

Test statistic

Probability

Critical value

One-tailed test

Two-tailed test

Type 1 error

Type 2 error

The observed value calculated using a specific inferential statistic to analyse the data collected

Rejecting a null hypothesis that is actually true

Data that is ordered in some way where the difference between each interval is not the same, for example the height of participants

Type of test used when the study has a directional hypothesis

Usually set at 0.05, meaning there is a 5% possibility results did occur by chance

Data that has a true zero point - most physical quantities have this

Data grouped into separate categories such as smoker, non-smoker

▶ Lesson notes p.87

Correlations and Spearman's Rho

Research aim: Choose (highlight or circle) one of the following:

- To investigate the relationship between exam stress and exam confidence.
- To investigate the relationship between the tastiness of chocolate and expense of chocolate.
- To investigate the relationship between index finger length and spelling ability.
- To investigate the relationship between time taken to peel an orange and shoe size.

Procedure: You will need to decide how you are going to **operationalise** these variables.

Covariable 1 = Covariable 2 =

Covariable 1 operationalised =

Covariable 2 operationalised =

Research hypothesis = Delete as appropriate Non directional/Directional

Null hypothesis =

Results: You will now need to calculate Spearman's Rho using the instructions from your textbook. You may wish to do this on a statistical software package (e.g. Excel) to make this easier. Or, try http://www.holah.karoo.net/stats.htm

Statistical value (Spearman's Rho) = Critical value =

Level of significance =

Statement results:

Conclusions:
What the results mean

▶ Lesson notes p.87

Researching warm and cold colours

The drug industry spends a lot of time choosing the colours of the drugs they produce. Drugs that fight illness may be warm colours like red and yellow. Those that calm your body may be white or blue (colder colours). Could a placebo effect exist based on the colour of a substance?

Are we subconsciously attracted by the colours we perceive?
Can we really detect a difference when we cannot 'see' the actual colour?

Hypothesis: There will be a difference in ability to correctly identify whether a chocolate bean's coloured shell is a warm colour or a cold colour.

Independent Variable: (identify which colours are warm, which are cold and record below)

Warm colours	Cold colours

Dependent Variable:

Procedure: Decision made	Justification given
Sampling method = *Opportunity sample. Sixth form students approached at a local secondary school.*	
Sample size = *25 participants will be approached*	
Sample age range = *17–18 years old*	
Research design = all participants try one bean. As each bean can only be correctly OR incorrectly identified, so independent measures design.	Each bean can only be recorded in one category: either correctly identified or incorrectly identified. They only give one score so it is an independent measures design.
Method = 1. Students are read standardised instructions that briefly explain the test and state the aim as researching our ability to taste different colours. 2. Each student is instructed to close their eyes. 3. Once their eyes are closed one bean is placed in their hand. 4. Keeping eyes closed students place the bean into the mouth where they are told to let it dissolve on their tongue, not chew it. 5. Once the bean is eaten students are asked to name the colour of the bean. 6. Students are told to open their eyes and thanked for their time. 7. A debrief is read out loud where the full aim is explained and participants asked if their data can still be used.	
Ethical measures = Right to withdraw and confidentiality assured before study. Under 16s have to give parental consent. Debrief given after to explain aim fully.	
Statistics test =	
Level of probability you will set $P < 0.05$	*Standard level set for psychological research. Likelihood results are due to chance is less than 5 in 100.*

▶ Lesson notes p.88

Testing the difference in cookies

Research aim: To investigate whether there is a difference in the amount of chocolate chips found in cookies of two different brands (i.e. value supermarket own brand vs. expensive brand name).

Procedure: Split the class in two. One half should have brand A, and the other brand B.

Brand A = ______ Brand B = ______

IV = ______

DV = ______

Experimental hypothesis = ______
Delete as appropriate
Non directional / Directional

Null hypothesis = ______

Stats test =
Looking for a difference / Looking for a relationship
Unrelated / Related data
Ordinal / Categorical data

Therefore use... *Spearman's Rho / Mann-Whitney / Chi-squared / Wilcoxon*

Results: You will now need to calculate the statistical value using the instructions from your textbook. You may wish to do this on a statistical software package (e.g. Excel) to make this easier. Or, try http://www.holah.karoo.net/stats.htm

Observed value = ______ Critical value = ______

Level of significance = ______

Statement results: ______

Conclusions:
What the results mean ______

▶ Lesson notes p.88

Wilcoxon *T* test investigation 1

LOW MOOD AND COMFORT-EATING

Garg *et al.* (2007) observed the food choices of 38 participants as they watched either an upbeat, funny movie (*Sweet Home Alabama*) or a sad, depressing one (*Love Story*). Participants were offered buttered popcorn and seedless grapes throughout the films.

Those watching the sad film consumed 36% more popcorn than those watching the upbeat film, but the upbeat film group ate far more grapes than the other group.

Garg *et al.* claim that people who feel sad or depressed want to 'jolt themselves out of the dumps', therefore they are more likely to go for a snack that tastes good to give them a sudden rush of euphoria. Happy people want to extend their upbeat mood and so choose healthy foods.

However, when participants were presented with nutritional information about the foods (among other information) prior to viewing, consumption of the relatively unhealthy foods dropped dramatically. Perhaps, suggest the researchers, when we eat to comfort ourselves, we would do well to check the nutritional information on the foods we indulge in!

Could it be that knowledge of nutritional information has an impact on our food choices? Food packaging now displays the fat, salt and calorie content of a product, often colour-coded red, amber or green. Is this information used by shoppers to inform their diet?

This investigation aims to identify whether a difference exists in how people rate unhealthy foods when nutritional information is presented compared to when no such information is given.

The independent variable is:

The dependent variable is:

The directional hypothesis is:

NB: The study has a directional hypothesis, therefore a one-tailed test is required.

The null hypothesis is:

Procedure:

1. Approach participant and read them standardised instructions.
2. Ask them to look at the three foods and rate each one on how appetising that food is on a scale of 1 (not at all appetising) to 10 (very appetising). No time limit is set but ask participants to give a 'gut reaction', do not think too long before answering.
3. Repeat Step 2 this time using the same three foods with the nutritional information displayed.
4. Record each participant's responses and add each rating together to produce a total score out of 30. Divide this score by 3 to find the mean appetising rating for the two conditions.
5. Debrief the participant.

You could counterbalance Steps 2 and 3 to reduce the risk of order effects impacting on validity.

Analysing the findings:

1. Record your findings on the data sheet.
2. You will be using a Wilcoxon *T* test to analyse the data because: the data was related (each participant took part in both conditions), ordinal data was collected (appetising ratings) and the study was looking for a difference between the two conditions (presence or absence of nutritional information).
3. Calculate the test statistic $T =$ ________________
4. Identify the critical value for $p<0.05 =$ ________________
5. State whether data is significant or not = ________________
6. State which hypothesis you will accept = ________________

▶ Lesson notes p.88

Wilcoxon *T* test investigation 2

Please rate how appetising you find the following foods on a scale of:

1 -- 10
(very unappetising) (very appetising)

100g of chocolate

100g of crisps

100g of pizza

Please rate how appetising you find the following foods on a scale of:

1 --- 10
(very unappetising) (very appetising)

100g of chocolate

525 calories
57.0g carbohydrates
29.8g fat
1.7g fibre
5.7g protein

100g of crisps

525 calories
33.0g carbohydrates
50.0g fat
4.0g fibre
6.5g protein

100g of pizza

259 calories
29.1g carbohydrates
10.1g fat
2.4g fibre
12.8g protein

Participant data

Participant	Appetising rating total for food shown alone	Appetising rating total for food and nutritional information	Difference (column 2 – column 3)	Rank:
1.				
2.				
3.				
4.				
5.				
6.				
7.				
8.				
9.				
10.				
11.				
12.				

T = Sum of ranks of the less frequent sign =

▶ Lesson notes p.88

Data decisions

Write the results of your class experiment here:

Condition A =

Condition B =

Mean =

Mode =

Median =

For this data, which is the best ***measure of central tendency*** and why?

Range =

Standard deviation =

For this data, which ***measure of dispersion*** is the best? What does it show?

Finished? Extension – which stats test would you use? Justify your decision.

▶ Lesson notes p.89

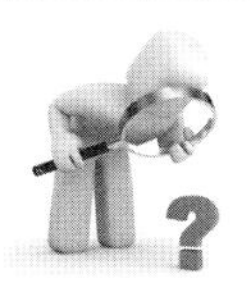

Qualitative crossword

ACROSS

9 Known as top-down approach. Qualitative data is coded using ideas and concepts from an existing theory. (T........ (8)A........(8))

11 Refers to views that are unaffected by personal biases. (O.....(9))

12 Acronym for Interpretive Phenomenological Analysis, which is concerned with understanding how people make sense of their own environment. (I... (3)).

DOWN

1 Method in which written or oral discourses are studied. (D... (9)A...(8))

2 Term for any data that is not in a numerical form. Data is summarised not counted (Q...(11) D...(4))

3 The observation of people in their natural environment. (E... (11))

4 The comparison of results from a variety of studies, who often employ different methods to study the same thing or person. (T...(13)).

5 Refers to the recognition that a researcher's attitudes and biases have an unavoidable influence on the research they are conducting. (R...(11))

6 Term for data that represents how much, long, many, etc., there is of something. Behaviour that is measured in numbers or quantities. (Q...(12)D...(4)).

7 Known as bottom-up approach. Codes emerge from the data collected rather than being generated by pre-existing views. (G...(8)T...(6)).

8 Views derived from personal views. (S...(10))

10 The process of identifying categories, themes, phrases or key words in a set of data. (C...(6))

▶ Lesson notes p.89

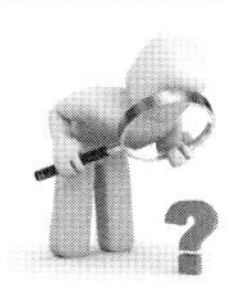

Qualitative crossword answers

Across:
- THEMATIC ANALYSIS
- OBJECTIVE
- IPA

Down:
- QUALITATIVE DATA
- DISCOURSE ANALYSIS
- ETHNOGRAPHY
- CODING
- QUANTITATIVE DATA
- GROUNDED THEORY
- TRIANGULATION
- REFLEXIVITY
- SUBJECTIVE

▶ Lesson notes p.89

Exam-style question 1

There are often concerns raised that there is a link between playing video games and aggression in young people.

A group of psychologists set out to investigate this claim.

With the permission of the headmaster, the psychologists went to a local primary school and asked parents if they would be willing to fill in a questionnaire as they waited for their children at the end of the school day. The questionnaire asked them to rate their child's behaviour in terms of aggressiveness and to report the hours spent playing video games.

The data shown are for children aged 8-11.

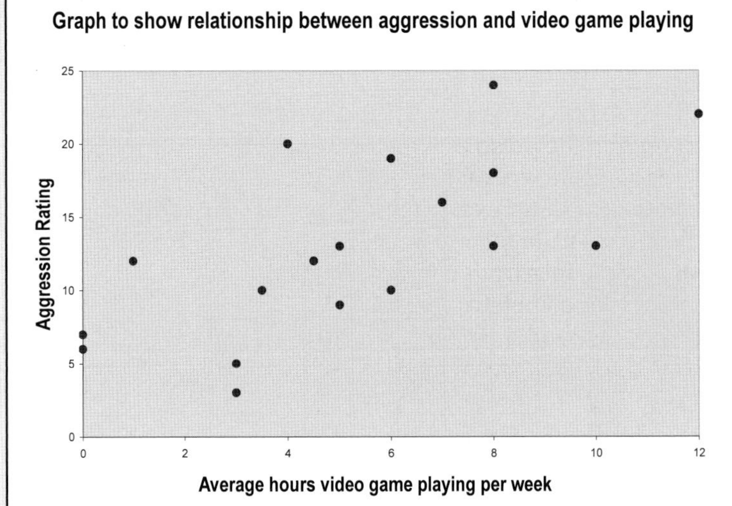

a) How were the variables aggression and video game playing habits operationalised? *(2 marks)*

b) i) Identify the research method of this study. *(1 mark)*
ii) Outline **one** weakness of this research method in the context of this study. *(3 marks)*

c) i) Identify the sampling method used. *(1 mark)*
ii) Outline **one** weakness of this sampling method in the context of this study. *(2 marks)*

d) i) Identify and explain **one** extraneous variable that could threaten the validity of this study. *(3 marks)*

ii) Explain how the psychologists might try and limit the impact of this variable. *(2 marks)*

e) Aggression of the children was measured using a scale. Describe how the reliability of this scale could be assessed? *(2 marks)*

f) Name an appropriate statistical test for analysing this data and justify your choice. *(4 marks)*

g) With reference to the graph above, describe the relationship between the two variables. *(2 marks)*

h) The relationship between the two variables was found to be significant at p=0.10. Identify and briefly explain whether a type 1 or type 2 error was more likely to have occurred. *(3 marks)*

i) The researchers decide that they need to determine a causal relationship between the variables. Design a study that will allow them to do this. You should include sufficient details to permit replication, for example a hypothesis, variables, details of design and procedure, sampling, etc. *(10 marks)*

▶ Lesson notes p.89

Exam-style question 2

Bosses at a financial office always try and limit the amount of stress their employees experience whilst they are at work. For the past month they have been playing classical music at low volumes to try and keep the employees relaxed. The bosses are unsure whether it has had an impact on their stress. In addition, they are unaware of any previous research in this area.

They decide to conduct an experiment in order to test whether classical music can de-stress their workers.

To do this they displayed an advert in their office to ask people whether they would be interested in taking part in an experiment for an extra £15 in their wages the following month. They recruited 48 participants from this advert and asked each of them to complete a stress questionnaire. They then randomly assigned them to one of two conditions. In the first condition participants worked for 4 days in a section of the office where classical music was playing. In the second condition participants worked for 4 days in a section of the office where no music was playing.

	Classical music condition	No music condition
Mean difference score (in ratings of stress given before and after the intervention)	-0.25	0.08
Standard deviation	7.65	3.77

Following this, each participant completed the stress questionnaire for a second time. Their score was subtracted from their original score from the first questionnaire. As such, a minus score showed that participant had 'de-stressed'. The results for each of the conditions were compared.

a) i) Identify the experimental design used. *(1 mark)*

ii) Explain **one** weakness of this design in the context of this study. *(3 marks)*

b) i) Write a suitable non-directional hypothesis for this study. *(2 marks)*

ii) Explain why a non-directional hypothesis would be used. *(2 marks)*

c) i) Identify the sampling technique used. *(1 mark)*

ii) Explain **one** potential weakness of this sampling technique with reference to this study. *(2 marks)*

d) Identify and explain a potential threat to the validity of this study (not previously been mentioned). *(3 marks)*

e) The before/after stress difference scores for the classical music condition were as follows: -10, -8, -7, 3, 8, 10, -12, -7, 14, -1, -3, -5, -1, -2, -3, -7, -8, -8, 3, 7, 6, 5, 4

i) Suggest **one** suitable method of central tendency to use with this data. *(1 mark)*
ii) Describe **one** advantage of using this measure of central tendency. *(2 marks)*

f) Discuss what the table of results shows about the two sets of data. *(4 marks)*

g) Name an appropriate statistical test for analysing this data and justify your choice. *(4 marks)*

h) Would a one- or two-tailed test be used with this data? *(1 mark)*

i) The results were significant at p=0.05. Explain what this means in the context of this study. *(3 marks)*

j) The financial company write up the results and submit a journal article for peer review. Describe this peer review process. *(6 marks)*

▶ Lesson notes p.89

Exam-style question 3

ECT is still used in cases of severe depression. One practitioner felt the extent of ECT and its methodology was a mystery to the general population, with opinions often based on knowledge from fictional films and novels. She decided to carry out research into public perceptions of ECT. She wondered whether Psychology students who have learnt about ECT as part of their A-level hold different views from those who have not learnt about this form of treatment.

She gave participants a table of adjectives that could be used to describe ECT. The table included words such as life saving, brutal, scientific, painful. She took care to ensure an equal amount of positive and negative words were included. Participants were asked to circle any words they felt described ECT. She recorded whether each participant chose more positive words or more negative words.

	Identified more positive words to describe ECT	Identified more negative words to describe ECT
A-level student studying Psychology	7	8
A level student not studying Psychology	3	12

(a) Identify the type of research design used in this study. *(1 mark)*

(b) The researcher took care to ensure there were an equal amount of positive and negative words. Why was it important she did this? *(4 marks)*

(c) Name an appropriate test of statistical significance for analysing this data. Explain why this would be a suitable test to use. *(4 marks)*

(d) Explain what is meant by $p \leq 0.05$. *(2 marks)*

(e) Give **one** reason why the researcher might use a two-tailed test. *(2 marks)*

(f) With reference to the data, outline and discuss the findings of this investigation. *(10 marks)*

(g) Following this study the researcher wished to investigate the impact of reading a case study of ECT, compared to watching a film clip of a patient's ECT experience. Design a suitable study. (12 marks).

▶ Lesson notes p.89